DEMCO

The World of Jewish Entertaining

MENUS AND RECIPES
FOR THE SABBATH, HOLIDAYS,
AND OTHER FAMILY CELEBRATIONS

Gil Marks

SIMON & SCHUSTER

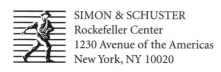

SIMON & SCHUSTER
Rockefeller Center
1230 Avenue of the Americas
New York, NY 10020

SIMON & SCHUSTER and colophon are registered trademarks
of Simon & Schuster Inc.

DESIGNED & ILLUSTRATED BY JILL WEBER

Manufactured in the United States of America

10 9 8 7 6 5 4 3 2 1

Library of Congress Cataloging-in-Publication Data

Marks, Gil.
    The world of Jewish entertaining : menus and recipes for the
Sabbath, holidays, and other family celebrations / Gil Marks.
        p.   cm.
    Includes index.
    1. Cookery, Jewish.   2. Holiday cookery.   3. Fasts and feasts—
Judaism.   4. Entertaining.   5. Menus.   I. Title.
    TX724.M3196   1998
    641.5'676—dc21   98-19913
                                                        CIP

ISBN 0-684-84788-4

Acknowledgments

SPECIAL THANKS to my editors at Simon & Schuster, Penny Kaganoff and Diana Newman, for their invaluable encouragement and suggestions.

My gratitude goes to the various talented and generous people who contributed to this work, including Sharon Friedman, Daniella Weiss, Eva Weiss, Diane Feldman, Stanley Allan Sherman (and his grandmother Bertha Sherman for her Salmon Gefilte Fish recipe), Claire Kaganoff, Michelle Comet, Faye Reichwald, Sharon and William Altshul, Shari and Jeffrey Marks, Aviva and Arthur Marks, Carol and Labby Vegh, and my parents, Beverly and Harold Marks.

To my nieces and nephews, who provide many opportunities for celebrating:
Efrat Zipporah, Asher Yaakov, Ora Rivka, Esther Chana, Aryeh Dov, Eliana
Bracha, Shlomo Yosef, Miriam Malka, Efrayim, Tehila, Ashira, Rivka, Moshe,
Leah, Shmuel, Ahron, Yeshai, Yakov, Chana Tzipora, Shifra Miriam, Avrohom
Boruch, Elisheva, Yisroel, Adina Rivka, Moshe Raphael, and Adira Tova.

Contents

Introduction

Great is hospitality; greater even than early attendance at the house of study or than receiving the Divine Presence. —TALMUD, SABBATH 127:A

Growing up in a home where the kitchen was not off-limits to the children, I enjoyed learning about food at an early age. Not that the paternal side of my family served as a positive role model when it came to cooking. My father rarely ventured into the kitchen, and my grandfather actually set his house on fire attempting to make instant coffee. My mother, however, was determined that none of her children should grow up to be so "culinarily" inept and gave us relatively free rein in the kitchen, encouraging experimentation and rarely making a fuss over the inevitable mess. As a result, all of my siblings can hold their own at the stove.

In addition to basic culinary skills, we were introduced early on to different types of food. My father's family, which emigrated from Romania to the United States in the 1880s, left a legacy of spicy Middle Eastern–influenced Ashkenazic dishes, as well as favorite American foods—my great-grandmother was renowned in her adopted home of Savannah, Georgia, for her lemon meringue pie and benne wafers (sesame cookies). My Ukrainian-born maternal grandfather so disliked the cooking of my Lithuanian grandmother that after dinner he would assume control of the kitchen and prepare the type of dishes dear to his heart, such as *lungen* (lung stew), *p'tcha* (calf's-foot gelatin), and *mamaliga* (cornmeal mush). As a southerner, I ate grits, spoon bread, and long before the movie, fried green tomatoes. In the Boy Scouts I learned to cook over an open fire and under genuinely adverse conditions—I still have my cooking merit badge somewhere. From fabulous home cooks I discovered an array of traditional Jewish dishes, many of which were incorporated into my first book, *The World of Jewish Cooking*.

A crucial aspect of my culinary education centered on entertaining, an integral part of my parents' home. In such a large family, rarely did a few months pass without a bar or bat mitzvah, brit, wedding, anniversary, or some other family event, always accompanied by food. Fish—in the form of pickled herring, whitefish salad, sable, and lox—was ubiquitous at morning affairs. Stuffed veal breast, stuffed turkey, stuffed cabbage, and stuffed guests seemed mandatory for soirees. New culinary customs also found their way to the table. The recent trend toward healthier living led to the inclusion of assorted muffins and more salads, while Hungarian in-laws contributed, somewhat incongru-

ously, baked goods such as *kakosh* (chocolate rolls) and *pogacha* (sour cream sugar cookies) to the dessert repertoire. Not all foods became standards. After years of whipping up his horseradish kugel, my brother-in-law still cannot find any takers other than himself. In honor of my brit, my mother, for the first time, made apple strudel from scratch (this was in the days before phyllo dough could be found in the grocer's freezer) and, justifiably proud, featured it on the buffet table. When one of the guests single-handedly devoured the entire large pastry, my mother was so shell-shocked that she never had the heart to make strudel again. On the other hand, for years no family baby naming, brit, birthday party, or *sheva brachot* was complete without some of my mother's rugalach, nut crescents, and florentines.

And, of course, there were the festivals. Some of my earliest and fondest memories revolve around the holiday table. My taste buds still tingle at the thought of the first bite of egg-rich challah, dill-laced chicken soup, and various sweet-and-sour appetizers, including meatballs, stuffed cabbage, and stuffed peppers. The smell and taste of Hanukkah's hot crispy potato latkes and Purim's freshly baked poppy-filled *hamantaschen* are ingrained in my memory. I remember the boisterous Passover Seders at my maternal grandparents' house in Cleveland, Ohio, and my parents' large homemade wooden sukkah in Richmond, Virginia, overflowing with relatives and friends. I recall the college students and other strangers who were always present at these occasions. And I remember the food.

Upon procuring my own place, I continued the family tradition of inviting guests to my table. Admittedly, my first attempt turned out to be less than successful. I prepared a large pot of *cholent* (traditional slow-simmered stew) for Sabbath lunch and placed it in a crockery pot set on a timer to turn off around noon. Instead, it went off at midnight, and the next morning, to my horror, I found an inedible gray mass. Thus, my first attempt at entertaining consisted of challah and cherry pie. I subsequently adopted my mother's philosophy of "being safe by overpreparing" so that even if the Israeli army on maneuvers stopped by, there would still be leftovers. As a result, I have never again come up short.

After the disaster of my first stab at entertaining, the only place to go was up. Fortunately, the results of my ensuing attempts proved more inviting. I always wanted to do a better job and prepare something different each time, so I constantly experimented with new dishes and various types of cuisine. I watched accomplished cooks in action, gleaning whatever tidbits I could from them. I read numerous cookbooks in search of ideas and information. And I learned to cope with the inevitable emergencies and frustrations. After a few years of entertaining at my New York City home, I earned a reputation in the neighborhood as a gourmet cook. When a highly regarded kosher caterer asked if I would be interested in occasionally moonlighting as her baker, I jumped at the oppor-

tunity. It proved a great learning experience. Eventually I found myself freelancing for several caterers and sometimes branching out on my own. Among my early productions were catering a health food wedding reception and baking 150 apple pies for a cooking spray promotion (in my small apartment with its tiny oven, this task took an entire day and every bit of available space).

Through word of mouth my culinary reputation spread, and I received an increasing number of requests to cater various affairs or consult on food-related matters. In 1986 I combined my interests in food, history, and writing to become editor of *Kosher Gourmet* magazine, a position I held for six years. I participated in several kosher-wine tastings for a major oenological magazine—smell, sip, swirl, and spit. I prepared traditional Jewish dishes in Macy's basement and performed the first Jewish cooking demonstration at Bloomingdale's flagship Manhattan store. One of my more unusual adventures came when a New York bank decided to turn its executive dining room kosher and asked me to supervise the transformation. (The most difficult part was dealing with a venerable French chef who considered me an interloper in his domain.) These activities enhanced my reputation as someone capable of synthesizing traditional Jewish foods with modern, sophisticated fare.

As my culinary experiences and reputation grew, I began giving cooking classes and demonstrations, which proved educational to me as well as, I trust, my students. Indeed, my very first class, for a ladies' auxiliary in Brooklyn, taught me a vital lesson. The contact person insisted that, because the women were generally young and inexperienced cooks, I should present only easy dishes. Walking into the hall, I was greeted by the sight of more than a hundred women, most of whom were Hungarian and old enough to have been cooking twice as long as I had been alive. To say that I was intimidated would be an understatement. Yet to my amazement, they were fascinated by what I considered to be simple dishes, including a raspberry-orange soup and chocolate-dipped strawberries. Although experts on the foods that their mothers handed down, they were basically unaware of anything outside their world. While subsequently giving cooking classes not only throughout the United States but also in Australia and Canada, I discovered a universal common denominator: cooks are eager to add unfamiliar and interesting dishes to their repertoire.

The Jewish year offers numerous occasions to make use of tasty recipes. Historic national experiences are observed annually through the various Jewish holidays. There are three basic categories of Jewish holidays: the Pilgrim Festivals (in the time when the Temple stood, Jews made their way to Jerusalem to celebrate these occasions)—Passover, Shavuot, and Sukkot; the High Holidays—Rosh Hashanah and Yom Kippur; and the minor festivals—Rosh Chodesh (the New Moon), Hanukkah, Tu b'Shevat, Purim, and Lag b'Omer. Family milestones—*me shebarach* (naming of a female child), *shalom*

zakhar (celebration held on the Friday night following the birth of a male, in recognition of the upcoming circumcision), *brit milah* (circumcision), *pidyon haben* (ceremonial redemption of a firstborn son on the thirty-first day following his birth), bar mitzvah and bat mitzvah (ceremonial recognition of religious maturity), chuppah (wedding canopy), and shivah (mourning period)—are commemorated at any time during the year as circumstances dictate. *Smachot* (Jewish celebrations) are designed to be observed in public, never in solitude, thereby reinforcing the bonds of community. An example of the role of public celebration in Jewish life is the period immediately following a wedding. While the standard American postnuptial activity is for the couple to take a honeymoon by themselves, in Jewish tradition the newlyweds spend the week following the wedding participating in feasts called *sheva brachot*. Jewish celebrations are, by design, communal acts.

In Judaism food, entertaining, and religion are intertwined. Thus, integral to every holiday and *simcha* (celebration) is a *seudat mitzvah* (celebratory meal), establishing and enhancing the spirit of the occasion. These feasts are much more than an opportunity to eat, although plenty of food is the rule. Among the most important roles of the *seudat mitzvah* is one of education. Indeed, the sages structured the best-known *seudah*, the Passover Seder, to serve as a pedagogic tool, and its continuing popularity illustrates just how incredibly successful the ancient rabbis were at achieving their goal.

Although no other *seudat mitzvah* is as highly ritualized as the Seder, all of them offer unparalleled opportunities for learning in an informal atmosphere. After all, these meals provide one of the increasingly rare occasions when various generations are represented and connected. In an atmosphere that encourages them to ask questions and observe social interactions, children learn about customs, terminology, and family roles, as well as how to interpret nonverbal social cues (who sits at the head of the table, when it is time to be quiet, what is considered appropriate humor). They discover how people interact. Indeed, it is at such occasions that young children learn the power of speech as they observe food being passed or diners breaking out in laughter in direct response to someone speaking. Perhaps the greatest benefit of a *seudat mitzvah* is the development of an emotional attachment to Judaism, which has been the key to its continuing survival.

Each Passover I prepare all sorts of fancy desserts for my family, often experimenting with adaptations of sophisticated modern fare. Yet every year I repeat one particular dish, *chremslach* (tiny matza meal pancakes in honey). The recipe I use is scribbled in my grandmother's handwriting on a yellowed, wine-splattered index card. (Although I am told that my grandmother was a fantastic cook, I cannot confirm it from personal experience, as she stopped cooking after her children left the nest and I never saw her in a kitchen. Thus this card is my sole contact with her culinary knowledge.) I scrupulously follow the directions, making certain that the pancakes are no larger than a quarter. Any

errant ones are immediately dispatched to a waiting niece or nephew. Each year as my father sneaks a sample of the finished product with the excuse of "quality control," he remarks on how they take him back to his childhood and the ones his mother used to make. Thus, the mere act of sampling a piece of fried ground matza in honey actually transcends time, linking generations. It is the patriarch Abraham offering a lavish meal to three strangers, setting the standard in hospitality for his descendants. It is the lentil soup Jacob prepared in memory of the passing of his grandfather, Abraham—a dish still served more than three thousand years later in Jewish households in mourning. It is why the patriarch Isaac asked his son Esau to prepare Isaac's favorite dish of venison stew in order that he could bless his eldest son. The acts of serving and consuming food can be an expression of who we are, as well as a spiritual experience.

I once read a book claiming that there is no true altruism, that even when there is no monetary or other physical compensation involved in a seemingly unselfish act, a person still receives some form of honor, satisfaction, or emotional reward from his or her actions. Entertaining is like that. Cooking and serving special meals provide me with the ego stroking that I failed to secure in a previous incarnation running a high school guidance department; the more compliments I receive for my culinary efforts, the more I want to outdo myself the next time. Yet even more important than the praise are the intangible dividends involved in the act of transforming and enhancing an occasion through the dishes that I prepare. When you serve a cake made by your own hands, even if it turns out less than perfect, it somehow proves more gratifying than a store-bought item, for the host as well as the guests.

For this reason, more and more people are opting to cook for various *smachot* themselves or to share the task with a group rather than hiring a caterer or purchasing take-out food. Besides saving one third or more off the cost, a do-it-yourself affair has a personal touch, makes the occasion unique, and ensures that it will be done the host's way. There exists a great deal of dissatisfaction with many commercially prepared foods, which all too often lack panache as well as flavor. People attend so many affairs at which the same old things are prepared without much thought or care that they consume the food without anticipation or pleasure. My culinary clients and students inevitably express a common sentiment as to what they want for their entertaining: exciting, sophisticated, and tasty fare.

Understandably, few people want to take on the daunting task of catering a wedding or other large event. If you have the desire, this book will provide assistance and motivation. Most prospective hosts, however, relish the thought of contributing to a family celebration or enjoying the satisfaction of throwing a dinner party. To those who feel intimidated by such prospects, I hope this book will help them overcome such fears. As I learned from my parents and taught my students in my guidance department days,

once you master the basic skills and feel comfortable in a subject, you can accomplish most anything. And space, or lack thereof, is not an acceptable excuse. Since I did much of my cooking in my stereotypically tiny Manhattan apartment (yes, even for parties of a hundred or more), I know it can be done in any home kitchen. When performed with organization and planning, entertaining is not a matter of drudgery or turbulence but one of grace and pleasure. Entertaining is about the host expressing his or her personality. Style is a matter of what the host is comfortable with. This book will serve as inspiration and guidance.

The World of Jewish Entertaining draws on my experiences and experiments. As I planned the book, I had in mind all the family members, friends, *Kosher Gourmet* subscribers, and students who, over the years, have sought my advice on culinary questions or asked for suggestions on what to serve for various celebrations. The result is an extensive collection of contemporary and classic recipes, primarily arranged in a menu format, for both informal and elegant occasions. Each section commences with a suggested menu for a particular occasion; those items listed in bold type have recipes following. The ensuing wine suggestions are keyed primarily to the entrée, but feel free to add appropriate vintages for any other course.

Most of the recipes in the family celebrations section offer quantities for both small and large gatherings. In many instances the larger amount is not proportionately increased but adjusted to my experiences. Following my first several catering jobs, I was surprised to discover greater amounts of leftovers than anticipated. This was partially due to the fact that most recipes provide a conservative portion amount and therefore leave an excess of food corresponding to the increase. In addition, the larger the crowd, the less you need, as there are usually more people who take smaller amounts. And since larger affairs generally have a more extensive menu, people take less of each item.

The recipes in this book were chosen not only for their taste and appearance but also for their shelf life—most can be prepared well in advance and stored in the refrigerator or freezer. These menus are not written in stone; the various dishes are meant to be interchangeable as the needs and preferences of the host dictate. In the same vein, the menus are hardly restricted to the ascribed categories. It is the aim of this book to transform your meal or party into a personal yet relaxed occasion and to offer many enticing possibilities to add to your culinary repertoire. With *The World of Jewish Entertaining* as a guide, even a timid host can create memorable events, whether small gatherings or large affairs.

A Guide for
the Perplexed Host

*W*hat produces a memorable occasion? Sharing good times, good conversation, and good food. The key to successful entertaining is making your guests feel comfortable. Therefore, disregard any strict rules about entertaining and remember that *entertaining* and *elaborate* are not synonymous. Your party and presentation should be a personal statement representing your individuality within the bounds of common sense. This uniqueness ensures that your event will be special.

One evening I watched an unusual sight in front of my window, unusual even for New York City. A knight sporting large feathers on his scarlet armor and a flaming horn in the middle of his head and sitting atop a bright pink horse galloped down the street through waves of mist. This scene was repeated again and again while a movie crew explored different angles and possibilities, technicians fine-tuned cameras and sound machinery, and assistants busily attempted to move the public out of sight. It was well after midnight before the director was satisfied with the results and left my block in relative peace. All this work was done for only a few moments of actual film time.

What is true in the movie business is true with any production: there are numerous details to remember and an extensive amount of planning to do. If the job is organized and done right, your guests will never be cognizant of all the details involved and the effort put forth behind the scenes. Therefore, the most important thing you can do in organizing a party is to make lists, including ones of guests, purchases (such as food), recipes, rentals, and things to do. Making lists may take a little time, but it can save you from potential disasters. On more than one occasion, checking a list of ingredients averted me from forgetting to obtain necessary items. Following are suggested schedules for planning both formal and informal affairs.

PLANNING A FORMAL OR LARGE PARTY

I. Several months before the party

Decide on the basic logistics of your party:

- Date.

- Time. The time of day influences the type of party, the setting, and the type of food served.

- Location. Will the party be held at your home, a friend's or relative's house, a public area such as a park, or a rented space such as a synagogue, community center, or other private facility? Will you stage the party indoors or outdoors and in what area of the house or garden? The dining room is appropriate for formal occasions; you may want to consider the kitchen or patio for less formal events. The number of guests is a factor in determining the location.

Make a guest list. You should be able to comfortably accommodate the number of guests in your chosen setting. For smaller parties you may want to keep a name or two in reserve in case of last-minute cancellations.

Decide on the type of party. The basic logistics and the number of guests influence whether you give a dinner party, buffet, or cocktail party.

Create a budget. Be liberal in your calculations, as emergency expenses tend to pop up.

Pick out the invitations, styling them to fit the event. Engraved invitations are necessary only for very formal occasions. Allow up to a month for ordering and printing invitations. Use whimsical or homemade cards for less formal affairs.

II. Several weeks before the party

Mail the invitations. Allow at least six weeks for formal events and about four weeks for less formal ones. If guests have not answered the RSVP, it is better to track them down for a reply than to face the unexpected.

Develop your theme and plan your decor. Keep in mind the color scheme, flowers, and centerpieces.

Write out the menu and recipes. Make a list of all ingredients.

Make a list of utensils, serving pieces, and furniture to be used, including tables and chairs, linens (tablecloths and napkins), serving platters, china, silverware, chafing dishes and burners, drinking glasses, coffee cups, trays, pot holders, toothpicks, can openers, paper towels, plastic wrap, foil, garbage bags, and waste containers. Commonly used bar items include wine and cocktail glasses, punch bowl, cocktail shakers, pitchers, stirrers, cocktail napkins, corkscrews, paring knives, cutting boards, ice tongs, and ice tubs.

Begin purchasing any missing equipment and ordering rental supplies such as tables, chairs, and linens. Some rental companies will rent new glassware, flatware, and china for an extra charge, which is useful for those who require kosher dishes. (Busy firms are constantly replacing broken and lost items.)

At least four weeks before the party, hire any help, including waiters and bartenders. Do this even earlier at holiday time.

Make a list of your items that need to be cleaned.

Purchase nonspoilable items, including sugar, coffee, spices, flour, canned goods, and paper goods.

Begin preparing foods that can be frozen.

III. A week before the party

Order bread and rolls.

Order flowers.

Purchase liquor and wine.

Purchase decorations.

Check if your party clothes require dry cleaning.

Check your linens. Do you have enough? Are they clean and pressed?

Check to ensure that all items on the inventory list are accounted for.

Reconfirm earlier orders, including rentals and help (such as waiters, bartenders, and housekeepers).

Finish preparing most foods that can be frozen.

IV. A few days before the party

Clear out all leftovers and nonessentials from your refrigerator and freezer.

Shop for perishable foods except fish, bread, and salad greens.

Make up place cards.

Begin cleaning the house.

Begin preparing any foods that can be refrigerated without detrimental effects.

V. The day before the party

Clear out or rearrange furniture to accommodate your guests. For buffets, arrange chairs in an arc or L shape to facilitate conversation.

Set up coat racks with hangers.

Set the table. If possible, do this even two or three days before the party. This not only saves valuable time later on but also enables you to check your supplies. If you set the table early, invert the plates and glasses.

Set up a table in a nontrafficked space on which to lay out all finished dishes that do not require refrigeration, thereby freeing much-needed space in your work area.

Finish cleaning the house, paying special attention to the bathrooms. People do notice.

Polish any tarnished silver or brass.

Finish most decorations.

Set up the bar. Do not forget corkscrews.

Fill salt and pepper shakers and sugar bowls.

Thaw most frozen foods except quick-thawing items such as cookies and mousses.

VI. The day of the party

Pick up ice, flowers, fish, bread, and salad greens.

Do any touch-up cleaning, including the kitchen. People do notice.

Finish any last-minute cooking.

Chill wine and soda two hours before the guests arrive.

Prepare coffee and hot water.

Put out the nosh. You should have something for the early arrivers to nibble on and drink while you see to any last-minute details or wait for the other guests to arrive.

Check your lists to ensure that everything has been done.

Allow yourself at least one hour for last-minute items and to relax before your guests arrive.

Welcome your guests.

PLANNING AN INFORMAL OR SMALL PARTY

Invitations to a small or casual affair such as a Sabbath dinner or life-cycle celebration (except bar or bat mitzvahs and weddings) are usually extended by telephone or personal conversation up to a few days before the function.

I. At least a week before the party

Plan your menu and decor.

Purchase nonspoilable items, including sugar, coffee, spices, flour, canned goods, paper goods, and wine.

Begin preparing foods that can be frozen.

Buy, borrow, or rent special utensils or equipment you will need.

II. A few days before the party

Shop for perishable foods except fish, bread, and salad greens.

Begin preparing foods that can be refrigerated.

Do the major cleaning.

Check that the linens are clean and pressed.

Polish any tarnished silver or brass.

For smaller affairs, plan the seating arrangements.

III. The day before the party

Wash plates, flatware, and glasses.

Set up the buffet or dinner table.

IV. The day of the party (on the Sabbath and Yom Tov, these would be done on the previous day)

Pick up ice, flowers, fish, bread, and salad greens.

Do any touch-up cleaning, including the kitchen and bathrooms.

Finish any last-minute cooking.

Chill wine and soda two hours before the guests arrive.

Prepare coffee and hot water.

Check your lists to ensure that everything has been done.

Allow yourself at least one hour for last-minute items and to relax before your guests arrive.

Welcome your guests and wish them mazel tov, good Shabbos, or good Yom Tov.

THE TIME

When scheduling and preparing for a party, keep in mind local attitudes and ethnic dispositions toward time. New Yorkers tend to arrive late, while southerners often show up early. Groups such as Germans and Syrians tend to be rather punctual, while eastern Europeans are less expeditious and Hasidim even more so. I know of some Syrians who actually make two sets of invitations—one with the actual starting time for their fellow Syrians and one stating an earlier time for Ashkenazim. Most affairs have no stated ending time, although invitations to cocktail parties and open houses generally state both when the party begins and when it ends.

BASIC PARTY TIMES

Breakfast: before 11:00 A.M.

Brunch: 10:00 A.M to 2:00 P.M.

Lunch: 12:00 noon to 3:00 P.M.

Tea: 3:00 P.M. to 5:00 P.M.

Cocktail party: 6:00 P.M. to 8:00 P.M.

Dinner party: 7:00 P.M. to 9:00 P.M.

Dessert: from 9:00 P.M.

PLANNING THE MENU

The type of event, the time of day, the time of year, and your sense of taste will be deciding factors in determining the menu. There is no rule stating that everything served at your party must be prepared from scratch. If you can, *kol ha'kavod* (more power to you). There is nothing wrong, however, with getting friends and relatives to help by sharing the tasks or asking them to bring a particular dish. Parts of some dishes can be prepared by separate individuals ahead of time, then assembled at the party. Delegation, after all, is the key to successful administration. Additionally, if there is a good-quality bakery or deli in town, buy items there to supplement what you make. I rarely go to the bakery for bread or rolls, which I can turn out relatively easily and to my specifications at home, but it seems sensible to purchase items that require a lot of *potchka* (effort) and with which I am less proficient, such as croissants and bagels. Knowing and compensating for your strengths and weaknesses is the best way to ensure success in any field.

If you are doing all or most of the cooking for your party, plan an easy menu with no more than one or two complicated dishes. A soufflé may be attractive, but the obvious complications make it inappropriate fare for these occasions. Plan dishes that can be prepared ahead of time and either reheated or served cold. This allows you more time to deal with those inevitable last-minute details and to serve as a relaxed host. Plan to have leftovers. It is always better to have extra than to run short.

Keep in mind the available oven, refrigerator, and freezer space. If you have only one oven at your disposal, most of the hot dishes should have the same cooking temperature or be served at different times. Portable ice chests offer a way of temporarily expanding refrigerator space. Check with neighbors and relatives to see if you can usurp some of their freezer space. For large affairs it may be necessary to rent an extra refrigerator or freezer or even a refrigerator truck.

Take into account the availability of seasonal produce. Fresh cranberries are generally unobtainable in the summer, as are cherries and plums during the winter. Although some greengrocers may offer asparagus after the spring, the price or quality will probably serve as a deterrent to its inclusion in a menu. Summertime fare should be cooler and lighter than that of cold weather. Save stews and robust dishes for winter entertaining.

It is advisable to ask your guests in advance whether they have any special dietary requirements, such as food allergies, health restrictions, or vegetarianism. In this way you can shape the menu or provide separate fare to meet their needs.

The key to menu planning is balance. The menu should be coordinated around the main course. One entrée is sufficient for a party of forty or less. For larger gatherings a choice of two or three entrées is an option. The type of meat or fish, as well as how you prepare it, will determine how much you need. Allow 6 to 8 ounces of boneless meat

roasts such as prime rib (12 ounces bone in) per person; as little as 4 ounces boneless meat per person for stews; and as little as 3 ounces for cold cuts. One 3- to 4-pound chicken will serve four people when roasted but nearly double the number when cut up and cooked in a sauce. Allow 4 to 6 ounces boneless poultry per person; 12 ounces bone in. If fish is your only entrée, allow 8 ounces bone in (4 to 6 ounces boneless) per person, especially if it is a popular variety such as salmon. If you are offering alternative entrées, reduce the amount to about 4 to 5 ounces boneless per person. The nature of the main course usually determines the wine selection, unless you want to offer a variety.

Once you have decided on the main course, select a first course/appetizer and side dishes that balance it in color, texture, and flavor. Even highly esteemed ingredients like caviar would quickly lose their cachet if they dominated all of the courses. Cauliflower, turnips, and plain white rice are not the most eye-catching accompaniments to chicken breast. Similarly, you would not want an all-red meal of rare roast beef, beets, and red cabbage. Nor would you want to offer an assortment of too many or only creamy textures or bland items.

A first course may consist of one large item—a meat pâté, vegetable terrine, stuffed vegetable, knish or other pastry, smoked fish, or pasta—or several hors d'oeuvres arranged on a plate. Appetizers are generally the most time-consuming part of a meal to prepare yet offer the host an opportunity to demonstrate his or her best culinary skills. Appetizers should be charming, colorful, flavorful, and attractive, and complement the meal to follow. They should not fill guests up. A simpler appetizer would better serve a fancy main course and vice versa. The primary ingredients of the appetizer should be different from those in the rest of the meal. Nor should the first course overpower the entrée; it would be inappropriate to serve a curry or highly seasoned dish before a delicate food such as fillet of sole.

Every crowd responds differently to specific types of food, so consider the nature of your guests. The general rule of thumb is to offer one starch (rice, pasta, or potato) and one to three vegetables (including salads). Estimate about 4 ounces of a side dish per person. Certain vegetables such as asparagus and wild rice tend to go more readily. At buffets most starches evoke little enthusiasm as diners concentrate on meats or more exotic items, so figure about half a potato per person and 2 ounces of rice or pasta per person. When the starch is in the form of a kugel or salad, it proves more popular. Remember, the larger the choice, the less people will take from each dish.

You may want to provide printed or handwritten menus to let your guests know what to expect.

PRESENTATION AND DECORATIONS

The presentation of the room, tables, and food is almost as important to the success of the party as the food itself. This is where your creativity and sense of style come into play. Use complementing and contrasting colors, shapes, forms, and volumes of food and serving vessels. A sense of drama helps to enliven the festivities, while simplicity can heighten the effect. Keep in mind scale; a stately centerpiece works in a cavernous space but overwhelms in a small room. With a complex centerpiece, use simple linens and china. Although flowers have traditionally served as centerpieces, edible items such as breads, fruits, or crudités are becoming popular alternatives. Baskets, cobalt glass bowls, and cake stands provide an interesting base on which to build a centerpiece. A cornucopia of autumn produce, including winter squash, pomegranates, and apples arranged with brightly colored dried leaves or straw, provides an attractive alternative for that season. At child-friendly affairs such as a baby naming, use stuffed animals and bright colors. Helium-filled balloons anchored to a base (you can rent a tank and fill them yourself) provide an inexpensive and colorful centerpiece for informal occasions. For a bar mitzvah my sister Sharon assembled baskets of food and grape juice for the centerpieces, then distributed them to the needy.

Ribbons and streamers provide an easy way to add color and flair. To set a sophisticated mood, use a mirror as the base of your centerpiece and top it with items of varying heights and shapes, such as candles, a single flower in a brandy snifter or ceramic vase, pine branches, and colorful stones. For an Italian setting, use miniature stone arches surrounded by Mediterranean fruit and vegetables. Pine branches and cones reflect a winter theme. A single bare branch accompanied by several pomegranates resting on an unusual plate bespeak a stark beauty. Incorporate appropriate holiday and ritual symbols in the theme: for example, edible (chocolate or cake) *tefillin* or *tallit* (prayer shawl) for a bar mitzvah, gold-wrapped chocolate coins for Hanukkah, and roses and honey for Shavuot. Whatever you choose, remember that restraint is generally best, as centerpieces and other decorations are intended to complement the food, not overwhelm it. People need to converse, and centerpieces should not block the interaction.

Color-coordinate decorations, flowers, dishes, tableware, napkins, and paper goods with the food and mood of the affair. For a contrasting effect, use napkins of a different color from the tablecloth. For formal occasions, use white or pastel linens; for festive and casual affairs, colors add pizzazz. Black and white project elegance. Silver and white are romantic. Pale greens and yellows are spring colors. Orange and brown bespeak autumn. For Mexican meals, use vibrant hues such as turquoise, orange, yellow, and purple. Red and gold are common Chinese colors. Pale blue, bright yellow, and terra-cotta create a Mediterranean atmosphere. Deep blue, gold, white, and browns resonate with a Middle

Eastern feeling, while red, gold, and black bespeak the Maghreb. Blue and white create an Israeli theme.

Serving vessels are an excellent way to enliven the table and show off the food. A general rule of thumb is to serve food in dishes of contrasting colors: dark-colored foods in light-colored dishes and vice versa. Glass bowls are best for multicolored or layered dishes. Use silver and copper trays and chafing dishes for formal occasions. Serve hearty dishes such as stews and thick soups in earthenware vessels. Baskets provide the perfect backdrop for breads and crudités, so buy a variety of inexpensive baskets and wicker trays; line with foil or lettuce for crudités and fruits. Use hollowed-out vegetables such as bell peppers and cabbages as containers for dip. (Afterward, grate them for coleslaw.) In the same vein, hollow out loaves of bread to make attractive containers for cheese spreads and chicken, fish, and egg salads. Wooden cutting boards are ideal for cheeses and fruit. Insert a piece of velvet or other cloth in a large picture frame and use as a tray to highlight the food.

Lights help to enhance the table, room, and mood. Candles and dim lighting create a romantic atmosphere. You can float a single candle in a glass bowl or group candles for a dramatic presentation. Colored strands of tube lights create an art deco mood. Strings of tiny white lights hung from the ceiling project an image of twinkling stars. Small lights under a floral centerpiece can enhance its appearance. Other types of lights include paper lanterns, plug-in spotlights, and kerosene lanterns.

Flowers are one of the most popular decorations, the type and arrangement a matter of personal taste. Avoid overly aromatic blossoms that compete with the food. If fresh flowers are expensive, one or two blooms in a small vase or floating in a bowl provide an attractive alternative. Ferns, palm leaves, rhododendron leaves, and other greenery are relatively inexpensive as well as beautiful. Check out your local flower district; if you buy in volume and pay in cash, many florists will sell at wholesale.

Many florists also sell oasis, a block of foam that helps to keep greenery fresh without a vase. To use the oasis, cut it to the desired size and soak in water. Wrap the bottom and sides with heavy-duty aluminum foil and insert the flowers into the foam.

HIRING HELP

A small dinner or cocktail party does not inherently require any paid serving or cleaning help, although you may want to arrange some assistance in setting up and cleaning up. Parties of more than twenty call for some backup, whether friends or hired help. Large events require service staff, and it will prove practical to hire someone to do the cleaning.

Arrange for the service staff at least four weeks before the event, earlier if it falls in a holiday season. College and high school students are a source of relatively inexpensive help. Since they tend to be inexperienced, for large or complex affairs be sure to have a reliable captain to supervise them. I once catered a large bar mitzvah for which the captain hired college friends as waiters and then proved reluctant to prod or push them to maintain the proper level of service. Party agencies, culinary art schools, employment agencies specializing in the restaurant business, and some colleges provide professional waiter and bartending services, most requiring a three- to five-hour minimum. Specify the type of dress, such as tuxedo, white waiter's jacket and dark slacks, suit, or a theme-related outfit. Have the service staff arrive about an hour before the party and utilize them to help with the setup and, if they are capable, with setting out and garnishing the food.

CLEANUP HINTS

- Place tubs or trash cans filled with soapy water in the kitchen to soak dirty dishes throughout the party. This frees up the sink and gives a head start on cleanup.

- Wash all pots and utensils that will possibly be used again for another task as soon as each stage of preparation is completed.

- Strategically place garbage containers or bags near the party area for collecting used disposable items during the party. Have plenty of large garbage bags handy for a quick and efficient cleanup afterward.

DINNER PARTIES

A dinner party, whether formal or informal, is the best way to entertain a small number of guests or to observe ceremonious occasions. Usually smaller than other forms of entertaining, dinner parties lend themselves to conversation and intimacy. Some dinner parties are preceded by a cocktail hour in which the guests mingle and nosh on light snacks and sip drinks. Dinners progress at an orderly pace, ranging from four courses—appetizer, salad, entrée accompanied by a starch and one to two vegetables, and dessert—to six courses, including soup and fish. The courses usually grow increasingly larger as the meal progresses, except for dessert. The general rule is to serve per person 2 ounces of appetizer, 6 to 8 ounces of soup, 2 ounces of fish, one large handful of salad, 4 to 6 ounces of entrée, and 2 to 3 ounces of dessert. When serving a smaller number of courses, increase the portion size.

The food at a dinner party should be special. It need not be overly elaborate and therefore ostentatious and unapproachable. Rather, what makes a meal interesting is food that looks and tastes good. A spicy first course should be followed by a palate-cleansing dish before the arrival of the entrée, so as not to dominate the latter. An appropriate wine is served with the main course, but different wines can also accompany the appetizer, fish, and/or dessert.

Since elegance is the key to dinner parties, the decor should be correspondingly elegant yet understated. This is a chance to use your best china, silver, and glassware. For casual occasions, disposable plates are acceptable. Formal dinners have guidelines for the table setting: the tablecloth should hang at least 9 inches below the edge of the table; the rim of the dinner plate and the flatware should be 1 inch from the edge of the table; and there should be 24 inches between the centers of dinner plates. The rule for forks and spoons is to place them in relation to when they will be used: the first used is the farthest from the plate. Forks go to the left of the dinner plate; knives, blades facing the plate, and spoons to the right.

It is best to figure out the seating arrangements ahead of time. Place cards make seating easy for small dinner parties and are necessary for a crowd of twelve or more. Since my family tends to have rather large Passover Seders, we find that place cards make the start smoother and quicker. Assigning the task of making the place cards to the kids gives them an opportunity to contribute to the occasion and keeps them occupied.

There are three types of service traditionally used at sit-down dinners: American, English, and French. With American service the food is arranged on the plates in the kitchen, then placed before the diners. This method not only is efficient but allows the host to set the plate attractively. With English service the food is served on platters that are passed and the guests help themselves. With French service the host or waiter holds a platter while placing the food on the plates in front of the guests. The latter is generally reserved for large, formal affairs and requires an abundance of waiters, at least one for every ten guests. For formal affairs the rule is to serve on the left and remove from the right. For casual sit-down gatherings, pass platters of food.

BUFFETS

A buffet is like Hemingway's Paris, a movable feast. Although a sit-down dinner may be the most elegant and intimate style of dining, it is rather impractical for a large number of guests, as it requires plenty of table space and the additional expense of waiters. A buffet is generally appropriate for more than fifteen people. Since the guests come to the

food rather than vice versa, it is the easiest way to manage a large crowd. A buffet also provides the opportunity for a wider selection of foods, both hot and cold.

There are two basic types of buffets: lap-style and sit-down. At a lap-style buffet the guests help themselves to food displayed on one or more tables, then sit or stand wherever they find space or feel comfortable. Meat should be presliced and deboned, and vegetables should be bite-size. Avoid using too many sauces and gravies or serving awkward foods like spaghetti. Although lap-style buffets are uncomfortable—diners must juggle their plates on their knees and find a resting spot for their glasses—they are frequently necessary, as many homes lack sufficient table space.

At a sit-down buffet the guests serve themselves from the buffet table, then take their seats at a set table. Individual servings are appropriate for sit-down buffets, as this more formal atmosphere allows for a larger variety of food and the guests do not have to balance plates on their laps. If you have a sit-down buffet, you may want to have an appetizer, a soup, or a salad on the tables when the guests arrive. Otherwise, it may be best to serve only breads and rolls, a main course, side dishes, and a dessert. For a crowd of sixty, plan on one linen napkin for each guest plus a dozen extra.

There are two types of service at buffets: self-service and waiter service. No waiter service is necessary for groups of less than twenty-five. For larger crowds you may want to consider some serving help. A buffet for sixty requires a wait staff of no more than four and, depending on the type of bar, possibly one or two bartenders. A server is especially advisable for the entrée and other expensive dishes, since too many people take more than they can eat. This is being wise, not miserly. It is better to let the guests come back for seconds than to waste food. Be sure to divide more expensive items into smaller portions and to use smaller spoons to serve them to control the amount and speed at which they are dispersed. Otherwise, you could find a dish used up before all of your guests are served. The general rule is to prepare per person a 6- to 8-ounce entrée when guests are serving themselves; 5 to 7 ounces when a waiter serves.

Whatever type of buffet you use, the food must be easy to reach and, to avoid backtracking, arranged in a logical manner so the guests receive first a plate, then the food, and finally the eating utensils. This is key to keeping the traffic flowing smoothly. If the table is located in the center of the room, the items can be orchestrated in a circular pattern, with a logical and noticeable starting and stopping point. For large groups a double-line buffet is preferable, providing access routes on both sides of the table moving in either the same or opposite directions. To prevent congestion, it is advisable not to start the buffet line from both ends of the table and meeting in the center. If there is not enough room on the table, the dishes and flatware may be placed on a separate table or, in the case of a sit-down buffet, on the dining tables. Beverages are frequently placed in a separate location as well.

A buffet table is generally arranged in the following order:

Dinner Plates → Entrée → Starch → Vegetables and Salads → Bread → Napkins → Flatware

Do not overdecorate the buffet table, as the food should dominate. Place serving utensils next to each dish. Allow enough room between or in front of the serving platters for the guests to set down their plates. Leave the serving dishes uncovered while the guests help themselves. To save time, prepare extra platters of food in advance to replace depleted or empty ones.

On more than one occasion I have suffered from severe stomach troubles after attending a party (fortunately, never one that I catered). To prevent food-borne illnesses, make sure that everything the food touches—including hands, cutting boards, counters, and serving utensils—is clean. Do not leave hot or cold food at room temperature for more than two hours. To keep foods hot, serve them in chafing dishes or on electric hot trays. When everyone has been served, you can cover those dishes that need to be kept warm. Serve cold foods, especially those containing meat, poultry, fish, and eggs, in medium-size quantities and replace when needed. Be especially careful on hot days. To keep crudités, salads, and other foods on the tables fresh-looking, cover them with damp towels that you then remove just before the guests arrive. Refrigerate any leftovers immediately.

If someone will be serving your guests, place the table toward the side of the room. If your guests will be helping themselves, place the table toward the center of the room so that they can reach all sides. An 8-foot table (96 by 30 inches) with access from both sides will serve up to fifty people for a buffet; use two or three tables for a larger crowd. To

cover the table, use a 120- by 54-inch linen cloth plus 14 feet of skirting (leaving one side open).

Dessert may be served on a separate table or on a rolling cart to reduce congestion. Place the dessert table near an electrical outlet so that coffee and hot water urns can be placed on or near it. If you are using the same table for the entire buffet, have a few napkins available to cover the inevitable spills.

COCKTAIL PARTIES

In the 1920s during Prohibition, Americans instituted a new form of entertaining at which guests were served finger food appetizers and spirits while standing, which enabled them to make a quick exit if necessary. Today the cocktail party is an effective way of hosting a large number of people at one time while providing the most conducive form of social interaction. At times a cocktail party may precede dinner and last up to one hour; on other occasions it constitutes the entire party, lasting two to three hours. In either case, the menu should include an interesting variety of hors d'oeuvres.

Cocktail parties are appropriate for groups of fifteen or more. In figuring the number of guests who will fit in the available space, estimate 5 square feet of floor space per person to prevent congestion. About a week before the party, telephone any invitees who have failed to respond in order to better gauge the turnout. You will need at least one waiter for a crowd of fifty, more if you intend on having some of the hors d'oeuvres passed.

Planning for a cocktail party is a balancing act, as hors d'oeuvres are generally the most time-consuming items to prepare and a wide variety is the norm. Keep in mind the amount of time required for each item. The more items that can be prepared in advance or frozen and baked or assembled on the day of the party, the better. Consider the available oven space in determining the number and quantity of hot hors d'oeuvres.

Hors d'oeuvres at cocktail parties should have a balance of colors, flavors, temperatures, and food groups—fish, meat, poultry, and vegetables or dairy, fish, and vegetables. The hors d'oeuvres should be bite-size and boneless, and have little or no sauce. The primary ingredients of each appetizer should differ from those of the rest. Milder foods should be served if wine is the only spirit; spicier ones if hard liquor is available. There should be a mixture of cold and hot items; hors d'oeuvres remain warm for about 5 minutes. Not all of the hors d'oeuvres must be expensive or intricate.

Canapés have a major disadvantage over other hors d'oeuvres—the bread base can become soggy. To avoid this problem, spread the bread with butter or margarine to pro-

tect it from the topping, allow the guests to spread the topping on the base themselves, or have waiters serve the canapés from a tray.

The arrangement of hors d'oeuvres on a serving plate or tray creates a visual effect that enhances the appearance of the food. The trays should be simply and attractively garnished and uncluttered. Replenish the trays frequently to maintain the look.

If serving hors d'oeuvres before a dinner, estimate three to four per person. For cocktail parties lasting about two hours, plan on seven to ten per person. For those lasting more than two hours, plan on eight to twelve per person. For crudités, plan on five to six pieces per person, and for spreads and dips, plan on 1 to 2 ounces per person. Of course, the more extensive the selection, the less is required of each food. The more popular tidbits tend to go more quickly, so they should not be set out at the beginning of the party or at one time. Estimate two to three drinks per person for a two-hour cocktail party.

PASSING THE BAR

When I first began catering, I sought advice for ordering liquor from various books. Inevitably, I was left with vast quantities of leftover spirits, and if I had followed the advice on the amount of food, I would have been sorely lacking. In estimating the correct amount of liquor for a particular party, take into account the ethnicity, age, and preferences of the guests and the type of affair. People generally drink more at cocktail parties than at a brit. One 750-ml bottle each of vodka, scotch, and rum, with optional bottles of bourbon and/or gin, plus 6 liters of seltzer will be sufficient for a crowd of forty or fewer. More liquor is necessary if there is a bartender preparing mixed drinks. You will also need mixers such as club soda, ginger ale, and cola—allow 1 pint per person. Estimate 3 liters of soft drinks and 3 quarts of juice (such as orange, tomato, grapefruit, and cranberry) for a party of twenty-five; 5 liters of soft drinks and 4 quarts of juice for forty. The average drink contains 1½ ounces of liquor, 3 to 4 ounces of mixer, and two to three ice cubes.

Bar supplies include bar fruit (lemons, limes, oranges, maraschino cherries, and olives), a cutting board, corkscrews, stirrers, bottle openers, ice containers, and a bar rag. Prepare mixes such as Bloody Marys and whiskey sours in advance. Since many people use a clean glass when refreshing their drink, allow two to three glasses per person. A standard 12-ounce wineglass is appropriate for all drinks. A full-service bar may also include cocktail (martini), old-fashioned (short), and highball (tall) glasses. Figure four cocktail napkins per person. In addition, you will need at least 1 pound of ice per person plus another bag for cooling the wine and beer.

In consideration of today's taste, place more emphasis on wine and beer than on hard liquor. Serve 5 to 6 ounces of wine per glass. For a group of fifteen, estimate three bottles of white wine, one of red wine, and eight 12-ounce bottles of beer; for a party of forty, estimate eight bottles of white wine, three of red wine, and fourteen 12-ounce bottles of beer (preferably several varieties). For larger parties, consider obtaining a keg or more of beer, possibly several varieties, from a local microbrewery.

The easiest and least expensive bar setup is self-service. If you are serving mixed drinks, you might consider hiring a bartender. A professional bartender's duties include setting up the bar, cutting the fruit, tending bar, and breaking down the bar. To avoid the cost of hiring a professional, ask a capable friend to assume the responsibility. One competent bartender can serve fifty people.

HOW MUCH?

(Suggested amounts for 20 people. Double the amount for 40 and so forth.)

CRUDITÉ TRAY AND SALADS

Broccoli	1 small head, cut into small florets
Carrots	1 pound, cut into 3-inch slices
Cauliflower	1 small head, cut into small florets
Celery	1 pound, cut into 3-inch slices
Cucumber	1 medium, cut into 3-inch slices
Green beans	½ pound
Green bell pepper	1 medium, cut into thin slices
Red bell pepper	1 medium, cut into thin slices
Yellow bell pepper	1 medium, cut into thin slices
Cherry tomatoes	1 pint
Zucchini	1 medium, cut into 3-inch slices
Tossed salad	2½ gallons
Salad dressing/dips	2 cups (2 tablespoons per person)

FRUIT PLATTER

Watermelon	1 small (about 6 pounds)
Cantaloupes	2 medium, peeled and sliced
Honeydews	2 medium, peeled and sliced
Blueberries	2 pints
Strawberries	2 pints
Grapes	1 to 2 pounds

Pineapples	2 medium, peeled and sliced
Oranges	4 medium, peeled and sliced
Grapefruit	4 medium, peeled and sliced

BREADS AND SPREADS

Rye or white bread	2 loaves/20 slices per loaf (2 slices per person)
Rolls	30 (1½ per person)
French bread	1 pound
Crackers	1 pound (4 to 6 per person)
Butter or margarine	8 ounces (1½ pats per person)
Mayonnaise	1 cup (2 teaspoons per person)
Mustard	½ cup (1 teaspoon per person)

BARBECUE OR PICNIC

Meat, with bone	10 pounds (8 ounces per person)
Meat, boneless	5 pounds (4 ounces per person)
Cold cuts	3 to 4 pounds as appetizer (2 to 3 ounces per person); 5 to 7 pounds as main course (4 to 5 ounces per person)
Beef, ground	5 pounds
Chicken	12 pounds
Hot dogs	4 pounds
Baked beans	2½ pounds; 2½ quarts (½ cup per person)
Potatoes, mashed	6 pounds (½ cup per person)
Potato salad	3½ quarts (¾ cup per person)
Coleslaw	3½ quarts (½ cup per person)
Pickles	1 quart (1 per person)

MISCELLANEOUS

Potato chips	20 ounces (1 ounce per person)
Pretzels	20 ounces (1 ounce per person)
Mixed nuts	20 ounces (2 tablespoons per person)
Cheese	2 pounds as side dish (2 to 3 ounces per person); 6 pounds as center of attention

Olives	3 cups (3 per person)
Cookies	5 dozen (3 per person)
Cakes	2 (13- by 9-inch) single-layer cakes or 2 (9-inch) layer cakes
Paper napkins	3 to 5 per person

BEVERAGES

Coffee, ground	½ pound (yields 1¼ gallons; 1 cup coffee per 2½ quarts water)
Sugar (for coffee)	½ pound
Cream (for coffee)	1 pint (2 teaspoons per person)
Milk	3 quarts (⅔ cup per person)
Juice	3 quarts (⅔ cup per person)
Soft drinks (soda)	15 liters
Punch	1 gallon (4 to 8 ounces per person)
Ice	20 to 40 pounds (you will need nearly twice as much ice in summer than in winter)

BAR
(3 drinks per person)

Dry white wine	4 (750-ml) bottles
Dry red wine	1 (750-ml) bottle
Champagne (brut)	4 (750-ml) bottles (4 ounces per serving/6 servings per bottle)
Beer	8 (12-ounce) bottles
Vodka	1 liter
Scotch	1 liter
Bourbon	1 (750-ml) bottle
Rum	1 (750-ml) bottle
Dry vermouth	1 fifth
Seltzer	5 liters
Crème de cassis	1 fifth
Tonic water	3 liters
Mineral water	3 liters
Ginger ale	1 liter
Cola	1 liter
Orange juice	1 quart

| Grapefruit juice | 1 quart |
| Tomato juice | 1 quart |

Garnishes (3 limes, 2 lemons, and 1 orange for wedges and peels; celery sticks for Bloody Marys; 1 small bottle green olives and cocktail onions for martinis; 1 small bottle maraschino cherries)

TABLES

8-foot rectangular table	seats 10
6-foot rectangular table	seats 8
72-inch round table	seats 12
60-inch round table	seats 10

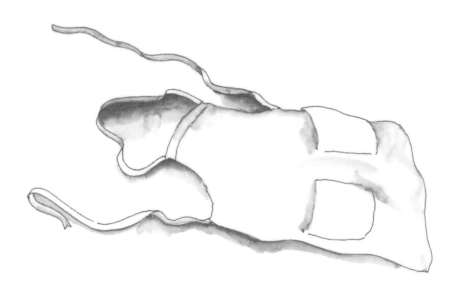

The Holiday and Sabbath Table

A Traditional Rosh Hashanah Dinner

SERVES 8

*R*osh Hashanah (literally, Head of the Year), a two-day holiday falling on the first two days of the month of Tishri, marks the creation of the world. The ten days from Rosh Hashanah through Yom Kippur are called Yamim Noraim (Days of Awe), a period of concentrated introspection, prayer, and inner transformation. According to tradition, it is during these days that the fate of all people is determined for the coming year. We greet one another with a special phrase, *L'shanah tova tikataiv* (May you be inscribed for a good year). Yet despite its poignancy, Rosh Hashanah is also an occasion of joy and feasting, for in the words of the Talmud, God declares, "On Rosh Hashanah I look upon all of you as if you had been created for the first time."

At this time of the year, the performance of symbolic acts is of special significance and food plays a vital role. The Talmud (Keritot 6:A) mentions five foods to eat on Rosh Hashanah—gourds, black-eyed peas, leeks, beets, and dates. Each of these foods is specified because of a similarity between its name and another word, thereby signifying a wish for the coming year. The Hebrew word for "gourd" (*kraa*) is similar to *yikara* (to be called out), suggesting that our good deeds are called out at this time of judgment. The Aramaic word for "black-eyed peas" is *rubiya,* which also means "abundance" and "increase." The Hebrew word for "leek" (*karti*) is similar to *yikartu* (to be cut off), signifying that the Jews' enemies should be cut off. The word for "beet" (*selek*) is reminiscent of *she'yistalqu* (that they will be removed), referring to the Jews' enemies. Similarly, *tamar* (the Hebrew word for "date") sounds like *yitamu* (to be removed).

Other Rosh Hashanah foods are symbols of fertility and plenty, including seeds and fruits and vegetables that contain many seeds. In many Sephardic homes a cornucopia of symbolic fruits and vegetables is served in a basket called a *trashkal,* the head of the family removing one item at a time and reciting an appropriate verse. An ancient custom is to eat a new fruit—one not yet sampled that season—on the second night of Rosh Hashanah while reciting the blessing *Shehechiyanu* (Who has preserved us).

The most popular and widespread Rosh Hashanah tradition is the dipping of apple slices in honey while reciting the phrase "May it be Your will to inaugurate for us a good and sweet year." This custom has many layers of meaning: honey is a food in the Bible associated with the land of Israel as well as being an ancient symbol of immortality and truth; in mystical literature an apple orchard is frequently pictured as a symbol of the Divine Presence; the Song of Songs (2:3) attests to the apple's sweetness, and Proverbs (25:11) to its beauty; and the sweetness of both the honey and the apple serves as a wish for a sweet year to come. In this vein Rosh Hashanah dishes are commonly sweetened, particularly with honey and fruits.

There are foods traditionally avoided on Rosh Hashanah. Eastern Europeans eschew nuts as well as any sour food, even sweet-and-sour dishes. In North Africa foods that are black, a color associated with mourning—including olives, raisins, eggplant, coffee, and chocolate—are banned from the table, although some permit these items on the second day.

The following meal combines an assortment of traditional Ashkenazic and Sephardic dishes.

FRUITED CHALLAH
APPLE SLICES WITH HONEY
SEPHARDIC LEEK SOUP
MOROCCAN DATE-STUFFED BAKED FISH
VEAL WITH FIGS
MIDDLE EASTERN YELLOW RICE
CARROT RING
SPINACH AND FRUIT SALAD
HONEY COOKIES
PLUM TART
TEA AND COFFEE

 Wine Suggestions: Dry Riesling, Gewürztraminer, or Chenin Blanc

Fruited Challah
2 LARGE OR 3 MEDIUM LOAVES

*T*he large amount of egg, fat, and sugar gives this bread a rich flavor, golden color, soft crust, and tender, fine crumb. Challah for Rosh Hashanah and Sukkot is traditionally kneaded with raisins or other dried fruits, a symbol of sweetness and the harvest. Traditional Rosh Hashanah shapes include a round (symbolizing continuity, with no beginning and no end), a spiral (symbolizing a person's eventual ascent to heaven), and a crown (symbolizing the King of the universe). On Rosh Hashanah the challah is traditionally dipped in honey rather than salt, a custom that many families continue during Sukkot.

2 (¼-ounce) packages (about 5 teaspoons total) active dry yeast or 1 (1-ounce) cake fresh yeast
2 cups warm water (105 to 115 degrees for dry yeast; 80 to 85 degrees for fresh yeast)
⅔ cup sugar or honey
3 to 4 large eggs
½ cup vegetable oil
1 tablespoon table salt or 5 teaspoons kosher salt
About 8 cups unbleached all-purpose flour
1½ cups raisins (or ¾ cup raisins and ¾ cup coarsely chopped dried apricots or dates)
Egg wash (1 large egg beaten with 1 tablespoon water)
About 3 tablespoons poppy seeds or sesame seeds (optional)

1. Dissolve the yeast in ½ cup of the warm water. Add 1 teaspoon of the sugar and let stand until foamy, 5 to 10 minutes.
2. Stir in the remaining water, remaining sugar, eggs, oil, salt, and 3 cups of the flour. Beat in enough of the remaining flour, ½ cup at a time, until the mixture holds together.
3. Place on a lightly floured surface and knead until smooth and elastic, about 10 minutes. Knead in the raisins. Place in a greased large bowl, turning to coat. Cover loosely with plastic wrap or a towel and let rise in a warm, draft-free place until double in bulk, about 1½ hours, or in the refrigerator overnight.
4. Punch down the dough and divide in half or thirds. Firmly pat the dough into rectangles, roll up jelly-roll style, then shape into balls. Place on greased baking sheets and flatten slightly. Cover loosely and let rise at room temperature until double in

bulk, about 45 minutes, or in the refrigerator for up to 1 day. (Let stand at room temperature for about 30 minutes before baking.)
5. Preheat the oven to 350 degrees.
6. Brush the challah with the egg wash and, if desired, sprinkle with the poppy seeds. (The egg produces a soft, shiny crust as well as helping the seeds to adhere to the surface.) Bake until the bread is golden brown and sounds hollow when tapped on the bottom, about 35 minutes for medium-size challahs or 45 minutes for large ones. Transfer to a rack and let cool.

Sephardic Leek Soup (*Sopa de Prasa*)
8 SERVINGS

¼ cup olive or vegetable oil
10 medium (about 2 pounds) leeks, trimmed, sliced, and well washed
   (or 5 leeks and 2 large yellow onions)
2 large baking potatoes or 3 medium carrots, peeled and grated
1 bunch fresh parsley, chopped
8 cups chicken broth or water
About 1½ teaspoons salt
About ¼ teaspoon ground black pepper
Pinch of grated nutmeg (optional)

1. Heat the oil in a 6-quart pot over medium heat. Add the leeks and potatoes and sauté until softened, 5 to 10 minutes.
2. Add the parsley, broth, salt, pepper, and if desired, the nutmeg. Bring to a boil, cover, reduce the heat to low, and simmer until tender, about 40 minutes. Adjust the seasonings. Serve the soup as is or puree in a food processor. Serve warm or chilled.

Moroccan Date-Stuffed Baked Fish
8 SERVINGS

*T*here is an ancient custom of displaying the head of a fish or lamb on the Rosh Hashanah table as a sign that "we will be the *rosh* [head] and not the tail" (the reverse of Deuteronomy 28:44), a play on the word *rosh,* signifying that in the coming year we should progress, not regress. For this reason, dishes made from lamb or calves' brains were once common Rosh Hashanah offerings. Fish and lamb also contain other meanings: fish is a symbol of fruitfulness, the Jewish people, and the Leviathan to be served at the feast following the arrival of the messiah; lamb is a reminder of the ram substituted for Isaac as a sacrifice and of the shofar.

Alsatians enjoy *carpe à la Juive aux raisins* (sweet-and-sour carp); Germans prepare a similar dish characteristically flavored with gingersnaps; and Italians serve the classic *pesce all'Ebraica,* a sweet-and-sour fish studded with pine nuts. Turkish and Greek Jews commonly stew their holiday fish in sauces made from tomatoes, greengage plums, or prunes. Indian Jews offer versions vibrantly flavored with curry or wrapped in lettuce leaves.

Date-stuffed fish, a traditional northwest African dish, utilizes several prominent Rosh Hashanah symbols, including fish, rice, and dates.

STUFFING
1 pound pitted dates, coarsely chopped (about 3 cups)
3 cups cooked rice
½ cup sugar or honey
¼ cup (½ stick) unsalted margarine, melted
1 teaspoon ground cinnamon
¾ teaspoon ground black pepper
½ teaspoon ground coriander
About ½ teaspoon salt

2 (4- to 5-pound) whole red snapper, sea bass, or grouper,
*   or 8 brook trout, cleaned but head and tail intact*
Salt to taste
Ground black pepper to taste
2 medium onions, sliced
About ⅓ cup vegetable oil or melted margarine

1. Preheat the oven to 400 degrees. Brush a large baking pan with oil or margarine.
2. Combine all the stuffing ingredients.
3. Rinse the fish inside and out and pat dry. Sprinkle with salt and pepper. Fill the cavities with the stuffing and sew up the opening or skewer with toothpicks.
4. Scatter the onions in the prepared pan. Place the fish in the pan and brush with a little oil. Cut several parallel slashes in the skin of each fish. (This prevents the skin from shrinking.)
5. Bake, brushing occasionally with oil, until the fish are tender and the flesh loses its translucency, 30 to 40 minutes. Remove the thread or toothpicks. If desired, serve with lemon wedges.

HINT: To prevent sticking when chopping dates, lightly oil the knife blade or kitchen shears.

Veal with Figs
8 SERVINGS

*T*he fig figures prominently in Jewish literature and tradition; the only fruit or vegetable mentioned more often in the Bible and Talmud is the grape. Fig dishes are popular additions to Rosh Hashanah fare, and this one reflects the eastern European love of meats cooked with sweeteners.

1 (6-pound) boneless veal shoulder, rolled and tied with twine
1½ to 2 pounds fresh, dried, or canned figs
1 cup dry white wine
1 cup water
½ cup honey
1 teaspoon ground cinnamon
1 teaspoon ground coriander or 1 tablespoon grated orange zest
About ½ teaspoon salt
¼ teaspoon ground black pepper or 10 whole peppercorns
1 bay leaf

1. Preheat the oven to 375 degrees.
2. Place the veal and figs in a large roasting pan. Combine the remaining ingredients and pour over the top.
3. Bake, basting occasionally and adding more water if necessary to keep the figs moist, until the veal is tender and browned, about 1½ hours.
4. Remove the veal to a cutting board or platter, cover loosely with aluminum foil, and let stand for at least 15 minutes. Remove the twine and cut the veal into slices. Serve with the figs and cooking liquid.

Middle Eastern Yellow Rice
8 SERVINGS

*M*iddle Eastern Jews prepare rice in three basic ways: plain white, red (with tomatoes), and for special occasions, yellow.

2 tablespoons vegetable oil
1 teaspoon turmeric
2 teaspoons ground cumin (optional)
2½ cups long-grain white rice
5 cups chicken broth or water
About 1¼ teaspoons salt

1. Heat the oil in a large saucepan over medium heat. Add the turmeric and, if desired, the cumin and stir for 1 minute. Add the rice and sauté until opaque, about 3 minutes.
2. Add the broth and salt. Bring to a boil, cover, reduce the heat to low, and simmer until the rice is tender, about 18 minutes. Remove from the heat and let stand, covered, for about 10 minutes. Fluff with a fork. To make a rice mold: Lightly pack the hot cooked rice into an oiled 8-cup ring mold or bowl, allow to stand for 1 minute, place a serving plate over top, then invert and lift off the mold.

Carrot Ring

8 SERVINGS

*T*he carrot is a popular eastern European Rosh Hashanah food partially because of its name: in Yiddish, *mehren* (multiply or increase), and in Hebrew, *gezer* (tear), which is similar to *gezayrah* (decree), indicating that any unfavorable decrees should be torn up. In addition, the carrot's sweetness fits in with the holiday's theme. And carrots have an additional attribute—when sliced they resemble gold coins.

2½ cups all-purpose flour
1 teaspoon baking soda
¾ teaspoon baking powder
1 teaspoon salt
1 teaspoon ground cinnamon or grated lemon zest
½ teaspoon ground ginger or nutmeg
1 cup vegetable shortening or softened unsalted margarine
1 cup packed brown sugar
4 large eggs
2 tablespoons fresh lemon juice
2 tablespoons water
2 cups (about 12 ounces) grated carrots
½ cup raisins or chopped dates (optional)

1. Preheat the oven to 350 degrees. Grease a 10-inch ring mold or large loaf pan.
2. Combine the flour, baking soda, baking powder, salt, cinnamon, and ginger. Beat together the shortening and sugar until light and fluffy. Beat in the eggs, one at a time. Add the lemon juice and water. Stir in the flour mixture, then the carrots and, if desired, the raisins.
3. Pour into the prepared pan. Place in a larger baking pan and add water to reach halfway up the sides of the filled pan. Bake until golden brown and a tester inserted in the center comes out clean, about 50 minutes. Serve warm or at room temperature.

Spinach and Fruit Salad
8 SERVINGS

*S*pinach salads, long popular in the Mediterranean region and Near East, are ideal fare for Rosh Hashanah. The similarity between *silkah,* the Aramaic word for "spinach" and "beet greens," is similar to the Hebrew *silake* (to remove), expressing the wish that our enemies be removed. According to tradition, each pomegranate contains 613 seeds, corresponding to the number of commandments in the Torah. Other seasonal fruits contribute additional symbolism.

20 ounces fresh spinach, torn into bite-size pieces
2 to 3 apples, cored and diced
½ cup pomegranate seeds
½ cup raisins, chopped figs, or chopped pitted dates
Sunflower or pumpkin seeds, hulled (optional)

DRESSING
¼ cup fresh lemon juice, red wine vinegar, or white vinegar
½ teaspoon dry mustard
About ½ teaspoon salt
About ½ teaspoon ground black pepper
½ teaspoon curry powder (optional)
½ cup olive or vegetable oil

Combine the spinach, apples, pomegranate seeds, and raisins in a large bowl. Combine the lemon juice, mustard, salt, pepper, and if desired, the curry powder. In a slow, steady stream, whisk in the oil. Drizzle over the salad, tossing to coat. If desired, sprinkle with the sunflower seeds.

Honey Cookies

ABOUT THIRTY 4-INCH OR SEVENTY 2½-INCH COOKIES

*F*or Rosh Hashanah I like to cut these cookies into the shapes of shofars (ram's horns), scales of justice, fish, and apples.

½ cup vegetable shortening
½ cup honey
2¼ cups all-purpose flour
1 teaspoon baking soda
¼ teaspoon salt
¼ teaspoon ground allspice
¼ teaspoon ground cinnamon
¼ teaspoon ground cloves

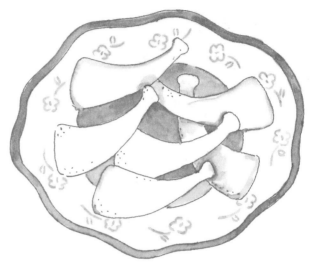

1. Bring the shortening and honey to a boil over medium heat and boil for 1 minute. Let cool.
2. Sift together the flour, baking soda, salt, and spices. Stir into the honey mixture. Form into a ball, wrap in plastic, and chill until firm, at least 1 hour.
3. Preheat the oven to 350 degrees.
4. Divide the dough in half. On a lightly floured surface, roll the dough to a ⅛-inch thickness, cut into desired shapes, and place on an ungreased baking sheet. Or shape tablespoons of the dough into balls, place on a baking sheet, and flatten with the bottom of a glass.
5. Bake until lightly colored, about 12 minutes. Let the cookies stand until firm, about 1 minute, then remove to a wire rack and let cool completely.

Plum Tart
8 TO 10 SERVINGS

*C*entral European Jews made use of seasonal plums to make this much-beloved treat.

PÂTE SABLÉE
¾ cup (1½ sticks) unsalted margarine, softened
⅓ cup sugar
1 large egg or 2 large egg yolks
½ teaspoon salt
2 cups all-purpose flour
Ice water as needed

FILLING
3 pounds ripe firm plums, preferably Italian (Lombard),
*   pitted and quartered*
About ¼ cup sugar
2 tablespoons unsalted margarine

1. To make the pastry: Beat the margarine and sugar until smooth and creamy. Add the egg and salt. Gradually blend in the flour. (The dough should have the consistency of a sugar cookie dough. If it is too stiff, add a little ice water.) Form into a ball and flatten into a disk. Cover with plastic wrap and refrigerate for at least 1 hour and up to 1 week.
2. On a lightly floured surface, roll out the dough into a ¼-inch-thick round about 12 inches in diameter. Transfer to a 10-inch springform pan or tart pan. Refrigerate for at least 30 minutes.
3. Preheat the oven to 400 degrees.
4. Arrange the plums, cut side up, in tight concentric circles in the pastry shell. Sprinkle with the sugar and dot with the margarine.
5. Bake until the fruit is tender and the pastry is golden brown, about 30 minutes. Let the tart cool for at least 10 minutes before removing the outer rim of the pan. Serve warm or at room temperature.

VARIATIONS

Streusel Plum Tart: Combine 1 cup all-purpose flour, ⅔ cup sugar, ⅛ teaspoon salt, and 1½ teaspoons ground cinnamon or grated lemon zest. Cut in ½ cup (1 stick) unsalted margarine to produce coarse crumbs. Sprinkle over the top of the plums.

German Plum Tart: Brush the inside of the pastry with 2 tablespoons lekvar (plum jam) or roll out 8 ounces of marzipan and press into the bottom of the shell.

A Healthy New Year Dinner

SERVES 8

*A*shkenazic food has a reputation—alas, one all too frequently warranted—for being unhealthy. Like other forms of cooking developed under conditions of extreme poverty, eastern European fare consists primarily of starches. Although starchy foods are not inherently bad, Ashkenazic cooks, to make up for the dearth of herbs and spices available to them, added copious amounts of schmaltz, sugar, and salt to impart flavor. The results certainly taste good—no mean feat considering the limited number of ingredients available—but these dishes tend to conflict with modern ideas of healthful eating. As more and more people have adopted diets higher in vegetables and fiber and lower in saturated fats, cholesterol, sodium, and refined sweeteners, they have adapted traditional Jewish fare to fit into their healthier lifestyles. Thus, "healthy Jewish cooking" is no longer an oxymoron.

HONEY WHOLE-WHEAT CHALLAH
APPLE SLICES WITH HONEY
MOCK CHOPPED LIVER
MOROCCAN PUMPKIN SOUP
SEPHARDIC BAKED FISH WITH VEGETABLES
SPINACH-STUFFED CHICKEN BREASTS
BROWN RICE PILAF
ZUCCHINI RINGS WITH JULIENNE OF VEGETABLES
INDIVIDUAL APPLE-CRANBERRY STRUDELS
TEA AND COFFEE

 Wine Suggestions: Dry Riesling, fruity Chardonnay, or Chenin Blanc

Honey Whole-Wheat Challah

2 LARGE OR 3 MEDIUM LOAVES

*W*hole-wheat flour, ground from whole milled wheat kernels, is a valuable source of natural nutrients as well as fiber. Although for those accustomed to white flour, whole wheat's earthy flavor and heavier texture may take a little getting used to, it can prove a healthful and flavorful addition to the diet. I sometimes make this challah for cooking classes (I arrive early and prepare another batch in order to give it time to rise), and students who swear they don't like whole-wheat products find it delicious. (Of course, coming hot from the oven also helps.) Since this bread contains no eggs, it is cholesterol-free.

2 (¼-ounce) packages (about 5 teaspoons total)
  active dry yeast or 1 (1-ounce) cake fresh yeast
2¼ cups warm water (105 to 115 degrees for
  dry yeast; 80 to 85 degrees for fresh yeast)
⅓ to ½ cup honey
¼ cup vegetable shortening or oil
1 tablespoon table salt or 4½ teaspoons kosher salt
3¼ cups whole-wheat flour
About 3¼ cups unbleached all-purpose flour
1 cup raisins or dried currants (or ½ cup raisins and
  ½ cup chopped dried apricots or dates) (optional)

1. Dissolve the yeast in ½ cup of the warm water. Stir in 1 teaspoon of the honey and let stand until foamy, 5 to 10 minutes.
2. Stir in the remaining water, remaining honey, shortening, salt, and whole-wheat flour. Beat in enough all-purpose flour, ½ cup at a time, to make a workable dough.
3. Place on a lightly floured surface and knead until smooth and elastic, 10 to 15 minutes. (Lightly oiling your hands before kneading makes whole-wheat dough more manageable.) Knead in the raisins if desired.
4. Place in a greased large bowl, turning to coat. Cover loosely with plastic wrap or a towel and let rise in a warm, draft-free place until almost double in bulk, about 1½ hours.

5. Punch down the dough and divide in half or thirds. Shape into rounds, spirals, or crowns and place on greased baking sheets. Cover loosely and let rise until double in bulk, about 1 hour.
6. Preheat the oven to 375 degrees.
7. Bake until the bread is golden brown and sounds hollow when tapped on the bottom, 35 to 45 minutes. Transfer to wire racks and let cool.

Mock Chopped Liver
8 SERVINGS

Chopped liver, one of the best known of all Jewish dishes (probably thanks to repeated references by Jewish comics), is a favorite Ashkenazic appetizer served on the Sabbath, at festivals, and on other special occasions. For these more health-conscious times, here is a vegetarian version. The meaty flavor of the mushrooms contributes to the deception, as does the liverlike grayish color. And unlike mock livers made from beans or peas, this version is perfect for Passover and, to my palate, is tastier.

2 tablespoons unsalted margarine or vegetable oil
2 shallots, finely chopped
1 pound mushrooms, finely chopped
About ½ teaspoon salt
Ground black pepper to taste

1. Melt the margarine in a large skillet over medium heat. Add the shallots and sauté until softened, about 2 minutes.
2. Add the mushrooms and sauté until the moisture is evaporated, about 10 minutes.
3. Purée the mushroom mixture. Season with the salt and pepper. Serve with crackers, matza, or fresh vegetables.

Moroccan Pumpkin Soup (L'Hamraak Garagh)

8 SERVINGS

This soup is a traditional Rosh Hashanah and Sukkot dish among Moroccan Jews, expressing the wish that just as the pumpkin is protected by a thick rind, so God will protect us. Four cups of canned pumpkin puree can be substituted for the fresh pumpkin.

1 cup dried chickpeas
3 tablespoons vegetable oil
2 leeks (white and light green part only)
    or 2 large onions, chopped (about 1½ cups)
8 cups beef broth, chicken broth, or water
2½ pounds pumpkin, butternut squash,
    or other winter squash,
    peeled, seeded, and diced (about 6 cups)
2 to 4 tablespoons sugar or honey
1 (3-inch) cinnamon stick or 2 teaspoons ground cinnamon
⅛ teaspoon ground allspice or nutmeg or pinch of cloves
About 2 teaspoons salt
Ground black pepper to taste

1. Soak the chickpeas in water to cover overnight. Drain.
2. Heat the oil in a large saucepan over medium heat. Add the leeks and sauté until soft and translucent, 5 to 10 minutes.
3. Add the broth, pumpkin, chickpeas, sugar, spices, and salt. Cover and simmer until the chickpeas are tender, about 1¼ hours.
4. If using the cinnamon stick, discard it. If desired, transfer the soup to a blender or food processor and puree until smooth. Return to the pot and check the seasonings.

Sephardic Baked Fish with Vegetables *(Plaki)*
8 SERVINGS

*T*his dish, also called *capama* by Sephardim, is a traditional Sabbath dish but is particularly popular at Rosh Hashanah because of the many symbolic meanings of fish: symbol of fertility and prosperity, reminder of the creation of life marked by Rosh Hashanah, and intimation of the messianic age ushered in by the Meal of the Righteous, at which the large fish called the Leviathan plays a prominent part.

3 tablespoons olive or vegetable oil
3 medium onions, sliced
3 to 4 cloves garlic, crushed
3 cups (about 1 pound) peeled, seeded, and chopped plum tomatoes
3 medium baking potatoes or carrots, sliced
2 medium green bell peppers, seeded and sliced
½ cup chopped fresh parsley
About 1 teaspoon salt
Ground black pepper to taste
⅛ teaspoon sugar or honey
4 pounds cod, flounder, grouper, halibut, sea bass, snapper, trout, or other
   firm-fleshed fish fillets, or 8 steaks (about 6 ounces each)

1. Preheat the oven to 350 degrees.
2. Heat the oil in a large saucepan over medium heat. Add the onions and sauté until soft and translucent, 5 to 10 minutes. Add the garlic and sauté for 30 seconds.
3. Add the tomatoes, potatoes, peppers, parsley, salt, pepper, and sugar and simmer until the tomatoes begin to break down, about 15 minutes. (The sauce can be prepared ahead, covered, and stored in the refrigerator for up to 2 days. Reheat before continuing.)
4. Spread half of the sauce in a large baking dish, add the fish in a single layer, and top with the remaining sauce.
5. Cover and bake until the fish is tender, about 1 hour. Serve warm or at room temperature.

Spinach-Stuffed Chicken Breasts

8 SERVINGS

The spinach filling creates an attractive contrast to the flesh when the chicken rolls are sliced.

SPINACH STUFFING

1 tablespoon vegetable oil
1 large onion, chopped (about ¾ cup)
1½ pounds fresh spinach, cooked and chopped, or 1 (1-pound)
    bag frozen chopped spinach, thawed and drained
¾ cup matza meal or bread crumbs
1 large egg, lightly beaten
About 1½ teaspoons salt
⅛ teaspoon grated nutmeg
Pinch of ground black pepper

8 chicken cutlets (4 skinned, boned, and halved chicken breasts)
Vegetable oil or melted margarine

1. Preheat the oven to 375 degrees. Lightly grease a shallow baking pan.
2. Heat the oil in a medium skillet over medium heat. Add the onion and sauté until soft and translucent, 5 to 10 minutes. Remove from the heat and stir in the remaining stuffing ingredients.
3. Place the cutlets between 2 sheets of wax paper. Using a meat mallet or heavy skillet, lightly pound the cutlets to an even ¼-inch thickness.
4. Spread about 3 tablespoons of the stuffing over each cutlet and roll up jelly-roll style. Place, seam side down, in the prepared pan and brush with oil or margarine.
5. Bake until tender, about 40 minutes. If desired, slice into pinwheel medallions. Serve warm or at room temperature.

Brown Rice Pilaf
8 SERVINGS

2 tablespoons vegetable oil or unsalted margarine
1 large onion, chopped (about ¾ cup)
2 cups long-grain brown rice
4 cups water
1 cup dried currants or raisins
1 (3-inch) cinnamon stick or ½ teaspoon ground cinnamon
About ½ teaspoon salt
¼ teaspoon ground black pepper
¼ cup chopped fresh parsley

1. Heat the oil in a medium saucepan over medium heat. Add the onion and sauté until soft and translucent, 5 to 10 minutes.
2. Add the rice and stir until well coated, about 3 minutes.
3. Add the water, currants, cinnamon, salt, and pepper. Bring to a boil, cover, reduce the heat to low, and simmer until the rice is tender, about 40 minutes.
4. Remove from the heat and let stand, covered, for 5 to 10 minutes. Fluff with a fork. If using a cinnamon stick, discard it. Stir in the parsley. (The pilaf can be prepared ahead, covered, refrigerated for up to 2 days, and reheated.) To make rice timbales: Pack the cooked rice mixture into timbale molds or custard cups and invert onto serving plates.

Zucchini Rings with Julienne of Vegetables
8 SERVINGS

This makes a very colorful presentation.

2 large (about 10 ounces each) zucchini
1 pound carrots, cut into sticks

1 pound green beans
Unsalted margarine or olive oil
Salt to taste
Ground black pepper to taste

1. Remove lengthwise strips of peel from the zucchini, leaving on equal-size strips of peel to create a striped effect. Cut the zucchini crosswise into 1- to 1½-inch pieces. Using a melon baller or spoon, hollow out the zucchini rounds, leaving ¼-inch-thick sides.
2. Cut the carrots and green beans to the same length, about 4 inches. Tightly pack into the center of the rings.
3. Bring a large pot of lightly salted water to a boil. Add the vegetables and cook until tender-crisp, about 5 minutes. Immerse the vegetable rings in ice water or rinse under cold running water to stop the cooking. Drain. (The rings can be stored in the refrigerator for 1 day.)
4. Preheat the oven to 300 degrees.
5. Top the vegetables with a little margarine and sprinkle with the salt and pepper. Cover and place in the oven until reheated.

Individual Apple-Cranberry Strudels
8 SERVINGS

This version transforms the classic dessert into individual portions.

1¼ pounds (about 3 medium) cooking apples, such as Golden Delicious,
  Jonathan, or Granny Smith, peeled, cored, and coarsely chopped
1 tablespoon fresh lemon juice
⅓ cup coarsely chopped, or dried, cranberries
About ½ cup sugar
¼ cup dry bread crumbs
¾ teaspoon ground cinnamon
8 sheets phyllo dough (each about 18 by 16 inches)
Cooking spray or ¼ cup (½ stick) unsalted margarine, melted
Confectioners' sugar (optional)

1. Preheat the oven to 375 degrees. Grease a large baking sheet.
2. Toss the apples with the lemon juice. Add the cranberries, sugar, bread crumbs, and cinnamon.
3. Place a phyllo sheet on a flat surface and lightly spray with the cooking spray or brush with the margarine. Fold in half from the shorter side. Spray with the cooking spray or brush with the margarine. Mound ½ cup of the filling along a short edge, leaving a 1-inch border on 3 sides. Fold over the sides of the phyllo, then roll up from the filling end.
4. Place, seam side down, on the prepared baking sheet and spray with the cooking spray or brush with the margarine. Bake until golden brown, about 30 minutes. (The strudels can be prepared 1 day in advance, covered loosely, stored at room temperature, and reheated at 400 degrees.) If desired, sprinkle with confectioners' sugar.

After the Fast

*T*radition relates that on the tenth day of the month of Tishri, Moses returned from Mount Sinai with the second set of tablets of the Ten Commandments and informed the people that they had been forgiven for the incident of the golden calf. Ever since, that day has been observed as Yom Kippur, the Day of Atonement. This twenty-five-hour fast, the culmination of a ten-day period that begins with Rosh Hashanah, is the most profoundly moving day on the Jewish calendar. Judaism believes that everyone has the power within to change, and through this day of physical self-denial, a person is able to look deep within his or her self to reach new spiritual heights. Yom Kippur, however, brings pardon only for those sins committed against heaven. Any wrong that a person inflicts upon others can be rectified only through appropriate reparation—hence, the ancient custom of asking friends and acquaintances for forgiveness and settling all disputes before the commencement of the fast.

As it is a fast day, there are, obviously, no traditional Yom Kippur foods. The meals before and after the fast, however, have developed their own traditions. The eve prior to the fast has a festive character. The table is set in the same way as for the Sabbath, and diners wear white clothes or their usual Sabbath clothing. Ukrainian Jews developed the custom of forming the challahs for the meal before the fast into images of ascension: birds (Isaiah 31:5), symbolizing that all sins should fly away and our prayers soar to the heavens; or ladders, reminiscent of Jacob's dream (Genesis 28:10–22). Dishes in the prefast meal are relatively bland so as not to increase thirst during the fast. Because of this, fish is avoided.

Kabbalists, noting that *gever,* the Hebrew word for "rooster," also means "man," viewed the link between men and chickens as mystical. Chicken, usually stewed, is the most common entrée, dating back to the medieval ritual of *kaparot,* whereby a person symbolically substituted a chicken for his sins. Moses Maimonides (1135–1204), the Spanish codifier, philosopher, and physician, recommended poultry soup for the weak and sick. In order to maintain their strength during the fast, Sephardim and Ashkenazim serve chicken soup, usually accompanied by rice, at the meal preceding Yom Kippur. Ashkenazim commonly serve chicken soup with kreplach (mystics compare the wrapping of dough with the divine envelopment of mercy and kindness and its triangular shape representing the three Patriarchs—Abraham, Isaac, and Jacob—through whose merit their descendants are forgiven).

The dishes served at the meal following the fast are included for their purported restorative powers, their symbolic significance, or since they should preferably be prepared before the holiday, simply their ability to keep. The break-the-fast can be as simple or elaborate as desired but is usu-

ally dairy, its whiteness befitting Yom Kippur's theme of purity. Although the pre–Yom Kippur meal rarely contains a dessert, it is customary to include some pastry when breaking the fast.

One year as I was leaving my apartment for the pre–Yom Kippur service, I turned the knob on the front door and the lock broke. Finding myself trapped in my apartment with Yom Kippur fast approaching, I telephoned several locksmiths before finding one who claimed he would "be there in less than an hour." He lied. The doorbell finally rang around midnight, after I had already retired for the evening. Fortunately, what to eat was not among my worries. To be sure, a fast day passes a lot more quickly when you are not trapped in your apartment, as do services without a *chazan* (cantor). I seemed to appreciate the post-fast meal more that year than in other years, perhaps because I postponed it until after I had arranged for another locksmith.

Fortunately, I had no guests scheduled that year. If you have guests coming to break the fast and your doors work, the following recipes should prove the right opening.

BAGELS OR ROLLS
YOGURT AND CUCUMBER SOUP
SYRIAN BAKED ZUCCHINI WITH CHEESE
FISH SALAD
TABBOULEH
SAVORY CHEESE PUDDING
ALMOND COFFEE CAKE
IRAQI CARDAMOM COOKIES
ORANGE JUICE, TEA, COFFEE, AND MILK

Yogurt and Cucumber Soup

8 SERVINGS

*Y*ogurt soup, popular fare in the Middle East, Central Asia, and the Balkans, makes a refreshing way to start a light meal.

6 cups regular or low-fat plain yogurt
1½ cups milk
Salt to taste
2 pounds cucumbers, peeled and diced or shredded (6 cups)
¾ cup chopped scallions (about 12)
¾ cup chopped fresh mint or cilantro or ¼ cup chopped fresh dill
5 to 6 cloves garlic, crushed

Blend together the yogurt, milk, and salt. Add the cucumbers, scallions, mint, and garlic. Refrigerate for at least 1 hour. Serve chilled.

HINT: If you find that yogurt is too tart for your taste, blend in some nonfat dry milk—the lactose sweetens it.

Syrian Baked Zucchini with Cheese (Calavasa al Horno)

8 SERVINGS

*S*yrians also serve this dish as a filling baked between layers of phyllo pastry.

2 pounds (about 6 medium) zucchini, peeled and coarsely grated
½ cup milk
2 tablespoons vegetable oil
1 large onion, chopped (about ¾ cup)
10 ounces (about 2½ cups) grated kashkeval or
  Muenster cheese (or 1½ cups kashkeval and 1 cup
  grated Muenster, mozzarella, or Gruyère cheese)
6 large eggs, lightly beaten
About 1 teaspoon salt
Ground black pepper to taste
¼ teaspoon sugar
3 tablespoons chopped fresh parsley or dill (optional)

1. Preheat the oven to 350 degrees. Grease an 8-inch-square or 11- by 7-inch baking pan or two 8-inch pie plates.
2. Squeeze out any excess liquid from the zucchini. Bring the zucchini and milk to a low boil and simmer for 5 minutes. Drain.
3. Heat the oil in a medium skillet over medium heat. Add the onion and sauté until golden, about 15 minutes.
4. Combine the zucchini, onion, 2 cups of the cheese, the eggs, salt, pepper, sugar, and if desired, the parsley. Spoon into the prepared pan and sprinkle with the remaining ½ cup cheese.
5. Bake until golden brown, about 25 minutes. Serve warm or at room temperature.

Fish Salad
8 SERVINGS

*S*erve this salad on a bed of lettuce, in hollowed-out tomatoes, or in sandwiches.

2 cups water
1 medium onion, sliced
2 stalks celery
2 tablespoons fresh lemon juice, dry white wine, or white vinegar
About 1 teaspoon salt
Pinch of ground black pepper
3 pounds white-fleshed fish fillets, such as cod, haddock, or halibut

DRESSING
1 cup mayonnaise
3 to 4 tablespoons fresh lemon juice
About 1 teaspoon salt
Ground white pepper
¼ cup sour cream (optional)
1½ cups chopped celery, ½ cup chopped sweet pickles,
    ½ cup sliced green olives, or ¼ cup capers
2 scallions, chopped

1. Bring the water, onion, celery, lemon juice, salt, and pepper to a boil. Reduce the heat to low and simmer for 5 minutes.
2. Add the fillets, cover loosely with greased parchment or wax paper, and poach over low heat until the fish is cooked through, 8 to 12 minutes, depending on the thickness of the fillets. Remove the fish from the poaching liquid and let cool.
3. Combine all the dressing ingredients. Flake the fish. Add the dressing, tossing to coat. Chill well.

VARIATIONS

Russian Fish Salad: Add 3 cups cooked and cubed potatoes, 3 cups cooked and cubed beets, ¾ pound cooked green beans, and 2 to 3 tablespoons prepared horseradish.
Curried Fish Salad: Omit the lemon juice and add about 2 teaspoons curry powder.

Tabbouleh

8 SERVINGS

*T*his variation on the classic Middle Eastern salad is designed to macerate in the refrigerator overnight. Americans tend to prefer a higher proportion of bulgur to parsley in this salad, while the opposite is true in the Middle East, where it is practically a parsley salad with bulgur.

2 cups (about 12 ounces) fine- or medium-grain bulgur
1½ cups water
1½ cups tomato juice
¾ cup fresh lemon juice
½ cup extra-virgin olive oil
1 to 3 cups chopped fresh parsley
1 cup seeded and chopped tomatoes
¾ cup finely chopped carrots
¾ cup finely chopped celery
½ cup finely chopped green bell pepper
½ cup finely chopped red bell pepper
½ cup finely chopped yellow bell pepper
4 to 6 scallions, chopped
⅓ to ⅔ cup chopped fresh mint or 2 tablespoons dried (optional)
About 1 teaspoon salt
Ground black pepper to taste

Combine all the ingredients. Cover and refrigerate overnight. Serve cold or at room temperature. Tabbouleh is commonly served with romaine lettuce leaves or pita bread.

Savory Cheese Pudding

8 SERVINGS

2 pounds farmer, pot, or ricotta cheese (or 1 pound farmer,
*   pot, or ricotta cheese and 1 pound softened cream cheese)*
6 large eggs, lightly beaten
6 tablespoons all-purpose flour
½ teaspoon baking powder (optional)
About ½ teaspoon salt
2 cups heavy cream or milk

1. Preheat the oven to 350 degrees. Grease a 13- by 9-inch baking pan or 8-inch spring-form pan.
2. Beat the cheese until smooth. Beat the eggs with the flour, baking powder, and salt. Stir in the cream. Blend into the cheese. Pour into the prepared pan.
3. Bake until golden brown, about 30 minutes. Turn off the heat and let the pudding cool in the oven.

VARIATION

Sweet Cheese Pudding: Add I cup sugar, 2 teaspoons vanilla extract, and if desired, I cup toasted almonds.

Almond Coffee Cake

1 LARGE OR 2 MEDIUM CAKES

DOUGH

1 (¼-ounce) package (2½ teaspoons) active dry yeast
1 cup warm water (105 to 115 degrees) or ¼ cup warm water and ¾ cup warm milk
¼ to ⅓ cup sugar
⅓ cup unsalted butter or margarine
1 large egg
1 teaspoon table salt or 2 teaspoons kosher salt
About 4 cups bread or unbleached all-purpose flour

ALMOND FILLING

½ cup (1 stick) unsalted butter or margarine, softened
1¼ cups (about 12 ounces) almond paste (page 361)
¼ to ½ cup granulated or packed brown sugar
1 teaspoon almond extract

Egg wash (1 egg beaten with 1 tablespoon water)

1. Dissolve the yeast in ¼ cup of the warm water. Stir in 1 teaspoon of the sugar and let stand until foamy, about 5 minutes.
2. Add the remaining water, remaining sugar, butter, egg, and salt. Blend in 1½ cups of the flour. Add enough of the remaining flour, ½ cup at a time, to make a workable dough.
3. On a lightly floured surface or in a mixer with a dough hook, knead the dough, adding more flour as needed, until smooth and springy, about 5 minutes. Place in a greased bowl, turning to coat. Cover loosely with a towel or plastic wrap and let rise in a warm, draft-free place until nearly double in bulk, about 1½ hours, or in the refrigerator overnight. Punch down the dough.
4. To make the filling: Beat the butter until smooth, about 1 minute. Gradually beat in the almond paste. Add the sugar and almond extract and beat until smooth.
5. On a lightly floured surface, roll the dough into an 18- by 12-inch rectangle about ¼ inch thick. Or divide the dough in half and roll each half into a 12- by 8-inch rectangle. Spread evenly with the filling, leaving a 1-inch border on all sides. Starting from a long side, roll up jelly-roll style, pinching the seams to seal. Place, seam side down,

on a lightly greased baking sheet and bend into a horseshoe shape or ring. Cover and let rise until nearly double in bulk, about 45 minutes.

6. Preheat the oven to 350 degrees.

7. Brush the cake with the egg wash. Bake until it is golden brown and sounds hollow when tapped on the bottom, about 40 minutes. (If the cake looks as if it is starting to burn, cover loosely with foil, dull side down.) Let cool on the baking sheet for 10 minutes, then transfer to a rack.

Iraqi Cardamom Cookies *(Hadgi Badah)*
ABOUT 6 DOZEN COOKIES

A favorite of Iraqi Jews, these cookies are served on Purim and at the meal following Yom Kippur.

2 cups all-purpose flour
1 teaspoon ground cardamom
½ teaspoon salt
¼ teaspoon baking powder
1⅓ cups sugar
4 large eggs
2 cups (about 10 ounces) ground blanched almonds
Rose water (optional)
About 6 dozen whole almonds

1. Preheat the oven to 350 degrees. Grease several large baking sheets.

2. Sift together the flour, cardamom, salt, and baking powder. Beat the sugar and eggs until light and creamy. Stir in the flour mixture, then the ground almonds.

3. Form the dough into 1-inch balls, moistening your hands with rose water, if desired. Place on the prepared baking sheets and flatten slightly. Press a whole almond into the center of each cookie.

4. Bake until lightly browned, about 12 minutes. Transfer to a wire rack and let cool. Store in an airtight container at room temperature.

A Sukkah Party

SERVES 8

*F*our days after Yom Kippur falls the eight-day holiday (seven days in Israel) of Sukkot. This festival represents the trek of the Israelites through the wilderness following the Exodus from Egypt, as well as the final harvest of the agricultural year. In remembrance of the Lord's protection during the forty-year transitional period in the desert, the family dines and sometimes sleeps in a sukkah (booth), a structure with a temporary roof consisting of branches or other forms of vegetation.

The most common Sukkot dishes are filled foods, particularly stuffed vegetables and pastries, symbolizing bounty and the harvest. Many of the dishes are prepared in the form of casseroles or thick stews, which are easy to shuttle outside to the sukkah. Preserved vegetable dishes such as pickles, eggplant spreads, and cucumber salads, representing the harvest, are also traditional Sukkot foods.

The seventh day of Sukkot, called Hoshanah Rabbah, is regarded as the day on which the divine verdicts of judgment decided on Yom Kippur are sealed. Therefore, as an extension of the Day of Atonement, foods traditional for the meal before the fast, such as kreplach, are served.

SHAPED BREAD
UKRAINIAN HOT BEEF BORSCHT
MIDDLE EASTERN LEMON-SESAME CHICKEN
INDIAN RICE AND VEGETABLE CASSEROLE
SYRIAN STUFFED CARROTS
ITALIAN PEAR CAKE
ETROG COOKIES
TEA AND COFFEE

 Wine Suggestions: Sauvignon Blanc, Chenin Blanc, or Soave

ENHANCING THE SUKKAH

Sukkah decorating is an eclectic art. The walls of my parents' sukkah in Richmond are typically covered with the year's batch of Rosh Hashanah cards alongside artwork created by children and grandchildren. No favoritism exists in this realm, as crude drawings receive equal prominence with professional-looking creations. Each year my parents also hang a seemingly incongruous item on the sukkah wall, an old dish towel featuring a map of Florida surrounded by marlins and palm trees. What makes this rather tacky item special is that it includes a city located just north of the Florida-Georgia border, Brunswick. That little-known town holds particular significance for the Marks family, as both sets of my father's grandparents lived there more than a century ago. Thus, sukkah traditions can derive from the most unexpected sources.

The sukkah roof also offers a canvas for expressing one's creativity. Many people hang a medley of gourds and fruit; increasingly popular is plastic fruit, which neither rots nor attracts insects or squirrels. Other common ceiling decorations include brightly colored autumn leaves, Indian corn, paper chains, origami, Chinese lanterns, and tinsel. Some sukkah decorators prefer a sparser look with only a few items attached to the roof and walls.

The sukkah table is generally simple, as there is always a chance of rain as well as an understandable reluctance to shlep things outdoors. Ease and practicality are key. Paper and plastic plates are definitely acceptable. My sister Sharon wraps individual serving utensils in a napkin and ties them with a ribbon.

Shaped Bread: *Epi* (Shaft of Wheat)
8 SERVINGS

*A*n *epi* is a baguette cut to resemble a shaft of wheat. You can also form the dough into the shape of one large sheaf of wheat or an etrog (citron) and lulav (palm branch).

1 recipe (3 pounds) Teddy Bear Bread dough (page 235)
  or Challah dough (page 40, leaving out the raisins)
Egg wash (1 egg beaten with 1 teaspoon water)

1. Divide the dough in half. Place on a lightly floured surface and roll into two 14- by 6-inch rectangles. (The dough should be at least 1 inch shorter lengthwise than the baking sheet). Starting from a long end, tightly roll up jelly-roll style halfway, pinching the edges as you roll. Repeat rolling from the opposite direction. Pinch the edges together to seal. Roll the ends gently between your hands to taper.
2. Place each loaf on a large baking sheet lined with parchment paper. Using a pair of kitchen shears, make a 2-inch-long cut almost through at one end of the loaf and pull that piece in the opposite direction. Cut the dough every 2 inches for the entire length of the loaf, turning the sections alternately to the right and left. Cover and let rise until puffy, about 30 minutes.
3. Preheat the oven to 350 degrees.
4. Brush the dough with the egg wash. Bake until the bread is golden brown and sounds hollow when tapped on the bottom, about 30 minutes. Let cool on the baking sheet for 10 minutes, then carefully transfer to a rack and let cool completely.

Shaped Bread: Cornucopia
8 SERVINGS

*M*ake a large bread cornucopia for a centerpiece or individual ones for each place setting.

⅓ recipe (1 pound) Teddy Bear Bread dough (page 235)
Egg wash (1 egg beaten with 1 teaspoon water)

1. Preheat the oven to 350 degrees.
2. Ball up pieces of aluminum foil to form a large curved horn of plenty. Wrap with parchment paper.
3. Roll out the dough to a thin rectangle and cut into 1½-inch-wide strips. Starting at the tip of the mold, begin wrapping the dough, overlapping the strips. When all of the mold has been covered, place it on a large baking sheet, brush with the egg wash, and let stand for 10 minutes.
4. Bake until the bread is golden, about 40 minutes. Let cool on the baking sheet for 10 minutes, then carefully transfer to a rack and let cool completely.

Ukrainian Hot Beef Borscht
8 SERVINGS

*B*orscht is commonly served with another mainstay of the eastern European diet, boiled potatoes.

3 pounds beef short ribs or brisket
8 cups water
9 medium (about 2 pounds) beets, peeled and chopped
2 medium yellow onions, chopped (about 1 cup)
1 to 2 cloves garlic, minced
¼ cup barley, 1 pound (1 small head) shredded cabbage,
  ¾ pound (4 large) coarsely grated carrots, or any combination
2 tablespoons tomato paste
About 2 tablespoons fresh lemon juice, cider vinegar,
  or red wine vinegar
1 to 3 tablespoons granulated or packed brown sugar
About 1½ teaspoons salt
Ground black pepper to taste
6 to 8 (2 to 2½ pounds) medium boiling potatoes, cooked

1. Place the meat and water in a heavy 6-quart pot. Bring to a boil, cover, reduce the heat to low, and simmer, skimming the foam from the surface occasionally, for 1 hour.
2. Add the beets, onions, garlic, and barley. Cover and simmer for an additional 1 hour.
3. Stir in the tomato paste, lemon juice, sugar, salt, and pepper. Simmer until the meat is tender, about 30 minutes. (The soup can be cooled and stored in the refrigerator for up to 3 days. Skim the fat from the surface before reheating.)
4. Remove the meat and slice, discarding any gristle. Return the meat to the soup. Serve hot with boiled potatoes.

Middle Eastern Lemon-Sesame Chicken

8 SERVINGS

In the Middle East chicken is reserved for special occasions. The nutty flavor of sesame seeds and the zing of fresh lemon make this dish even more distinctive.

¼ cup vegetable oil
¼ cup (½ stick) unsalted margarine or olive oil
1 cup fresh bread crumbs, matza meal, or flour
½ cup sesame seeds
1½ teaspoons paprika
1½ teaspoons salt
1 teaspoon ground black pepper
2 (3-pound) chickens, each cut into 8 pieces
2 large eggs beaten with ¼ cup water (optional)
1 cup dry white wine or white vermouth
6 tablespoons fresh lemon juice (optional)
⅓ cup minced scallions (optional)

1. Preheat the oven to 375 degrees. Combine the oil and margarine in a large roasting pan and heat in the oven.
2. Combine the bread crumbs, sesame seeds, paprika, salt, and pepper. (A large plastic bag makes this task easier and neater.) If desired, dip the chicken pieces into the egg mixture. Add the chicken to the crumb mixture, tossing to coat.

3. Place in the prepared pan, skin side up, and bake for 30 minutes.
4. Sprinkle with the wine and, if desired, the lemon juice and/or scallions. Bake until golden brown, about 30 additional minutes.

Indian Rice and Vegetable Casserole (Bireani)
8 SERVINGS

*T*he first Jewish settlement appeared in India more than two thousand years ago. Eventually three distinct Jewish communities sprang up in three different parts of the subcontinent: the Bene Israel of Bombay in the west; the Jews of Cochin on the Malabar coast in the southwest; and in the east the Baghdadis of Calcutta. The last group, consisting primarily of Middle Easterners who arrived in the early nineteenth century, adapted the local cuisine, synthesizing it with Middle Eastern fare. The result is a unique form of Jewish cooking that includes such dishes as this spicy, colorful casserole traditionally served on Sukkot.

RICE LAYER
½ cup (1 stick) unsalted margarine or vegetable oil
2 cups long-grain white or brown rice
4 cups water
2 teaspoons turmeric
½ teaspoon salt
⅔ cup raw slivered almonds
⅔ cup raw cashews
⅔ cup golden raisins

VEGETABLE LAYER

¼ cup (½ stick) unsalted margarine or vegetable oil
1½ teaspoons mustard seeds
1 teaspoon poppy seeds
2 teaspoons turmeric
About 1 teaspoon curry powder
½ teaspoon ground coriander
¼ teaspoon cayenne pepper
1 large eggplant, peeled and diced
1 large zucchini, diced
1 large red bell pepper, seeded and diced
1 cup lima beans
2 cups tomato puree
1 teaspoon sugar
About 1 teaspoon salt

1. Preheat the oven to 350 degrees. Grease a 13- by 9-inch baking dish.
2. To make the rice layer: Heat ¼ cup of the margarine in a large saucepan over medium heat. Add the rice and sauté until opaque, about 3 minutes. Add the water, turmeric, and salt. Bring to a boil, cover, reduce the heat to low, and simmer until the liquid is absorbed, about 17 minutes for white rice, 40 minutes for brown rice.
3. Heat the remaining ¼ cup margarine in a small saucepan over medium heat. Add the nuts and sauté until golden. Stir in the raisins. Remove from the heat.
4. To make the vegetable layer: Heat 1 tablespoon of the margarine in a large saucepan over medium-high heat. Add the mustard seeds and sauté until they begin to pop. Reduce the heat to low and stir in the poppy seeds, turmeric, curry powder, coriander, and cayenne.
5. Add the remaining 3 tablespoons margarine to the spices. Increase the heat to medium-high, add the eggplant, zucchini, and bell pepper, and sauté for 2 minutes. Add the lima beans, tomato puree, sugar, and salt. Bring to a boil, cover, reduce the heat to low, and simmer until the vegetables are tender-crisp, about 10 minutes.
6. Spread half of the rice in the prepared baking dish and top with the vegetables. Combine the remaining rice with the nut mixture and spread over the casserole.
7. Cover with foil and bake for 30 minutes. Serve warm.

Syrian Stuffed Carrots *(Djezar Mehshi)*
8 SERVINGS

*S*yrian Jews love to entertain and take as much pride in the planning, presentation, and serving of the food as in the preparation, all of which are subsumed under the general term *suffeh*. Holidays and other special occasions offer Syrian cooks suitable opportunities to demonstrate their culinary and decorative abilities. Stuffed carrots are typical of Syrian culinary ingenuity. By adding a stuffing, a simple dish is transformed into something fancy without being expensive.

16 fat, short carrots

STUFFING
1½ pounds ground beef or lamb
¾ cup long-grain white rice
About 1 teaspoon salt
¾ teaspoon ground allspice

SAUCE
3 cups water
6 tablespoons tomato paste or tomato sauce
3 tablespoons temerhindi (see Note)
2 to 3 cloves garlic, minced
About 1¼ teaspoons salt
1 teaspoon dried mint (optional)

1. To prepare the carrots: Let the carrots stand at room temperature for 24 hours. Cut off the stems. Using a vegetable peeler or paring knife, scoop out the center, reserving the pulp.
2. To make the stuffing: Combine all the stuffing ingredients.
3. Stuff the meat mixture ⅔ full into the carrots, leaving room for expansion. Form any excess meat mixture into meatballs and set aside.
4. Spread the reserved carrot pulp in a large saucepan and arrange the carrots on top. Combine all the sauce ingredients and pour over the carrots. Cover and bring to a boil. Add any meatballs at this time. Cover, reduce the heat to low, and simmer until the carrots are tender, about 1 hour.

NOTE: Temerhindi, also called *ooht,* is a tangy Syrian sauce made from tamarind and used as a souring agent in sweet-and-sour dishes. It is available in Middle Eastern and Asian food markets. Substitute equal amounts of apricot butter and prune butter for the temerhindi.

Italian Pear Cake *(Torta di Pera)*
8 TO 10 SERVINGS

1¼ cups plus 2 tablespoons all-purpose flour
1 teaspoon ground cinnamon
1 teaspoon baking powder
¼ teaspoon salt
½ cup (1 stick) unsalted margarine, softened, or vegetable shortening
1¼ cups sugar
3 large eggs
⅓ cup almond milk (see Note) or nondairy creamer
1½ teaspoons vanilla extract or 1 tablespoon brandy
3 Bosc or Bartlett pears, peeled, cored, and diced
½ cup dried currants or raisins
½ cup pine nuts, chopped almonds, or chopped hazelnuts

1. Preheat the oven to 325 degrees. Grease an 8½-inch springform pan.
2. Sift together the flour, cinnamon, baking powder, and salt. Beat the margarine and sugar until light and fluffy, about 5 minutes. Beat in the eggs, one at a time. Add the almond milk and vanilla. Fold in the flour mixture. Add the pears, currants, and nuts.
3. Pour the batter into the prepared pan and smooth the top. Bake until a tester inserted in the center comes out clean, about 1 hour. Let cool in the pan for 10 minutes, then remove to a wire rack and let cool completely. Wrap tightly in plastic, then foil. (The cake can be stored at room temperature for up to 4 days or in the freezer for up to 2 months.)

NOTE: To make almond milk, bring 1 cup water and ¼ cup ground blanched almonds to a boil. Reduce the heat to low and simmer for 10 minutes. Let cool, then strain through several layers of cheesecloth.

Etrog Cookies
2 DOZEN COOKIES

*T*he etrog (citron), known in the Bible as *etz peri hadar* (fruit of the goodly tree), is one of the cuttings used in the Sukkot ritual of the Arbeh Minim (Four Species). According to one ancient legend, the citron was the Tree of Good and Evil in the Garden of Eden. This lemon-like fruit, which has a very thick rind and sparse pulp, has a limited number of culinary uses. It appears primarily in marmalade and as candied peel. In this recipe cookies are shaped to resemble this holiday symbol.

3 cups all-purpose flour
2 teaspoons ground cinnamon
1½ teaspoons baking soda
½ teaspoon salt
¾ cup vegetable shortening
1¼ cups granulated or packed brown sugar
1 large egg
⅓ cup unsulfured (light) molasses
2 teaspoons vanilla extract
24 pitted prunes, dates, or dried apricots

ICING
1 pound confectioners' sugar
Fresh lemon juice or water
Several drops yellow food coloring

1. Sift together the flour, cinnamon, baking soda, and salt. Beat the shortening and sugar until light and fluffy, about 5 minutes. Beat in the egg. Add the molasses and vanilla. Stir in the flour mixture. Form the dough into a ball, wrap tightly in plastic, and refrigerate until firm, at least 1 hour or up to 3 days.
2. Preheat the oven to 375 degrees. Grease 2 large baking sheets.

3. Sprinkle a flat surface lightly with flour or confectioners' sugar, roll out the dough to a ¼-inch thickness, and cut into 48 rounds. Or divide the dough into 48 equal balls and flatten into ¼-inch-thick rounds.

4. Place a prune, date, or dried apricot in the center of each round. Fold over the sides to enclose it and pinch the edges to seal. Place, seam side down, on the prepared baking sheets and pinch the ends to form an etrog shape.

5. Bake until the cookies are light golden, 20 to 25 minutes. Let them stand until firm, about 1 minute, then remove to a rack to cool completely.

6. To make the icing: Combine the confectioners' sugar with enough lemon juice or water to make a thick icing. Add a few drops yellow food coloring to create a lemon color.

7. To assemble: Spread a thin layer of the icing on the flat sides of 24 cookies and press against the flat sides of the remaining cookies to form 24 whole etrog shapes. Frost the outsides of the cookies and let stand at room temperature until dry.

A Simchat Torah Dinner

SERVES 8

*A*t the conclusion of Sukkot, a separate series of holidays begins: Shemini Atzeret and Simchat Torah. Shemini Atzeret is a two-day biblical festival (one day in Israel) concluding the extensive holiday period that began nearly a month earlier with Rosh Hashanah.

Simchat Torah (literally, Happiness over the Torah) is a relatively late creation, its source lying in the ancient and enduring Jewish tradition of publicly reading from a Torah scroll. Sections from the Five Books of Moses are read on all of the holidays as well as thrice weekly—on the Sabbath and the two ancient Jewish market days, Monday and Thursday. The custom in Judea was to read the complete Five Books of Moses in a triennial cycle, while in the Jewish community of Babylonia the reading was done in a single year. The Babylonian mode eventually won worldwide acceptance, and Shemini Atzeret was marked as the day on which the previous cycle ended. Simchat Torah, along with Purim, is one of the two most uninhibitedly joyful occasions on the Jewish calendar, replete with singing, dancing, and feasting.

Simchat Torah fare, similar to that of Sukkot, is intended to reflect the bounty of the harvest and includes thick soups and stews incorporating seasonal produce and filled foods—including stuffed poultry and veal breast, filled pastries, and especially stuffed vegetables—symbolizing abundance.

FRUITED CHALLAH (PAGE 40)
CARROT-DILL SOUP
SWEET-AND-SOUR STUFFED CABBAGE
APPLE-GLAZED ROAST TURKEY WITH BIBLICAL FRUIT STUFFING
DOUBLE-POTATO TERRINE
SWISS CHARD WITH BLACK-EYED PEAS
FRESH CRANBERRY RELISH
CHOCOLATE PECAN PIE
TEA AND COFFEE

 Wine Suggestions: Sauvignon Blanc, Riesling, Chardonnay, or Beaujolais

---

Carrot-Dill Soup

8 SERVINGS

*T*his soup has a slightly sweet flavor and dazzling orange color. For a special presentation, ladle the soup into serving bowls and drizzle 1 to 2 tablespoons Red Bell Pepper Soup (page 326) or pesto into the center of the soup.

3 tablespoons vegetable oil
2 medium onions, chopped (about 1 cup)
2 pounds (about 14 medium) carrots, coarsely chopped
8 cups chicken broth or water (or 7 cups broth and 1 cup orange juice)
1 large boiling potato, peeled and chopped
2 bay leaves
About 1 teaspoon salt
Ground black pepper to taste
Pinch of sugar
3 to 4 tablespoons chopped fresh dill

1. Heat the oil in a large saucepan over medium heat. Add the onions and sauté until soft and translucent, 5 to 10 minutes. Add the carrots and sauté until slightly softened.
2. Add the broth, potato, bay leaves, salt, pepper, and sugar. Bring to a boil, cover, reduce the heat to low, and simmer until the carrots are very tender, about 45 minutes.
3. Discard the bay leaves. In batches, puree the soup. Return to the pot, add the dill, and heat through. If the soup is too thick, add more broth or, for a creamier consistency, a little soy milk or nondairy creamer. Serve warm or chilled.

Sweet-and-Sour Stuffed Cabbage

ABOUT 16 LARGE ROLLS

*W*henever my mother prepares an especially well received dish, she insists, "Enjoy it, since you'll never get it again." My mother is the type of cook who rarely follows direc-

tions but prefers to guess and experiment. One Sukkot she added wheat germ to the cabbage stuffing, the next year passion fruit to the sauce. Although the flavor was interesting, she forgot to remove the seeds before adding the passion fruit, and so we were spitting a lot while otherwise enjoying our appetizer.

Stuffed cabbage, symbolizing abundance, is a popular Sukkot, Simchat Torah, and Passover dish. It can also serve as a main course for eight people if you add eight quartered boiling potatoes to cook alongside the cabbage. You can double the recipe and place half in the freezer for future entertaining.

1 large head green cabbage (about 3 pounds)

STUFFING
1½ pounds ground beef
½ cup long-grain white rice or matza meal
1 medium onion, chopped (about ½ cup)
1 large egg
About 1 teaspoon salt
Ground black pepper to taste

SAUCE
4 cups tomato sauce or juice (or 3 pounds chopped undrained canned
  plum tomatoes and 1½ cups tomato sauce)
½ to ¾ cup granulated sugar, packed brown sugar, or honey
6 tablespoons fresh lemon juice or cider vinegar or ¼ teaspoon sour salt (citric acid)
6 tablespoons vegetable oil
2 bay leaves
About 1½ teaspoons salt
Ground black pepper to taste
1 cup raisins (optional)

1. Cut out the core of the cabbage. Parboil the head in a large pot of lightly salted water, occasionally turning the cabbage, until the leaves are pliable, about 5 minutes. Remove 16 large leaves, returning the head to the boiling water as necessary. (For bite-size appetizers, use about 32 smaller cabbage leaves.) Shred the extra cabbage leaves and place in the bottom of a deep pot or baking dish.
2. Combine all the stuffing ingredients.

3. To assemble: Place about ¼ cup of the stuffing in the center of each cabbage leaf. Fold the stem end over the stuffing, tuck in the sides of the leaf, and roll up. Arrange the cabbage rolls, seam side down, on top of the shredded cabbage.

4. Combine all of the sauce ingredients and pour over the cabbage rolls. Weight down with a plate. (The cabbage rolls tend to rise to the surface and unravel. Instead of weighting down the rolls, you can secure them with toothpicks or use half the amount of sauce.)

5. Bring to a boil, cover, reduce the heat to low, and simmer until the cabbage is very tender, at least 1½ hours. Or bake, covered, in a 350-degree oven for 1½ hours, then uncover and bake for an additional 30 minutes. If the sauce gets too thick, add a little water. (The stuffed cabbage can be cooled, then stored in the refrigerator for up to 3 days or in the freezer for several months. Thaw the cabbage rolls in the refrigerator overnight before reheating.)

Apple-Glazed Roast Turkey with Biblical Fruit Stuffing
8 SERVINGS

The various components of this stuffing are mentioned in the Bible.

GLAZE
4 cups apple cider
⅓ cup sugar
⅓ cup honey

STUFFING
¼ cup vegetable oil
2 medium onions, chopped (about 1 cup)
2 medium stalks celery, chopped (about ⅔ cup)
4 cups (about 8 ounces) croutons or dry bread cubes
2 cups cored and chopped apples

1 cup chopped pitted dates
1 cup chopped fresh or dried figs
1 cup dried currants or raisins
1 to 1½ cups coarsely chopped almonds or walnuts
½ cup chopped fresh parsley
1 teaspoon dried sage or ground cinnamon
Salt to taste
Ground black pepper to taste
2 large eggs, lightly beaten (optional)
About ½ cup chicken broth, dry white wine, orange juice, or apple cider

TURKEY
1 (8- to 12-pound) turkey, thawed if frozen
Salt to taste
Ground black pepper to taste
¼ cup vegetable oil or melted unsalted margarine

1. To make the glaze: Cook the cider, sugar, and honey over medium heat, stirring occasionally, until reduced to about 1 cup, about 40 minutes. Set aside. (The glaze can be prepared up to 2 days ahead and stored in the refrigerator.)

2. To make the stuffing: Heat the oil in a large skillet over medium heat. Add the onions and celery and sauté until softened, about 10 minutes. Remove from the heat and stir in the croutons, apples, dates, figs, currants, almonds, parsley, sage, salt, and pepper. Toss to coat. If desired, add the eggs. Stir in enough of the broth to moisten. Let cool before using.

3. Preheat the oven to 325 degrees.

4. Rinse the turkey inside and out. Pat dry. Season inside and out with salt and pepper. Loosely fill the cavity with the stuffing. Skewer or sew the neck end closed, then tie the legs together.

5. Place the turkey, breast side down, on a wire rack in a shallow baking pan. Rub with the oil. Roast for 60 minutes, basting occasionally. Turn the turkey onto one side and roast for 30 minutes. Turn the turkey to the other side and roast another 30 minutes.

6. Turn the turkey breast side up and brush with the glaze. Continue roasting, brushing with the glaze every 25 to 30 minutes, until the juices in the inner thigh run clear when pricked with a fork and the meat in the deepest part of the thigh registers 165 degrees on a meat thermometer, 15 to 20 minutes per pound or 1½ to 2½ hours. (The turkey takes 3½ to 4½ hours total roasting time.)

7. Remove the stuffing immediately after cooking. For a moister bird and easier carving, let the turkey stand for at least 15 minutes. After removing from the oven, do not leave the turkey at room temperature for more than 2 hours. To carve, hold the bird with a carving fork and remove the legs by cutting through the joints between the breast and thigh. Cut off the drumsticks. Cut off the wings at the joint attaching them to the body. Remove the top breast in one piece by cutting along the breastbone. Carve thin slices diagonally from the breast. Place the turkey pieces on a warm serving platter.

Double-Potato Terrine

8 TO 10 SERVINGS

WHITE POTATO LAYER

2 tablespoons vegetable oil
1 large onion, chopped (about ¾ cup)
2 cups (about 1 pound) mashed cooked white potatoes
2 large eggs, lightly beaten
2 tablespoons unsalted margarine, melted
2 tablespoons nondairy creamer
Salt to taste
Pinch of ground white pepper

SWEET POTATO LAYER

2 cups (about 1 pound) mashed cooked sweet potatoes
2 large eggs, lightly beaten
2 tablespoons brown sugar
2 tablespoons apple juice
2 tablespoons unsalted margarine, melted
1 teaspoon fresh lemon juice
½ teaspoon ground cinnamon or ginger
Pinch of salt

1. Preheat the oven to 350 degrees. Grease a 9- by 5-inch loaf pan, line the bottom with wax paper, and grease the wax paper.

2. To make the white potato layer: Heat the oil in a large skillet over medium heat. Add the onion and sauté until soft and translucent, 5 to 10 minutes. Puree the onion and combine with the remaining ingredients for the white potato layer.

3. To make the sweet potato layer: Combine all the ingredients.

4. Spread half of the sweet potato mixture in the prepared pan and top with half of the white potato mixture. Repeat the layers with the remaining sweet potato mixture and remaining white potato mixture. Cover with a piece of greased wax paper.

5. Place the loaf pan in a larger pan and add hot water to come partway up the sides of the loaf pan. Bake for 1 hour.

6. To serve, remove the wax paper from the top of the terrine. Invert onto a serving platter and remove the pan and wax paper from the bottom. Cut into slices. Serve warm or at room temperature.

Swiss Chard with Black-eyed Peas
8 SERVINGS

*S*wiss chard, also called blette and silver beet, has an earthy flavor with a slightly bitter undertone.

2 pounds Swiss chard, washed well
3 tablespoons vegetable oil
4 to 5 scallions, chopped
2 to 3 cloves garlic, minced
1½ cups cooked black-eyed peas
¼ teaspoon turmeric
2 tablespoons fresh lemon juice
Salt to taste
Ground black pepper to taste

1. Separate the Swiss chard leaves from the stems. Cut the stems into ½-inch pieces and the leaves into 1-inch pieces.

2. Heat the oil in a large skillet or saucepan over medium heat. Add the scallions and garlic and sauté until softened.

3. Add the Swiss chard and black-eyed peas, cover, reduce the heat to low, and simmer until the Swiss chard is tender, about 20 minutes. Add the turmeric, lemon juice, salt, and pepper. Serve warm or at room temperature.

Fresh Cranberry Relish
ABOUT 3½ CUPS

*O*ne of my favorite food combinations is roast turkey and fresh cranberry relish.

12 ounces (about 3 cups) fresh cranberries
1 medium orange, quartered and seeded (not peeled)
1 medium apple, quartered and cored (not peeled)
About 1 cup sugar

In a food processor or grinder or by hand, chop the cranberries, orange, and apple. (I prefer the texture coarse, but you can chop finely if you wish.) Stir in sugar to taste. Refrigerate for at least 6 hours.

Chocolate Pecan Pie
8 TO 10 SERVINGS

*T*ransparent fillings are similar to custard but contain no milk or cream, so they have a soft, translucent, jelly-like consistency. Pecan pie differs from basic transparent pie by the addition of corn syrup, which produces a smooth, nongrainy filling. Dark corn syrup imparts a caramel-like flavor. Adding a little melted chocolate or bourbon cuts the cloying sweetness of the sugar in the filling.

PÂTE BRISÉE (FLAKY PASTRY)

1⅓ cups all-purpose flour
½ teaspoon salt
½ cup vegetable shortening (or 5 tablespoons vegetable shortening
    and 3 tablespoons chilled unsalted margarine)
3 to 5 tablespoons ice water

FILLING

1 cup (4 ounces) pecan halves or 1½ cups (6 ounces) coarsely chopped toasted pecans
4 large eggs, lightly beaten
1 cup light or dark corn syrup
¾ cup sugar
¼ teaspoon salt
¼ cup (½ stick) unsalted margarine, melted
2 to 3 ounces semisweet or bittersweet chocolate, melted
1½ teaspoons vanilla extract

1. To make the pastry: Combine the flour and salt. Using the tips of your fingers, a pastry blender, or 2 knives in a scissor motion, cut in the shortening until the mixture resembles coarse crumbs. Sprinkle 1 tablespoon of the ice water over a section of the mixture. Gently mix in with a fork to moisten that section. Push the moistened dough aside and continue adding and mixing in the water until the dough just holds together. Using your fingertips, lightly press and knead the dough into a ball. Do not overhandle. Cover with plastic wrap, flatten into a disk, and refrigerate for at least 30 minutes and up to 4 days.

2. On a lightly floured flat surface, roll out the dough to a 12-inch round about ⅛ inch thick. Transfer to a 9-inch pie plate, trim the excess dough against the rim of the pan, and flute or crimp the edges. Cover and refrigerate for at least 45 minutes.

3. Preheat the oven to 350 degrees.

4. Arrange the pecans in the pastry shell. Place the eggs in a bowl and beat in the corn syrup, sugar, and salt. Stir in the margarine, chocolate, and vanilla. Pour over the pecans. (They will rise to the surface.)

5. Bake until the filling is set and a knife inserted in the center comes out clean, about 40 minutes. (The filling firms as it cools.) Let cool at least 4 hours. (Pecan pie freezes well.)

A Hanukkah Party

SERVES 8

*I*n 168 B.C.E. the Hasmonean patriarch Mattathias and his five sons, better known as the Maccabees, launched a revolt against Emperor Antiochus IV and his Syrian-Greek forces, who were seeking to obliterate Judaism. Three years later the Jews chased their oppressors out of Jerusalem. The Temple, desecrated by the enemy, lay in a state of physical and spiritual disarray. Although the priests found but one small vial of untainted olive oil, enough to burn in the candelabra for only one day, the flame lasted for eight days.

Hanukkah ("dedication" in Hebrew) commemorates the rededication of the Temple by the Hasmoneans. Light is the preeminent theme of this eight-day festival, one that is particularly apropos at this time of the year, when daylight once again begins to increase. The central ritual of Hanukkah is the kindling of an eight-branched candelabra—called *hanukkiyah* by Sephardim and menorah by Ashkenazim—after sunset each evening. A single candle is lit on the first evening—using an extra candle called the *shamash*—and an additional candle is lit on each successive night, until a total of eight are burning on the final day. The lighting is accompanied by a short prayer, "Ha'Nerot Hallalu" (These Lights), and the singing of a thirteenth-century German hymn, "Ma'oz Tzur" (Mighty Rock) by Ashkenazim and Psalm 30 and various hymns by Sephardim.

Despite Hanukkah's prominent position in American Jewish life, before this century it was a rather minor festival, one whose story is not told in the Bible. There are no rituals in the synagogue, and only a few prayers are added to the services. The custom of giving Hanukkah presents is a modern American phenomenon derived from Christmas celebrations.

The candle lighting is usually followed by a festive meal. Perhaps because of Hanukkah's former minor status, the holiday never inspired many specific traditional dishes. Generally, foods were fried in recognition of the miracle of the oil. In eastern Europe, where oil was scarce and expensive, schmaltz (rendered poultry fat) was usually substituted. And since schmaltz could not be used with dairy products, Ashkenazic Hanukkah feasts were commonly meat.

ROLLS
SWEET POTATO AND PEAR SOUP
CALCUTTA FRIED CREPES
BAKED BRISKET
HONEY TURNIPS
POTATO LATKES
APPLESAUCE
GREEN BEANS WITH MUSTARD SEEDS
JELLY DOUGHNUTS
TEA AND COFFEE

 Wine Suggestions: Pinot Noir, red Zinfandel, or Cabernet Sauvignon

Sweet Potato and Pear Soup
8 SERVINGS

*F*lavor and nutrition make the sweet potato a delightful addition to any meal. For a creamier texture, add 1 cup nondairy creamer.

¼ cup (½ stick) unsalted margarine or vegetable oil
3 medium onions or 4 medium leeks (white and light green part only),
　　chopped (about 1½ cups)
1½ pounds (about 3 medium) sweet potatoes, peeled and diced
8 cups chicken broth or water
1 cup dry white wine or 1½ cups apple juice
About 1½ teaspoons salt
½ teaspoon ground white pepper
1 (3-inch) stick cinnamon or pinch of grated nutmeg (optional)
4 to 5 Bartlett, d'Anjou, or Comice pears, peeled, cored, and chopped

1. Melt the margarine in a large saucepan over medium heat. Add the onions and sauté until soft and translucent, 5 to 10 minutes.
2. Add the potatoes, broth, wine, salt, pepper, and if desired, the cinnamon stick. Bring to a boil, cover, reduce the heat to low, and simmer for 15 minutes.
3. Add the pears, cover, and simmer until very soft, about 15 minutes. If using the cinnamon stick, discard it.
4. In a blender or food processor, puree the soup until smooth. If serving hot, return to the pot and reheat. Serve warm or chilled, accompanied by Calcutta Fried Crepes (page 91).

Calcutta Fried Crepes *(Pantras)*

16 CREPES

FILLING
3 tablespoons vegetable oil
2 medium onions, chopped (about 1 cup)
1½ pounds ground beef or chicken
3 tablespoons chopped fresh cilantro or parsley
¾ teaspoon turmeric
¾ teaspoon grated fresh ginger (optional)
About ½ teaspoon salt
Ground black pepper to taste

CREPES
2 cups water
2 large eggs, lightly beaten
½ teaspoon salt
1½ cups all-purpose flour
Vegetable oil for frying

1. To make the filling: Heat the oil in a large skillet over medium heat. Add the onions and sauté until soft and translucent, 5 to 10 minutes. Add the beef and remaining filling ingredients and sauté until the meat loses its pink color and most of the liquid evaporates, about 5 minutes. Let cool.
2. To make the crepes: Whisk together the water, eggs, and salt. Gradually whisk in the flour to make a smooth, thin batter with the consistency of heavy cream. Strain if there are any lumps. Cover and let stand in the refrigerator for at least 2 hours or up to 2 days.
3. Heat a heavy 6-inch skillet over medium heat. Brush lightly with oil. Pour in about 2 tablespoons batter and tilt the pan until the batter just coats the bottom.
4. Cook until the edges begin to brown, about 1 minute, then flip the crepe onto a piece of wax paper. Repeat with the remaining batter. You should have about 16 pancakes. (The crepes can be stored in the refrigerator for up to 4 days or frozen for up to 2 months. Return to room temperature.)
5. To assemble: Place a crepe, browned side up, on a flat surface and place a heaping tablespoon of the filling near one end. Fold the edge over the filling, then fold over about ½ inch of the sides. Roll up like a cigar.
6. Deep-fry in about 1 inch hot oil or fry in a thin layer of oil in a skillet until golden brown on all sides. Drain on paper towels.

Baked Brisket

8 SERVINGS

In Alsace and Germany geese were inexpensive to raise from spring through fall, when grasses and grains were readily available. As winter approached and the geese became a liability, most of them were slaughtered. Their fat was rendered and much of it put away to be used as cooking fat. The surplus of geese at this time of year made the bird a natural Hanukkah dish in eastern and central European Ashkenazic communities. In eastern Europe, where geese were less common, cows, particularly older ones, were frequently slaughtered before the onset of winter, and brisket, a relatively inexpensive cut, became the most common Hanukkah meat. In either case, latkes fried in schmaltz served as an accompaniment.

1 (4- to 5-pound) first-cut beef brisket
Salt to taste
Ground black pepper to taste
Paprika (optional)
3 to 4 large onions, sliced
About 2 cups water (or 1 cup chicken broth and 1 cup dry red or white wine)
3 medium carrots, cut into chunks
3 to 5 whole cloves garlic
2 to 3 stalks celery, sliced (optional)
8 to 10 small new potatoes (optional)
1 tablespoon chopped fresh thyme or 1 teaspoon dried (or 1 teaspoon chopped
*   fresh rosemary or ½ teaspoon dried) (optional)*
1 bay leaf

1. Preheat the oven to 350 degrees.
2. Rub both sides of the meat with the salt, pepper, and if desired, the paprika. Spread half of the onions over the bottom of a shallow roasting pan. Place the brisket, fat side up, in the pan and top with the remaining onions. Add ¼ cup of the water. Bake, uncovered, basting occasionally, until the meat and onions begin to brown, about 1 hour.
3. Pour in enough of the remaining water to reach halfway up the sides of the meat. Add the remaining ingredients, cover, and reduce the heat to 300 degrees or place over low heat. Cook until the meat is fork-tender and the thickest part of the brisket registers

about 175 degrees on a meat thermometer, about 3 hours (1 hour per pound) total cooking time.

4. Cover the brisket loosely with foil and let stand for 20 minutes before carving. Slice the brisket diagonally against the grain about ⅛ inch thick. (The brisket can be prepared up to 2 days ahead and reheated in the gravy.) If desired, serve with horseradish or whole-grain mustard.

VARIATIONS

Brisket Tzimmes: In step 3, add 1 pound pitted prunes, 4 peeled and quartered large sweet potatoes, ¼ cup granulated or brown sugar, and 2 to 3 tablespoons fresh lemon juice.

Brisket with Cabbage: About 20 minutes before the brisket is done, add 1 medium head green cabbage, cut into 10 pieces.

Honey Turnips

8 SERVINGS

*T*he turnip and its cousin, the rutabaga, have a sharp flavor and coarse texture that complement beef roasts and duck.

2 pounds (about 6 medium) white turnips, peeled and diced
⅓ to ½ cup honey
¼ cup (½ stick) unsalted margarine
¼ teaspoon grated nutmeg
Pinch of salt

1. Bring a large pot of water to a boil over medium heat. Add the turnips, cover, reduce the heat to low, and simmer until tender, about 10 minutes. Drain.
2. Add the remaining ingredients and toss to coat.

Potato Latkes
ABOUT THIRTY-TWO 3-INCH PANCAKES

A few years ago my sister Carol thought she would make healthier latkes for her family by "frying" them in cooking spray. Much to her chagrin, no one would eat them. Some things simply cannot be changed, and to achieve the proper texture and flavor, potato latkes have to be fried in oil. However, if the temperature is high enough, the pancakes absorb very little fat. A larger amount of oil, about ¼ inch deep, is best for reaching and maintaining a high temperature, signified when the oil starts to shimmer. Do not, however, let the oil start smoking.

Crisp on the outside and tender on the inside, unadorned or smothered in a cool topping, this form of potato is irresistible. Since oblong-shaped baking potatoes (also called russet or Idaho potatoes) contain less moisture than boiling potatoes, they produce crisper latkes. Although these pancakes remain a favorite comfort food, I have seen miniature ones served as hors d'oeuvres at fancy affairs.

3 pounds (about 6 large) baking potatoes, peeled
1 large yellow onion, finely chopped (about ¾ cup)
3 large eggs, lightly beaten
About ¼ cup matza meal or all-purpose flour
About 1¼ teaspoons salt
About ¼ teaspoon ground black pepper
Vegetable oil for frying

1. Grate the potatoes coarsely or finely into the onion and stir to combine. (This keeps the potatoes from darkening.) Press out as much moisture as possible. If desired, puree part of the potatoes and stir back into the grated potatoes. Stir in the eggs, matza meal, salt, and pepper.
2. Heat about ¼ inch oil in a large skillet over medium-high heat until the oil shimmers.
3. In batches, drop the batter by ¼ cupfuls into the oil and flatten with the back of a spoon. Fry, turning, until golden brown on both sides, 3 to 5 minutes per side. Drain on paper towels. (The flavor and texture of latkes deteriorate rather quickly, but they can be reheated. Place the cooled or frozen latkes in a single layer on a baking sheet and reheat in a 375-degree oven until crisp, about 5 minutes per side for cooled, 8 minutes per side for frozen.) Serve with applesauce, jam, or for dairy meals, sour cream.

Applesauce
ABOUT 3 CUPS

*A*pples are traditional Greek Hanukkah fare, based on a legend that the Maccabees ate duck with apples at a feast in celebration of their victory.

2 pounds (6 to 7 medium) cooking apples (such as Golden Delicious, Granny Smith, Gravenstein, Jonathan, Pippin, Starr, Winesap, or any combination), peeled, cored, and sliced
½ cup water, apple cider, or apple juice
About 2 tablespoons fresh lemon juice
1 (3-inch) stick cinnamon or ⅛ teaspoon ground cinnamon (optional)
¼ to ½ cup granulated sugar, packed brown sugar, or honey
⅛ teaspoon ground cardamom, cloves, or nutmeg (optional)

1. Bring the apples, water, lemon juice, and if desired, the cinnamon stick to a boil. Reduce the heat to low, cover, and simmer, stirring occasionally and adding more water if necessary, until the apples are soft, about 20 minutes.
2. Stir in the sugar and, if desired, the cardamom and simmer until the juice becomes syrupy, 2 to 3 minutes.
3. For a chunky sauce, mash the apples with a potato masher. For a smooth sauce, puree in a food processor or food mill.

Green Beans with Mustard Seeds
8 SERVINGS

¼ cup vegetable oil
2 teaspoons mustard seeds
2 pounds green beans, sliced
2 medium onions, chopped (about 1 cup)
1 teaspoon ground cardamom
About ¼ teaspoon salt
Pinch of ground black pepper
3 tablespoons fresh lemon juice

1. Heat the oil in a large saucepan over medium-high heat. Add the mustard seeds and cook until they begin to pop.
2. Add the green beans, onions, cardamom, salt, and pepper and sauté for 3 minutes. Add the lemon juice, cover, reduce the heat to low, and simmer until the beans are tender-crisp, about 10 minutes. (The beans can be prepared up to 2 hours ahead and reheated.)

Jelly Doughnuts (*Sufganiyot*)
ABOUT 16 MEDIUM DOUGHNUTS

I spent my junior year of college studying in an Israeli yeshiva. The food was typically Israeli and generally more healthful than the American diet. Breakfast consisted of rolls, salads, yogurt, and cereal. Dinner was similar but with the addition of a main course such as pasta. Lunch was the main meal of the day, usually featuring chicken or turkey in some form. Partway through the year a new lunch cook appeared on the scene, a middle-aged Russian émigrée who did not quite grasp the concept of gastronomy. Her first lunch featured stewed *pupicks* (gizzards). Believe me, the following several attempts were no better. Such questionable fare naturally provoked complaints and grumbling from the student body. In frustration, the cook asked some students what types of foods Westerners ate for lunch and received various replies, including fish cakes. That Friday night

we bit into dessert and had a rude shock. The hapless cook had added salted fish to the cake batter! I suppose some cultural barriers prove impossible to span.

Fortunately, the dinner cook, a nice Moroccan woman, consistently demonstrated much greater competency in the kitchen than her lunchtime counterpart. However, she had never tasted, let alone cooked, a potato latke during her entire life. Instead, for Hanukkah she stood over a pot of boiling oil and fried up batches of delicious jelly doughnuts.

Jews in Poland adopted a traditional Polish doughnut filled with preserves, most notably prune or raspberry, called *ponchik*s (written *paczki* in Polish) as their favorite Hanukkah dish. Australian Jews, many of whom emigrated from Poland during the twentieth century, still refer to jelly doughnuts as *ponchiks*. When the jelly doughnut made its way to Israel, however, it took the name *sufganiyot*, a "spongy dough" mentioned in the Talmud. *Sufganiyot* subsequently emerged as the most popular Israeli Hanukkah treat, sold at almost every bakery and market. Today when my nieces and nephews urge me to make *sufganiyot* each Hanukkah, I still remember those turned out by that Moroccan cook.

1 (¼-ounce) package (about 2½ teaspoons) active dry yeast
½ cup warm water (105 to 115 degrees)
¼ cup sugar
½ cup milk or nondairy creamer (use the creamer for meat meals)
⅓ cup unsalted butter or margarine, softened (use the margarine for meat meals)
3 large egg yolks or 2 large eggs
1 teaspoon table salt or 2 teaspoons kosher salt
About 3¾ cups unbleached all-purpose flour
Vegetable oil, safflower oil, peanut oil, or shortening for deep-frying
About 1 cup jelly, whipped cream, custard, or pudding (use the jelly for meat meals)
Confectioners' or granulated sugar for dusting

1. Dissolve the yeast in the warm water. Add 1 teaspoon of the sugar and let stand until foamy, 5 to 10 minutes.
2. Stir in the milk, remaining sugar, butter, egg yolks, salt, and 2 cups of the flour. Beat in enough of the remaining flour to make a smooth, soft dough. Cover loosely with plastic wrap or a towel and let rise in a warm, draft-free place until double in bulk, about 1½ hours.
3. Punch down the dough. On a lightly floured surface, knead until smooth, about 12 times.

4. Roll out the dough until ¼ inch thick. Using a biscuit cutter or glass, cut out 2½- to 3½-inch rounds. Place the dough rounds in a single layer on a lightly floured baking sheet, cover, and let rise until double in bulk, about 1 hour.

5. In a heavy pot or deep-fat fryer, heat at least 1 inch of oil or shortening over medium heat to 375 degrees. (To test the temperature of the oil, use a candy thermometer or drop a cube of soft white bread into the oil; it should brown in 35 seconds.)

6. Using an oiled spatula, carefully lift the doughnuts and drop them, top side down, into the oil. (If you drop them bottom side down, the doughnuts will be difficult to turn.) Fry 3 or 4 at a time, without crowding the pan, until golden brown on all sides, 3 to 5 minutes. (The temperature of the oil should not drop below 350 degrees.) Remove with a slotted spoon and drain on paper towels.

7. Pierce the edge of each doughnut with a thin knife and pivot it back and forth to slit the insides and form a pocket. Place the jelly in a pastry bag with a 1¼-inch hole or nozzle tip and pipe it through the slit. Sprinkle with confectioners' sugar or roll in granulated sugar.

VARIATION

To make doughnuts without a pastry bag: Place 1 teaspoon of jelly in the center of half of the dough rounds. Brush the edges with egg white. (Save a white from the eggs used to make the dough.) Top with a second dough round and press the edges to seal.

Hanukkah Gelt (Chocolate Coins)
ABOUT 50 LARGE CANDIES

*R*ecently chocolate coins have fulfilled the role of Hanukkah gelt (the traditional gift of money to children). The following coins, not necessarily for children, are made from a rich chocolate mixture called a ganache.

GANACHE
1¼ cups plus 2 tablespoons heavy cream
4 tablespoons (½ stick) unsalted butter

12 to 14 ounces semisweet or bittersweet chocolate, chopped
3 tablespoons almond, hazelnut, orange, raspberry, or other liqueur
¾ teaspoon vanilla extract

COATING
2 pounds semisweet or bittersweet chocolate, chopped

1. You will need two 14- by 4-inch rectangular flan molds (bottomless metal molds about 1 inch high), which can easily be removed from the chocolate. Or you can make molds by cutting 2 large pieces of cardboard into ¾- to 1-inch-wide strips about 36 inches long, wrapping with aluminum foil, and bending into 14- by 4-inch rectangles. Line a large baking sheet with parchment paper and set the flan molds or homemade molds on top.

2. To make the ganache: Bring the cream and butter to a simmer in a medium saucepan over medium heat. Pour over the 12 to 14 ounces chocolate and stir until melted. (This can be done in a food processor with the machine running.) Stir in the liqueur and vanilla.

3. Spread the ganache evenly into the flan molds to a ½-inch thickness. Cover with plastic wrap and smooth the surface. Refrigerate until firm, at least 30 minutes.

4. Using a heated 1¼- to 2-inch biscuit or cookie cutter (or a metal can with the top removed), cut out rounds. Chill until firm, at least 2 hours.

5. To make the coating: In the top of a double boiler over barely simmering water or in a microwave, melt the chocolate, stirring until smooth.

6. Dip the ganache rounds into the chocolate, letting the excess drip off. Place on a parchment-lined baking sheet and refrigerate until firm, at least 1 hour. If desired, wrap the candy in pieces of gold- or silver-colored aluminum foil. Store in an airtight container in the refrigerator for up to 2 weeks or in the freezer for up to 2 months.

DREIDEL

 A custom developed in some areas for women not to do work while the Hanukkah menorah was lit. To help pass the thirty minutes to an hour until the lights burned out and dinner was served, the family played various games. Although some rabbis attacked this practice, the custom spread, and by the end of the Middle Ages, even card games such as a Hungarian version of blackjack called *kvitli* had become popular. So that the children could wager, parents gave them Hanukkah gelt (money) and candy.

The best known of these games of chance involves a four-sided top called a *dreidel* in Yiddish (*sevivon* in Hebrew), patterned after an old German game. On its sides are four Hebrew letters—*nun, gimmel, heh,* and *shin*—representing the phrase *nes gadol hayah sham* (a great miracle happened there). In Israel the last letter of the dreidel is a *peh*, "here" (instead of "there"). After each player antes up (using Hanukkah gelt, candy, nuts, or other tokens), participants take turns spinning the dreidel. If it falls to reveal the *nun*, the spinner nets *nisht* (nothing); *gimmel* gets *gantz* (all); *heh* receives *halb* (half); and *shin* results in *shtel* (put in). The game is over when one player wins everything or the participants tire of the competition, whichever comes first.

A Fruitful Tu b'Shevat

SERVES 8

*T*u b'Shevat (the fifteenth day of the month of Shevat) is a minor holiday sometimes referred to as Jewish Arbor Day and by the Talmud as Rosh Hashanah l'Ilanot (New Year for Trees). In Israel by early February, most of the year's rain has fallen, the sap starts to flow again, and the branches begin to show the first signs of budding. In agricultural-based ancient Israel, this was a meaningful occasion accompanied by singing and dancing. Sephardim manifested a deep devotion for the day, which they called Las Fructus (The Fruit). Among Ashkenazim, on the other hand, Tu b'Shevat was only marginally celebrated, probably because it falls in the dead of winter in northern Europe. Beginning in the late 1800s with the establishment of agricultural settlements in Israel, where there was a need to plant trees to rebuild the land, this holiday took on renewed significance.

The principal influence on Tu b'Shevat practices came from a group of sixteenth-century kabbalists living in Safed who developed a new liturgy and rituals including a "Seder." An expanded version of these prayers and a description of the Tu b'Shevat Seder were collected in the anonymous eighteenth-century work *Peri Etz Hadar* (Fruit of the Goodly Tree). In the Tu b'Shevat Seder, the first cup of wine is white—symbolizing the snows of winter—and is followed by fruits that have an inedible covering, including nuts, citrus fruits, pineapples, and pomegranates. The second cup is golden—symbolizing the sap beginning to flow in the trees—and is followed by fruits that have edible coverings but also contain large pits, including apricots, carob, cherries, dates, peaches, plums, and olives. The third cup is pink—symbolizing the blossoms that are just sprouting on the branches—and is followed by completely edible fruit or those with very small seeds, including apples, berries, figs, grapes, quinces, and pears. The fourth and final cup is a deep red, symbolizing the fertility of the land. Appropriate psalms and biblical verses referring to fruit and vegetables are recited during the Seder.

Although there are few specific Tu b'Shevat dishes, a common custom is to serve fare containing fruit, nuts, and wheat or barley.

FRUITED CHALLAH (PAGE 40)
PÂTÉ ON APPLE SLICES
DRIED FRUIT SOUP
CHERRY-GLAZED CHICKEN
SPICED WINTER SQUASH
ZUCCHINI CUPS WITH TINY PEAS
FRUITED BULGUR
FRESH FRUIT TART
TEA AND COFFEE

 Wine Suggestions: Dry Riesling, Gewürztraminer, or Chenin Blanc

Pâté on Apple Slices

ABOUT 45 PIECES

3 tablespoons fresh lemon juice
3 tablespoons water
3 to 4 eating apples, such as Yellow Delicious, Gala, Granny Smith, or McIntosh
2 cups chopped liver
Sliced olives, sliced cornichons, or parsley sprigs

1. Combine the lemon juice and water. Core the apples, cut in half, then cut each half into ¼-inch-thick crescents. Dip the slices into the lemon water to prevent browning.
2. Just before preparing, drain the apples and pat dry. Spread one side of the apple slices with a thin layer of chopped liver. Garnish with a slice of olive or cornichon or a parsley sprig.

Dried Fruit Soup

8 SERVINGS

*T*he world abounds with an untold number of edible fruits, the seed-bearing part of a plant. Although many of these once exotic items are becoming a common sight in Western markets, the old standards still retain their mass appeal. This soup makes a refreshing start to a meal, as well as a light finish. Vary the soup by adding assorted fresh fruit, such as berries, cherries, peaches, and plums.

2 pounds (about 7 cups) any combination mixed dried fruit, such as apples, apricots,
    blueberries, cherries, cranberries, figs, peaches, pears, prunes, and raisins
8 cups water
1 to 1½ cups sugar or honey
1 medium lemon, sliced
2 (3-inch) sticks cinnamon
1 whole clove (optional)
1 to 2 cups orange juice, grape juice, or dry white wine

1. Place the dried fruit and water in a large pot and let soak for at least 1 hour.
2. Add the sugar, lemon slices, cinnamon sticks, and if desired, the clove. Bring to a boil, cover, reduce the heat to low, and simmer until the fruit is very tender, about 40 minutes.
3. Stir in the juice. Serve warm or chilled.

Cherry-Glazed Chicken
8 SERVINGS

¼ cup (½ stick) unsalted margarine or vegetable oil
2 medium red or yellow onions, sliced
2 (3-pound) chickens, cut up, or 4 Rock Cornish hens, halved
Salt to taste
Ground black pepper to taste
About 1 cup all-purpose flour
1 cup dry white wine or white vermouth

SAUCE
About 3 tablespoons sugar
2 tablespoons cornstarch
2 (17-ounce) cans pitted cherries, with juice
½ cup brandy or dry red wine
Slivered almonds (optional)

1. Preheat the oven to 375 degrees.
2. Melt the margarine in a large roasting pan over medium heat. Add the onions and sauté until soft, about 10 minutes.
3. Sprinkle the chicken with salt and pepper and dredge with the flour. Arrange the chicken pieces, skin side up, in a single layer in the pan. Bake, uncovered, for 30 minutes. Add the wine and bake until the chicken is fork-tender, about 30 additional minutes.
4. To make the sauce: Combine the sugar and cornstarch in a medium saucepan. Stir in 1⅓ cups of the cherry juice (if needed, add roasting liquid from the pan to make 1⅓ cups) and brandy. Bring to a boil, reduce the heat to medium-low, and simmer, stir-

ring constantly, until thickened. Add the cherries and heat through, about 1 minute. Spoon the cherry sauce over the chicken and bake for several minutes. If desired, garnish with slivered almonds.

Spiced Winter Squash
8 SERVINGS

3 pounds butternut, acorn, or other winter squash, peeled, seeded, and cut into 1-inch pieces
¼ cup (½ stick) unsalted margarine
4 cardamom pods, hulled and ground, or 2 teaspoons cumin seeds
1 teaspoon turmeric
Salt to taste

1. Cook the squash in boiling water until tender, 20 to 30 minutes. Or cut the squash in half lengthwise, place on a baking sheet, cut side down, and bake at 375 degrees until tender, about 25 minutes; peel and cut into 1-inch pieces.
2. Melt the margarine in a large skillet over medium heat. Add the cardamom and turmeric and sauté for 1 minute.
3. Add the squash and sauté until heated through, 2 to 3 minutes. Season with the salt. (The squash can be refrigerated, then reheated over low heat.)

Zucchini Cups with Tiny Peas
8 SERVINGS

These attractive cups can also be filled with sautéed chopped zucchini or a vegetable puree.

4 large (about 10 ounces each) zucchini
2 cups frozen tiny green peas, thawed
About 3 tablespoons olive oil or melted unsalted margarine
Salt to taste
Ground black pepper to taste

1. Remove lengthwise strips of peel from the zucchini, leaving on equal-size strips of peel to create a striped effect. Cut the zucchini crosswise into 2- to 3-inch sections. Using a melon baller or spoon, hollow out the zucchini rounds, leaving ¼-inch-thick sides and a ½-inch-thick bottom.
2. Cook the zucchini in a large pot of lightly salted boiling water or steam until tender-crisp, about 4 minutes. Quickly plunge under cold water to stop the cooking. Invert onto paper towels and let drain.
3. Combine the peas, oil, salt, and pepper. Arrange the zucchini in a baking dish and fill with the peas. (The cups can be stored in the refrigerator for 1 day.)
4. Preheat the oven to 350 degrees.
5. Bake the zucchini until heated through.

Fruited Bulgur

8 SERVINGS

1½ cups boiling water
1 cup (about 6 ounces) fine- or medium-grain bulgur
⅓ cup fresh lemon juice
6 tablespoons extra-virgin olive oil
1 cup chopped fresh parsley
½ cup chopped scallions
¼ to ½ cup chopped fresh mint or 1 tablespoon dried
¼ cup chopped dried apricots
¼ cup dried currants or raisins
¼ cup chopped pitted dates
⅓ cup coarsely chopped almonds or pistachios
⅛ teaspoon ground cinnamon
Pinch of salt

1. Pour the boiling water over the bulgur and let stand until tender, 20 to 40 minutes, depending on the age and type of bulgur. Drain off any excess water.
2. Mix the lemon juice and oil, drizzle over the salad, and toss to coat. Stir in the remaining ingredients. Cover and refrigerate for several hours to let the flavors meld. Serve cold or at room temperature.

Fresh Fruit Tart
8 TO 10 SERVINGS

*U*se any soft fresh fruit or poached hard fruit for this tart, such as bananas, blackberries, blueberries, pitted cherries, seedless grapes, kiwis, mangoes, sliced nectarines, orange slices, papayas, peaches, poached pears, plums, raspberries, strawberries, or any combination.

PÂTE SABLÉE
¾ cup (1½ sticks) unsalted margarine, softened (for dairy meals,
*   you can substitute ¾ cup unsalted butter)*
⅓ cup sugar
1 large egg or 2 large egg yolks
½ teaspoon salt
2 cups all-purpose flour
Ice water as needed

PASTRY CREAM
1 cup nondairy creamer or coconut milk (for dairy meals, you can use 1 cup cream)
Pinch of salt
3 large egg yolks, lightly beaten
6 tablespoons sugar
2 tablespoons cornstarch or 3 tablespoons all-purpose flour
½ teaspoon vanilla extract

¼ cup apricot preserves, apple jelly, or red currant jelly, melted and strained
3 to 4 cups soft fresh fruit or poached hard fruit

1. To make the pastry: Beat the margarine and sugar until smooth and creamy. Add the egg and salt. Gradually blend in the flour. (The dough should have the consistency of a sugar cookie dough.) Form into a ball and flatten into a disk. Cover with plastic wrap and refrigerate for at least 1 hour or up to 1 week.
2. On a lightly floured piece of wax paper or flat surface, roll out the pastry to a ⅛-inch thickness. Line a 9- or 10-inch flat-bottom tart pan with the pastry and trim the

edges. Using the tines of a fork, prick the bottom and sides at ½-inch intervals. Cover with plastic wrap and refrigerate for at least 1 hour and up to 4 days.

3. Preheat the oven to 375 degrees.

4. Line the bottom and sides of the pastry shell with aluminum foil and fill with pie weights or dried beans, pressing against the sides. Bake until the pastry is set, about 10 minutes. Remove the foil and weights and bake until lightly browned, about 10 minutes. Let cool on a rack. (The crust can be prepared a day ahead, covered, and stored at room temperature.)

5. To make the pastry cream: In the top of a double boiler over medium heat, warm the creamer and salt until small bubbles appear around the edges. Meanwhile, beat the egg yolks and sugar until thick and creamy, about 5 minutes. Stir in the cornstarch or flour. (Cornstarch produces a lighter cream; flour, a sturdier cream.) Gradually beat in the warm creamer. Return to the double boiler and cook, stirring, until smooth and thickened, 6 to 10 minutes.

6. Strain into a medium bowl and stir in the vanilla. Whisk over a bowl of ice until cooled or press a piece of plastic wrap against the surface and refrigerate until chilled, at least 4 hours or overnight. (The pastry cream can be stored in an airtight container in the refrigerator for up to 3 days.)

7. It is preferable not to assemble the tart until a little before serving. Brush the bottom and sides of the cooled tart shell with about 2 tablespoons of the melted jam. Spread with the pastry cream, then arrange the fruit in concentric circles over the top. Brush with the remaining melted jam.

A Purim Feast

SERVES 8

*I*n 586 B.C.E. the emperor Nebuchadnezzar and his Babylonian forces destroyed Jerusalem and the First Temple, then exiled the upper and middle classes of Judea to Babylon. Forty-seven years later Babylon was conquered by Cyrus and the Jews suddenly found themselves part of the Persian Empire. It was during this era that the Purim story unfolded.

The events commemorated by the Festival of Lots are recorded in the Megillat Ester (Scroll of Esther). Ahasuerus, who ruled the Persian Empire from his capital in Shushan, promoted Haman to the position of prime minister. The new leader conspired to exterminate the entire Jewish population of the Persian Empire on the thirteenth day of the month of Adar. The plot backfired when it turned out that the new queen, Esther, was actually a Jew, and the villain and his allies were roundly routed.

In response to Haman's plot to physically annihilate the Jews, their descendants commemorate Purim through physical enjoyment and riotous celebration. There are four central Purim rituals: reading the Megillat Ester, sending *mishloach manot* (gifts of foods, more commonly pronounced *shalachmones*) to friends, giving money to the poor, and eating a *seudah* (feast). Numerous other traditions emerged over the centuries. During the Megillah reading, listeners make noise at every mention of Haman, literally blotting out the villain's name. Ashkenazim use traditional noise-makers called *groggers.* Children as well as many adults dress up in costumes, a custom that originated in Italy at the end of the fifteenth century, inspired by the masked entertainers of the Commedia dell'Arte. In the sixteenth century a custom emerged in Europe for students to perform humorous skits called *purimshpiel*s, giving them an opportunity to make good-natured fun of everyone. In accordance with the statement of the Babylonian scholar Rava that "a man is obliged to drink until he no longer knows the difference between cursing Haman and blessing Mordechai," alcohol is liberally enjoyed, a practice most strongly disapproved of during the rest of the year.

The *seudah* is traditionally held on Purim afternoon. Ashkenazic feasts begin with a *keylitch,* a large braided challah, symbolizing the rope on which Haman was hung. Many Purim dishes involve a filling, alluding to the many intrigues, secrets, and surprises unfolding in the Purim story. Reflecting a legend that Esther ate only vegetable dishes while living in the palace, chickpeas and fava beans are traditional fare.

Kabbalists compare Purim to another, seemingly unrelated holiday: Yom Kippur. The similarity in names was seen as no coincidence, and a parallel was drawn between the physical lots of Purim cast by Haman and the metaphysical lots of Yom Kippur. Indeed, the great kabbalist Yitzchak Luria referred to the Day of Atonement as Yom ke-Purim (Day like Purim). Thus foods

served on Yom Kippur eve, especially kreplach, which like *hamantaschen* have three corners, became traditional Purim fare.

I once prepared an elaborate Purim *seudah* in my apartment for a group of friends, one of whom brought along her visiting brother. This twenty-something gentleman failed to appreciate my handiwork, commenting that he preferred meat loaf to my stuffed veal and that the wine was not sweet enough. He also asked if the baked meringue layer in the mousse cake was stale bread. At least he seemed to favor the *hamantaschen,* which disappeared. As the cliché states, you can't please everybody. The following menu, however, should elicit delighted responses from your guests.

BRAIDED CHALLAH

ASPARAGUS SOUP

GREEK FISH IN GRAPE LEAVES

ROCK CORNISH HENS WITH RICE AND PINE NUT STUFFING

SAUTÉED CHERRY TOMATOES

SESAME BROCCOLI

LEMON–POPPY SEED CAKE

STRAWBERRY AND RHUBARB SORBET

SHALACHMONES (PAGES 119 TO 134)

TEA AND COFFEE

 Wine Suggestions: Oak-aged Chardonnay, Sauvignon Blanc, or slightly chilled Beaujolais

---

Asparagus Soup
8 SERVINGS

Since Purim falls at the onset of spring, seasonal produce such as artichokes and asparagus hold a prominent place on many Purim tables.

¼ cup vegetable oil
3 medium onions, chopped (about 1½ cups)
7 cups chicken broth or water
3 pounds asparagus, tips removed and stalks chopped
½ cup long-grain white rice or
    1 large boiling potato, peeled and diced
About 1 teaspoon salt
About ½ teaspoon ground white pepper
Pinch of grated nutmeg, ground cumin, or cayenne
⅓ cup dry white wine or
    1 cup nondairy creamer (optional)

1. Heat the oil in a large saucepan over medium heat. Add the onions and sauté until soft and translucent, 5 to 10 minutes.
2. Add the broth and bring to a boil. Add the asparagus tips and boil until just tender, about 3 minutes. Remove the tips with a slotted spoon and plunge into cold water to stop the cooking. Set the tips aside.
3. Add the rice or potato and return to a boil. Cover, reduce the heat to low, and simmer until very tender, about 20 minutes for the rice, 40 minutes for the potato.
4. Add the chopped asparagus stalks, salt, pepper, and if desired, the nutmeg. Bring to a boil, cover, reduce the heat to low, and simmer until the asparagus is tender, about 10 minutes.
5. Strain, returning the liquid to the pot. Puree the solids and return to the pot. If desired, stir in the wine. Serve warm or chilled. Garnish with the asparagus tips.

Greek Fish in Grape Leaves

8 SERVINGS

*W*rapping the fish in grape leaves helps it to keep very moist flesh.

1 (8-ounce) jar (24 medium) preserved grape leaves
2 pounds 1-inch-thick firm white fish fillets (such as flounder, grouper,
    halibut, orange roughy, or sole), cut into 24 pieces
2 tablespoons chopped fresh basil, marjoram, mint,
    or thyme or 1 tablespoon dried
About ⅓ cup fresh lemon juice
Salt to taste
Ground black pepper to taste
2 cups dry white wine

1. Preheat the oven to 350 degrees. Grease a large baking dish.
2. Unroll the grape leaves, rinse under cold water, and soak in water to cover for 5 minutes. Drain and pat dry. Carefully cut off the stems. Place the leaves, shiny side down and vein side up, on a flat surface. Place a piece of fish on each leaf and sprinkle with the basil, lemon juice, salt, and pepper. Fold over the sides of the leaves to enclose the fish. (The fish packages can be prepared several hours ahead and stored in the refrigerator.)
3. Place the fish packages, seam side down, in the prepared pan and add the wine. Bake, uncovered, for 20 minutes. Serve 3 packages per person.

VARIATION
Substitute 24 romaine lettuce leaves blanched in boiling water for the grape leaves.

Rock Cornish Hens with Rice and Pine Nut Stuffing

8 SERVINGS

*T*iny hens, if available, make delightful individual servings; split larger ones for two servings. With some difficulty, I was able to procure 150 of these tiny birds for my cousin Avi's wedding to Deborah. Since my Manhattan apartment could not possibly handle an affair of this size, I rented the kitchen of a nearby synagogue to do the advance preparations and store the food until the wedding day. The hens arrived frozen on Friday morning, and I figured that after a weekend in the refrigerator, they would be thawed and ready to stuff on Sunday. Wrong! The synagogue's refrigerator gauge went off kilter, and everything inside was frozen solid on Sunday morning. The birds were hardly much better by the time we reached the synagogue in New Jersey where the affair was being held. To be honest, I did what some experts caution against doing—I rinsed the hens under water until sufficiently pliable. Everything else went without a hitch, and in the end, the hens looked and tasted great.

STUFFING
3 tablespoons olive or vegetable oil
1 large onion, chopped (about ¾ cup)
1⅓ cups long-grain white rice
⅓ cup pine nuts
2⅔ cups chicken broth or water
1 teaspoon salt
¼ teaspoon ground black pepper
¼ cup brandy
2 tablespoons chopped fresh tarragon or 4 teaspoons dried

8 small or 4 medium Rock Cornish hens
½ cup (1 stick) unsalted margarine, melted, or olive oil

1. To make the stuffing: Heat the oil in a large saucepan over medium heat. Add the onion and sauté until soft and translucent. Add the rice and pine nuts and sauté until the rice is opaque, about 3 minutes. Add the broth, salt, and pepper, cover, and

bring to a boil. Reduce the heat to low and simmer until the liquid is absorbed, about 18 minutes. Stir in the brandy and tarragon and let cool.

2. Preheat the oven to 400 degrees.

3. Loosely fill the hens with the stuffing. Set on a rack in a shallow roasting pan, breast side down, leaving room between each bird. Brush with some of the margarine.

4. Roast for 15 minutes. Turn the hens onto one side, brush with margarine, and roast another 15 minutes. Turn onto the other side, brush with margarine, and roast 15 minutes. Turn the hens breast side up and continue roasting until browned and tender and the thigh meat registers 180 degrees on a meat thermometer, 10 to 30 additional minutes (about 1 hour total). Cut larger hens in half. Spoon the stuffing onto the serving plates and arrange the hen alongside.

Sautéed Cherry Tomatoes

8 SERVINGS

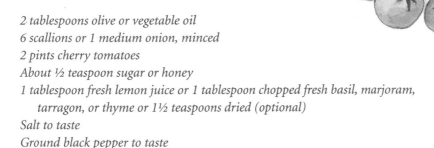

2 tablespoons olive or vegetable oil
6 scallions or 1 medium onion, minced
2 pints cherry tomatoes
About ½ teaspoon sugar or honey
1 tablespoon fresh lemon juice or 1 tablespoon chopped fresh basil, marjoram,
    tarragon, or thyme or 1½ teaspoons dried (optional)
Salt to taste
Ground black pepper to taste

Heat the oil in a large skillet over medium heat. Add the scallions and sauté until soft. Add the tomatoes, sugar, and if desired, the lemon juice and sauté until heated through, about 2 minutes. Do not overcook or the tomatoes will be mushy. Season with the salt and pepper.

VARIATION

Substitute 10 medium (about 6 ounces each) ripe tomatoes, peeled, seeded, and cut into slices or wedges for the cherry tomatoes.

Sesame Broccoli
8 SERVINGS

3 pounds (about 2 large bunches) broccoli, cut into florets
⅓ cup vegetable oil
2 to 3 cloves garlic, peeled
2 medium onions or 4 scallions, chopped
3 tablespoons sesame seeds, toasted
3 tablespoons soy sauce
3 tablespoons rice vinegar or white vinegar
Salt to taste
Ground black pepper to taste

1. Blanch the broccoli in lightly salted boiling water or steam for 3 to 4 minutes. Rinse under cold water and drain.
2. Heat the vegetable oil in a large skillet or wok over medium heat. Add the garlic and sauté until browned but not burned. Remove and discard the garlic.
3. Add the onions and sauté until soft and translucent, 5 to 10 minutes. Add the broccoli, sesame seeds, soy sauce, vinegar, salt, and pepper and sauté until the broccoli is tender-crisp and heated through, 2 to 3 minutes.

Lemon-Poppy Seed Cake
8 TO 10 SERVINGS

*T*he similarity of the German word for "poppy seed," *mohn,* to the villain of the Purim story, Haman (pronounced *hamohn* in Hebrew), led to its inclusion in many Ashkenazic Purim dishes, especially desserts.

2 cups cake flour or 1¾ cups all-purpose flour
1 teaspoon baking powder
½ teaspoon salt

1 cup (2 sticks) unsalted margarine or vegetable shortening
1⅓ cups sugar
5 large eggs, lightly beaten
1 tablespoon fresh lemon juice
1 teaspoon vanilla extract
4 teaspoons grated lemon zest
¼ cup poppy seeds

SYRUP
⅓ cup fresh lemon juice
⅓ cup sugar

1. Preheat the oven to 325 degrees. Grease the bottom and halfway up the sides of a 9-by 5-inch loaf pan or 9-inch tube or Bundt pan.
2. Sift together the flour, baking powder, and salt. Beat the margarine until smooth. Add the sugar and beat until light and fluffy, about 5 minutes. Beat in the eggs, one at a time. Add the flour mixture, lemon juice, vanilla, and zest. Stir in the poppy seeds.
3. Pour the batter into the prepared pan and tap to remove any air bubbles. Bake until the cake is lightly browned and a wooden tester inserted in the center comes out clean, about 1¼ hours.
4. To make the syrup: Simmer the lemon juice and sugar over medium-low heat until the sugar dissolves.
5. Remove the cake from the oven and let stand on a rack for 2 minutes. Pierce the surface of the hot cake in several places with the tines of a fork. Brush the top of the cake with the syrup until all of it is used up. Let the cake cool in the pan for 15 minutes, then turn out on a rack, place upright, and let cool completely.

VARIATION
Double the recipe and bake in a 10-inch tube or Bundt pan at least 4 inches deep.

Strawberry and Rhubarb Sorbet
8 SERVINGS

These seasonal fruits complement each other, producing a refreshing end to a meal.

2 pints strawberries, hulled
2 pounds rhubarb, cut into pieces
2 cups Gewürztraminer wine
1 cup sugar
1 cup light corn syrup

1. Stir all the ingredients over high heat until the sugar dissolves. Cover, reduce the heat to low, and simmer until the rhubarb is very tender, 15 to 20 minutes.
2. In a food processor or blender, puree the mixture until smooth. Pour into a shallow dish and let cool.
3. Place in the freezer until the mixture is nearly frozen, about 1½ hours. Break up and puree in the food processor or blender again. Return to the freezer until frozen.

Sophisticated *Shalachmones*

The Megillah declares, "They should make them days of feasting and gladness, of sending portions [*mishloach manot*] one to another and gifts to the poor." The obligation of *shalachmones* entails sending gifts of at least two ready-to-eat foods to at least two people. The most common Purim foods are sweets, a symbolic way to wish for a "good lot" or, in other words, a sweet future. It is for good reason that Muslims refer to Purim as Id-al-Sukkar (The Sugar Holiday).

Shalachmones has become a bit commercial lately, with many baskets containing the same assortment of bags of snack foods, chemically laden cakes and cookies, and candy bars. While store-bought foods certainly fulfill the letter of the law, they lack something in the spirit. Homemade goodies show special care and thought, and they generally taste better. Granted, many people are simply too busy to prepare their own *shalachmones*, and they should not feel guilty. But if you have the time and desire, prepare any or all of the following impressive treats. In addition, try making some classic cookies, muffins, or quick breads. Your *shalachmones* will not be the same old thing.

After you have gone to the trouble of making or purchasing special items for *shalachmones,* put them in something special. A cake pan or tart mold provides an appropriate base for baked goods. Insert a piece of velvet or other cloth in a large picture frame and use as a tray for a unique backdrop to your treats. (Your friends can then utilize the frame for its original intention.) Or use a large ceramic bowl. Baskets make charming containers and frequently can be purchased at bargain prices at discount and odd-lot stores.

Theme baskets can be an outlet for your ingenuity. Create an Italian motif with an assortment of pastas, homemade tomato sauce, pesto, balsamic vinegar, sun-dried tomatoes, salami, Italian bread or focaccia, biscotti, and a bottle of Italian wine. For a sushi basket, include some homemade sushi, short-grain rice, nori (seaweed sheets), rice vinegar, tamari, mirin (sweet rice wine), pickled ginger, wasabi (Japanese horseradish), salmon caviar, dashi (soup stock), sake, and Japanese tea and enclose instructions on how to use everything. For an English theme, choose Scones (page 381), an assortment of marmalades or jams, fresh strawberries, Cheddar cheese, rice pudding, pound cake, shortbread cookies, English ales and beers, and an array of teas. To create a Middle Eastern basket, include a medley of dishes from the *meze* section (pages 195–209). Of course, there is always the classic fruit basket.

A bottle of good kosher wine makes a welcome addition to your Purim gift. Use a mask (easy to make yourself using colored paper and elastic thread), candy money (to make your own gelt, see page 98), cards containing the music and words of popular Purim songs (you can find this infor-

mation at a Jewish bookstore), and/or a *grogger* (noisemaker) to enliven your presentation. You may want to add a note of explanation for those friends who are unfamiliar with the custom. If you are worried about the contents falling out or want to add a pretty effect, wrap the basket in cellophane and tie the top with a ribbon.

HAMANTASCHEN
PECAN TASSIES
INDIVIDUAL BAKLAVA
LEAF COOKIES
FORTUNE COOKIES
FLOWER SPRITZES
LEMON HALOS
ALMOND HORNS
SPICE SANDWICHES
SARAH BERNHARDTS
CHOCOLATE BELLS

Hamantaschen

ABOUT 40 SMALL PASTRIES

Shape is the underlying theme of traditional Purim pastries, symbolically erasing Haman's name or identifying with Esther and Mordechai. Winding the dough to produce ear-shaped pastries, the most widespread Purim sweet, comes from the medieval custom of cutting off a criminal's ear before execution, a reference to Haman's fate. Middle Eastern Jews eat a date-filled cookie variously called *menanas, ma'amoul,* and *makrud.* Turkish and Syrian Jews prepare ring-like pastries symbolizing Esther's jewelry, such as *ka'ak* (sesame rings) or *graybeh/koorabie* (butter cookies). Austrians and Hungarians make *kindli* (little children) resembling a baby wrapped in a blanket, a symbol of Haman's large family. Ashkenazim from western Europe bake gingerbread men, while those from the East favor the triangular *hamantaschen* (Haman's pockets).

Of the many versions of *hamantaschen* made with cookie dough, this is my favorite. If poppy seeds are not to your liking, substitute about 1½ cups lekvar (prune jam), *povidl* (plum preserves), or other filling.

DOUGH

11 tablespoons (1 stick plus 3 tablespoons) unsalted butter or margarine, softened
½ cup sugar
1 large egg
3 tablespoons fresh orange juice or water (or 2 tablespoons water
* and 1 tablespoon fresh lemon juice)*
1 teaspoon vanilla extract
¼ teaspoon salt
About 2¾ cups all-purpose flour

POPPY SEED FILLING

1½ cups (about 7 ounces) poppy seeds, ground in a food grinder or food processor
¾ cup water or milk
⅔ cup sugar or honey (or ⅓ cup each)
1 tablespoon fresh lemon or orange juice or ½ teaspoon vanilla extract
1 tablespoon unsalted butter or margarine
Pinch of salt
1½ teaspoons grated lemon or orange zest (optional)
⅓ cup raisins
¼ cup finely chopped almonds, walnuts, or pecans (optional)

1. To make the dough: Beat the butter or margarine until smooth, about 1 minute. Gradually add the sugar and beat until light and fluffy, about 5 minutes. Beat in the egg. Blend in the juice, vanilla, and salt. Stir in enough of the flour to make a soft dough. Wrap the dough in plastic wrap and chill until firm, at least 1 hour or up to 3 days.

2. To make the filling: Combine the poppy seeds, water, and sugar and simmer over medium-low heat, stirring frequently, until the mixture thickens, about 10 minutes. Remove from the heat and add the remaining ingredients. Let cool. (The filling can be stored in the refrigerator for up to 3 days.)

3. Preheat the oven to 375 degrees.

4. If the dough is too hard to roll out, let it stand at room temperature until malleable but not soft. For easy handling, divide the dough into 4 pieces. On a lightly floured surface, roll out each piece ⅛ inch thick. Using a 2½- to 3-inch cookie cutter or glass, cut out rounds. Reroll and cut the scraps.

5. Place 1 teaspoon of the filling in the center of each round. Pinch the bottom edge of the dough round to form a point. Continue pressing the edges together partway over the filling. Fold down the top of the dough round and pinch the corners together to form the other two points of a triangle. Press the edges of the dough together over the filling, leaving some filling exposed in the center. (The *hamantaschen* can be frozen at this point for several months. Thaw before baking.)

6. Place the *hamantaschen* 1 inch apart on ungreased baking sheets. Bake until golden brown, about 13 minutes. Transfer to a wire rack and let cool completely.

Pecan Tassies

ABOUT 2 DOZEN PASTRIES

*A*lthough pecan is the traditional filling for these southern tartlets, any pie filling can be substituted. For a pareve treat, substitute standard pâte brisée (flaky pastry, page 273) for the cream cheese pastry.

PASTRY

1 cup (2 sticks) unsalted butter or margarine, softened
8 ounces cream cheese, softened
½ teaspoon salt
2 cups all-purpose flour

FILLING

¾ cup packed brown sugar
1 large egg
1 tablespoon unsalted butter or margarine, melted
1 teaspoon vanilla extract
Pinch of salt
⅔ cup coarsely chopped pecans

1. To make the pastry: Beat the butter and cream cheese together until light and fluffy. Add the salt. Beat in the flour to form a smooth dough. Wrap in plastic and refrigerate for at least 1 hour or up to 4 days.

2. Preheat the oven to 350 degrees. Lightly grease 24 mini (1-ounce) muffin cups.

3. On a lightly floured surface, roll out the dough ⅛ inch thick. Cut out 3-inch dough rounds and press into the prepared muffin cups. Or divide the dough into 24 balls and press onto the bottom and sides of the muffin cups. Refrigerate while preparing the filling.

4. To make the filling: Beat together the brown sugar, egg, butter, vanilla, and salt. Divide the pecans evenly among the pastry cups and spoon about 1½ teaspoons of the filling on top.

5. Bake until the filling is set and the pastry is golden brown, about 25 minutes. Let cool in the pan for 30 minutes, then release the edges with a knife and transfer to a rack.

VARIATIONS

Almond Tassies: Omit the pecan filling. Beat together ½ cup granulated sugar and ¼ cup (2 ounces) almond paste (page 361). Beat in 2 large egg yolks, one at a time. Stir in 3 tablespoons all-purpose flour, 2 tablespoons light cream or nondairy creamer, and 1 tablespoon water. If desired, spoon ½ teaspoon seedless raspberry jam into the tarts before adding the filling.

Chocolate Pecan Tassies: Substitute ⅓ cup granulated sugar for the brown sugar and add 6 ounces melted semisweet chocolate, 1 tablespoon milk, and if desired, 1 teaspoon coffee liqueur to the filling.

Individual Baklava

ABOUT 2 DOZEN PASTRIES

*B*aklava, which means "sweet-of-a-thousand-layers," is a traditional Purim treat throughout the Middle East but is also enjoyed throughout the year. This version consists of individual pastries.

SYRUP

2 cups sugar
1 cup water
2 (3-inch) cinnamon sticks or 1 teaspoon ground cinnamon
2 tablespoons fresh lemon juice (optional)

FILLING

4 cups (about 1 pound) finely chopped almonds, walnuts,
*   pistachios, or any combination*
½ cup sugar
2 teaspoons ground cinnamon

PASTRY

1 pound phyllo dough, cut in half crosswise
About 1 cup (2 sticks) unsalted butter or margarine, melted

1. To make the syrup: Stir the sugar and water over medium-low heat until the sugar dissolves. Stop stirring, increase the heat to medium-high, and bring to a boil. Add the cinnamon and, if desired, the lemon juice and simmer until slightly thickened, about 10 minutes. Let cool and refrigerate for at least 8 hours.
2. To make the filling: Combine all the filling ingredients.
3. Preheat the oven to 375 degrees. Grease a large baking sheet.
4. To assemble: Place 1 phyllo sheet on a flat surface and brush with butter. Place 2 tablespoons filling near a short end, fold the long sides over the filling, and starting from the filling end, roll up jelly-roll style. (The pastries can be frozen for up to 3 months. Do not thaw; increase the baking time by about 10 minutes.)
5. Place the pastries, seam side down, on the prepared baking sheet about 2 inches apart and brush with butter. Bake until golden brown, about 20 minutes.
6. Drizzle the cooled syrup slowly over the hot pastry. Cover and store at room temperature or in the freezer.

VARIATION

Date, Chocolate, and Nut Baklava: For the filling, reduce the nuts to 2 cups and the sugar to 2 tablespoons and add 6 ounces (about 1 cup) coarsely chopped pitted dates and 6 ounces coarsely chopped semisweet chocolate.

Leaf Cookies

ABOUT FIFTY 2½-INCH OR THIRTY 4-INCH COOKIES

Y̶ou can purchase a leaf mold—most have two 2½-inch-long cutouts—in a kitchen specialty store or make your own mold by cutting a leaf shape out of a thick piece of plastic or cardboard.

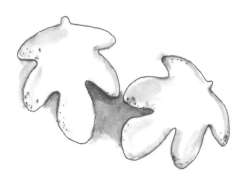

¾ cup all-purpose flour
⅓ cup finely ground almonds, hazelnuts,
    pecans, or walnuts
⅛ teaspoon salt
¼ cup (½ stick) unsalted butter
    or margarine, softened
⅓ cup superfine sugar
1 large egg or 2 large egg whites
½ teaspoon vanilla, almond, or orange extract

1. Preheat the oven to 350 degrees. Line a baking sheet with parchment paper or grease a large baking sheet.
2. Combine the flour, nuts, and salt. Beat the butter until smooth, about 1 minute. Add the sugar and beat until light and fluffy, about 5 minutes. Beat in the egg and vanilla. Stir in the flour mixture.
3. Place a leaf mold or stencil on the prepared baking sheet. Using a spatula dipped in cold water, spread a thin layer of batter in the mold (about 1 heaping teaspoonful for a 2½-inch-long mold), then carefully remove the mold. Wipe away any excess batter. Repeat, leaving about 1 inch between cookies.
4. Bake until the edges of the cookies are lightly colored, about 8 minutes. Set the baking sheet on a rack and let cool. Store the cookies in an airtight container at room temperature for up to 5 days or in the freezer for up to 3 months.

VARIATION

Chocolate-Dipped Leaf Cookies: Melt 12 ounces semisweet or bittersweet chocolate. Dip the tops of the cookies into the chocolate or spread the chocolate using a metal spatula. Place the cookies on a baking sheet lined with wax paper and let stand until set.

Fortune Cookies

ABOUT 16 COOKIES

*T*hese almond-flavored wafers are not an authentic Chinese food but were created by an enterprising San Francisco restaurateur who was looking for a way to keep his patrons occupied while they waited for the bill. You will need to prepare fortunes on small strips of paper. To help you get started, here are a few sample sayings:

Happy Purim!

The highest form of wisdom is kindness.—TALMUD BERACHOT 17:A

The beginning of wisdom is to desire it.—SOLOMON IBN GABIROL

Wisdom is to the soul as food is to the body.—ABRAHAM IBN EZRA

Happy is he who performs a good deed, for he may tip the scales for himself and the world.—TALMUD KIDDUSHIN 40:2

A man without friends is like a left hand without a right.—SOLOMON IBN GABIROL

6 tablespoons (about 5 large) egg whites
½ cup all-purpose flour
¾ cup sugar
1 tablespoon cornstarch
½ teaspoon almond extract
¼ teaspoon salt

1. Preheat the oven to 300 degrees. Grease a large baking sheet.
2. In a food processor or blender, process the egg whites for 30 seconds. Add the remaining ingredients and process until smooth. (This can also be done by hand.)
3. Drop by tablespoonfuls, 5 inches apart, onto the prepared baking sheet (3 to 4 at a time). Bake until the edges of the cookies begin to color, 13 to 15 minutes.
4. Remove from the oven and immediately place a fortune in the center of each cookie. Fold in half and pinch the edges together, holding for 1 minute to maintain the shape. (If the cookies harden too much to bend, return to the oven for a few seconds.) Let cool.

Flower Spritzes

ABOUT 5 DOZEN COOKIES

2 cups all-purpose flour
1 tablespoon unsweetened cocoa powder
1 cup (2 sticks) unsalted butter or margarine, softened
½ cup sugar
1½ tablespoons lightly beaten egg (about ½ large egg)
½ teaspoon vanilla extract
⅛ teaspoon salt

1. Preheat the oven to 350 degrees. Lightly grease several baking sheets.
2. Sift 1 cup of the flour with the cocoa. Beat the butter until smooth, about 1 minute. Add the sugar and beat until light and fluffy, about 5 minutes. Beat in the egg, vanilla, and salt. Divide in half. Add the cocoa mixture to half of the butter mixture and the remaining 1 cup flour to the other half.
3. Place the doughs in separate pastry bags fitted with ½-inch plain tips. For each cookie, pipe 5 to 6 dots of one type of dough in a circle on a prepared baking sheet. Pipe a dot of the other dough into the center. Space the cookies about 1 inch apart.
4. Bake the cookies until lightly golden, about 15 minutes. Let stand until firm, about 1 minute, then transfer to a wire rack and let cool completely.

Lemon Halos

ABOUT 4 DOZEN COOKIES

DOUGH
2 cups all-purpose flour
1 teaspoon baking soda
1 teaspoon salt
⅔ cup vegetable shortening
1 cup granulated or packed brown sugar
1 large egg
1 teaspoon vanilla extract

MERINGUE

3 large egg whites
¾ cup sugar
1 teaspoon vanilla extract

FILLING

3 large egg yolks
½ cup sugar
¼ cup fresh lemon juice
1 teaspoon grated lemon zest
3 tablespoons unsalted butter or margarine

1. To make the dough: Sift together the flour, baking soda, and salt. Beat the shortening and sugar together until light and fluffy, about 5 minutes. Beat in the egg and vanilla. Blend in the flour mixture. Wrap in plastic and refrigerate for at least 1 hour.
2. Preheat the oven to 300 degrees. Lightly grease a large baking sheet.
3. To make the meringue: Beat the egg whites on low speed until foamy, about 30 seconds. Increase the speed to high and beat until soft peaks form. Gradually add the sugar, beating until the whites are stiff and glossy. Fold in the vanilla.
4. To assemble: By level teaspoonfuls, form the dough into balls. Place on the prepared baking sheet and flatten into ⅛-inch-thick rounds. Spoon level teaspoonfuls of the meringue onto each dough round. Using the back of a small spoon dipped in cold water, hollow out the center of the meringues.
5. Bake until lightly colored, 10 to 12 minutes. Let the cookies stand until firm, about 1 minute, then transfer to a rack and let cool completely.
6. To make the filling: In a small saucepan, beat the egg yolks, sugar, lemon juice, and zest together and stir over medium-low heat until thickened, about 10 minutes. Do not boil. Remove from the heat and stir in the butter, 1 tablespoon at a time. Let cool.
7. Spoon or pipe ¼ teaspoon of the filling into the center of each halo.

VARIATION

Chocolate Halos: Substitute 2 cups ganache (page 132) for the lemon filling.

Almond Horns
ABOUT 5 DOZEN COOKIES

2 pounds (about 3½ cups) almond paste (page 361)
3½ cups sugar
1 large egg yolk
1 cup (8 to 9 large) egg whites
24 ounces (about 6 cups) thinly sliced almonds
18 ounces semisweet or bittersweet chocolate, melted (optional)

APRICOT GLAZE
1 cup sugar
¾ cup apricot preserves
½ cup light corn syrup

1. Cover a baking sheet with parchment paper or aluminum foil and place the baking sheet on top of a second sheet.
2. Beat the almond paste and sugar until well blended. Beat in the egg yolk. Gradually add the egg whites and beat until well blended.
3. Drop the batter by rounded tablespoons into the sliced almonds and shape into 4-inch lengths, coating well with the almonds. Place on the prepared sheet and shape into crescents. Let stand for 1 hour.
4. Preheat the oven to 400 degrees.
5. Bake the cookies until lightly colored, 12 to 15 minutes. Remove the bottom baking sheet and continue baking until golden brown, 3 to 5 minutes.
6. Meanwhile, make the glaze. Bring the sugar, preserves, and corn syrup to a boil, reduce the heat to medium-low, and simmer, stirring frequently, for 5 minutes. Brush the warm cookies with the warm glaze. Let cool, then place in the freezer until chilled.
7. If desired, dip the ends of the cookies into the melted chocolate, then place on a baking sheet lined with wax paper and freeze until set.

Spice Sandwiches
ABOUT 2 DOZEN COOKIES

DOUGH
2½ cups all-purpose flour
¾ teaspoon baking soda
¾ teaspoon ground cinnamon
¾ teaspoon ground ginger
½ teaspoon ground cloves
¼ teaspoon ground cardamom
½ teaspoon salt
½ cup (1 stick) unsalted butter or margarine
¾ cup packed brown sugar
½ cup unsulfured (light) molasses
1 large egg
1 tablespoon cider vinegar
2 teaspoons vanilla extract

FILLING
¼ cup (½ stick) unsalted butter or margarine, softened
2½ cups confectioners' sugar
1 teaspoon vanilla extract

1. To make the dough: Sift together the flour, baking soda, spices, and salt. Melt the butter with the brown sugar and molasses over low heat. Let cool to lukewarm. Add the egg, vinegar, and vanilla. Gradually stir in the flour mixture. Wrap in plastic and refrigerate for at least 2 hours.
2. Shape the dough into 1-inch balls. Place on greased and floured baking sheets, 3 inches apart, and flatten into 3-inch rounds. Refrigerate for several hours.
3. Preheat the oven to 325 degrees.
4. Bake the cookies until golden brown, about 14 minutes. With a spatula, gently flatten the cookies. Let cool.
5. To make the filling: Beat the butter until smooth, about 1 minute. Beat in the confectioners' sugar and vanilla.
6. To assemble: Spread 1 tablespoon of the filling on the bottom of half of the cookies and top with another cookie.

Sarah Bernhardts
ABOUT 2 DOZEN COOKIES

*T*hese elegant macaroons were named after the French actress.

MACAROONS
8 ounces (¾ cup plus 2 tablespoons) almond paste (page 361)
1 cup sugar
⅛ teaspoon salt
1 teaspoon almond extract
⅓ cup (about 3 large) egg whites, lightly beaten

GANACHE
1½ cups heavy cream
16 ounces semisweet or bittersweet chocolate, finely chopped or grated
1 teaspoon vanilla extract

GLAZE
6 tablespoons sugar
2 tablespoons water
1 tablespoon light corn syrup
½ tablespoon unsalted butter or margarine
2 ounces semisweet or bittersweet chocolate, chopped
2 tablespoons sliced almonds or chopped pistachio nuts

1. Preheat the oven to 350 degrees. Line a baking sheet with parchment paper or lightly grease the baking sheet.
2. To make the macaroons: Using your hands, work together the almond paste, sugar, and salt until well blended. Add the almond extract. Gradually beat in the egg whites to make a soft, dropable dough with the consistency of cooked oatmeal.
3. Place the almond paste mixture into a pastry bag fitted with a ⅜-inch or ⅝-inch plain tip and pipe onto the prepared baking sheet, making 1¼-inch rounds about ½-inch high.

4. Bake until the macaroons begin to color, about 13 minutes. Let stand until the parchment can easily be pulled off the cookies, about 2 minutes, then transfer to a rack and let cool completely.

5. To make the ganache: In a small heavy saucepan over medium heat, bring the cream just to a simmer, stirring occasionally. Place the chocolate in a medium bowl, pour the cream over it, and let stand for 30 seconds. Stir until the chocolate is melted and the mixture is smooth. Stir in the vanilla.

6. Pour the ganache into a medium bowl and refrigerate, stirring occasionally, until it stiffens to spreading consistency, about 2 hours. (The ganache can be refrigerated for up to 1 week. Let stand at room temperature to soften to spreading consistency, 30 to 45 minutes.)

7. Beat the ganache until light and fluffy. Using a pastry bag fitted with a ⅝-inch plain or star tip, pipe about 2 tablespoons of the ganache on top of each cookie. Refrigerate the cookies until the ganache is firm, at least 30 minutes.

8. To make the glaze: Stir the sugar, water, corn syrup, and butter over medium-low heat until the sugar dissolves. Increase the heat to medium-high and bring to a boil. Stop stirring and boil for 1 minute. Remove from the heat, add the chocolate, and stir until smooth. Let stand until the glaze begins to stiffen.

9. Place the cookies on a rack set over a baking sheet and spoon the chocolate glaze over the tops, allowing the excess to drip off (the excess can be melted and reused). Arrange several almond slices or pistachios on top. Store in the refrigerator.

Chocolate Bells
12 SERVINGS

6 tablespoons all-purpose flour
6 tablespoons cornstarch or potato starch
6 large eggs, separated
Pinch of salt
1 cup sugar
2 tablespoons fresh orange juice
1 tablespoon fresh lemon juice
2 cups chocolate mousse (page 369), ganache (page 132), or sweetened whipped cream

CHOCOLATE GLAZE
6 ounces semisweet or bittersweet chocolate, chopped
¼ cup sugar
¼ cup water
¼ cup (½ stick) unsalted butter or margarine, softened

1. Preheat the oven to 350 degrees. Grease the bottoms of 12 standard-size muffin cups.
2. Sift together the flour and cornstarch. Beat the egg whites on low speed until foamy, about 30 seconds. Add the salt, increase the speed to high, and beat until soft peaks form. Gradually add ½ cup of the sugar, 1 tablespoon at a time, beating until the whites are stiff and glossy, about 5 minutes.
3. Using the same beaters, beat the egg yolks to blend. Gradually add the remaining ½ cup sugar to the yolks and continue beating until they are thick and creamy, about 5 minutes. Blend in the juices. Stir in the flour mixture. Fold ¼ of the egg whites into the yolk mixture, then fold in the remaining whites.
4. Fill the prepared muffin cups ¾ full with the batter and tap the pan to release any air bubbles. Bake until the cakes spring back when lightly touched, 20 to 25 minutes. Invert the pan, support with glasses or bottles, and let cool completely.
5. To make the glaze: In the top of a double boiler, melt the chocolate with the sugar and water. Remove from the heat and stir in the butter. Let cool until slightly thickened, 15 to 30 minutes.
6. Line a baking sheet with wax paper. Loosen the sides of the cakes and remove from the pan. From the bottom, cut out the center of each cake, leaving ½-inch-thick shells. Fill the centers of the cakes with the mousse, mounding slightly.
7. Dip the cakes in the chocolate glaze to coat the filling and sides. Place on the wax paper and refrigerate until firm, at least 30 minutes.

An Ashkenazic Seder

SERVES 8

Passover is an eight-day holiday (seven days in Israel) commemorating the Exodus from Egypt. Like the other Pilgrim Festivals, Passover also has a connection to agriculture and nature, since it occurs at the onset of spring and the winter wheat harvest. In addition, it coincides with the time of year when the shepherds, goat herders, and cattle herders brought their animals in from winter pasturing in the wilderness for the birth of lambs, kids, and calves. A festival celebrating freedom is perfectly timed for this season of new life and renewed hope.

A ceremonial dinner called the Seder ("order" in Hebrew) is held on the first two nights of the festival. During the Seder the Passover story is recounted and relived through a progression of symbols and ceremonies as recorded in the Haggadah (literally, "retelling"). On the table are wine (each person's cup is filled four times), three whole matzas (part of which will become the *afikomen* eaten at the end of the meal), and six traditional symbols: *maror*—a bitter herb symbolizing the bitterness of the slavery experience; *charoset*—a fruit mixture devised to blunt the taste of the bitter herbs and symbolizing the mortar used to construct buildings while in slavery; *karpas*—a green vegetable, such as celery or parsley, representing spring and renewal; *chazeret*—lettuce used for the Hillel sandwich; *betzah*—a roasted hard-boiled egg representing the festival sacrifice; and *zeroah*—a roasted shank bone or poultry neck representing the paschal sacrifice.

Because of the holiday's various dietary regulations, Passover fare differs from that of the rest of the year. Over the centuries creative cooks have found ways to adapt some of their everyday dishes as well as create new ones to meet the special requirements of Passover.

MATZA

CHICKEN SOUP WITH MATZA BALLS
SALMON GEFILTE FISH
PÂTÉ-STUFFED VEAL BREAST
APPLE KUGEL
LEMON-GLAZED ASPARAGUS
CARROT PUREE
NUT TORTE
TEA AND COFFEE
AFIKOMEN

MATZA

During the entire holiday of Passover, matza is the only permitted form of bread. To eliminate any possibility of *chametz,* both Ashkenazim and Sephardim roll out the dough very thin, perforate it to prevent the formation of air bubbles, then bake it until very crisp. Matza can be made only from one of the Five Species—wheat, barley, spelt, rye, and oats. However, almost all matza is made from wheat.

The flour for making matza is safeguarded to prevent contact with moisture and therefore fermentation. *Shmurah* (guarded) matza has been watched from the moment of harvest. "Passover flour" is supervised from the time of milling. The water for making matza must stand for at least twenty-four hours. The entire matza-making process from exposure to moisture until baking must take place in less than eighteen minutes. Handmade *shmurah* matza generally comes in large, thin rounds and has a nutty taste, much more flavorful than machine-made matza.

To increase matza's utility, it is also ground to make matza meal or finely ground to make matza cake meal. Crumbled and ground matza is used to create an imaginative array of Passover dishes, including stuffings, puddings, casseroles, pancakes, fritters, dumplings, pastries, and cakes. Since matza meal has an intriguing nutty flavor, it is often used for binding and breading throughout the year as well as on Passover.

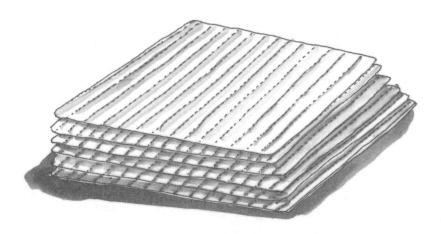

Chicken Soup with Matza Balls

ABOUT 2 QUARTS

*O*ne of the most anticipated concerns of the Seder is "How did the matza balls turn out this year?" Some are disappointingly small and hard; others crumbly or spongy. On occasion a promising surface hides a dense interior. In particularly disastrous years the matza balls disintegrate. The ideal matza ball should be feathery light throughout and mildly flavorful, yet rich and hearty—never bland, heavy, or rubbery. Served in a mellow bowl of chicken soup, matza balls make the ideal first course not only on Passover but throughout the year.

Classic chicken soup is golden in color and has a pronounced chicken flavor complemented by an underlying sweetness of vegetables and a subtle splash of dill. It is not only Jewish penicillin but the quintessential Ashkenazic dish, one served not only when someone feels ill but for the Sabbath, holidays, and weddings.

1 (4- to 5-pound) chicken, cut up
3 quarts cold water
3 to 4 medium carrots, cut into chunks
2 to 3 stalks celery, including leaves
2 medium yellow onions, sliced
2 to 3 medium parsnips, cut into chunks
6 sprigs fresh parsley
3 to 4 sprigs fresh dill
About 2½ teaspoons table salt or 5 teaspoons kosher salt
8 to 10 peppercorns or ¼ teaspoon ground black pepper
1 bay leaf

1. Place the chicken and water in a large pot. Bring to a boil, reduce the heat to low, and simmer for 30 minutes, occasionally skimming the foam from the surface.
2. Add the carrots, celery, onions, parsnips, parsley, dill, salt, peppercorns, and bay leaf. Partially cover and simmer until the chicken is very tender, at least 2 hours. (The soup can be stored in the refrigerator for up to 3 days or in the freezer for up to 3 months.) Serve the soup with the matza balls.

MATZA BALLS *(Knaidlach)*
ABOUT 16 DUMPLINGS

4 large eggs, lightly beaten
¼ cup schmaltz or vegetable oil
About 1½ teaspoons salt
¼ teaspoon ground black pepper
1 cup matza meal
¼ cup club soda, seltzer, chicken soup, or hot water

1. Beat together the eggs, schmaltz, salt, and pepper. Stir in the matza meal, then the club soda. Cover and refrigerate for at least 1 hour or up to 2 days.
2. Using moistened hands, form the matza mixture into 1-inch balls. (They expand during cooking.)
3. Bring at least 2 quarts of lightly salted water to a low boil. Drop in the matza balls, one at a time, and gently stir to prevent sticking. Cover, reduce the heat to low, and simmer until tender, about 40 minutes—do not uncover during cooking. Remove with a slotted spoon. (The *knaidlach* can be refrigerated for several days or frozen for up to 3 months. Freezing tends to improve the texture of heavy matza balls.)

Salmon Gefilte Fish
ABOUT 20 MEDIUM CROQUETTES

*B*uy the fish whole and have your fishmonger dress it for you: a 2-pound whole fish yields slightly less than 1 pound of flesh. Save the bones, heads, and tails to make the stock. Salmon and snapper are easy to grind, but pike tends to be a bit difficult.

Unlike the gefilte fish of Polish and Baltic Jews, this recipe from Bertha Sherman of Portland, Oregon, follows the Hungarian and German style of adding no sugar. For those who prefer sweeter gefilte fish, add 1 to 4 tablespoons sugar to the fish mixture and 1 to 3 tablespoons sugar to the stock. This recipe can be doubled or tripled.

STOCK
2 quarts cold water
Fish bones, heads, and tails
4 stalks celery, sliced
3 to 4 medium carrots, sliced
2 medium onions, sliced
About 2 teaspoons salt

CROQUETTES
1½ pounds fresh salmon fillets
½ pound fresh yellow pike fillets
½ pound fresh red snapper fillets
3 medium onions, chopped (about 1½ cups)
4 large eggs, lightly beaten
3 tablespoons matza meal
1 large carrot, grated
3 tablespoons chopped fresh parsley
About 1 tablespoon salt
Ground white or black pepper to taste

1. To make the stock: Put the stock ingredients in a large stockpot. Bring to a boil, reduce the heat to low, and simmer for 2 hours.
2. To make the croquettes: In a food grinder or food processor, finely grind the fish and onions. Stir in the eggs, matza meal, carrot, parsley, salt, and pepper. Place in the refrigerator until the stock is ready.

3. Moisten your hands with cold water (do this often while shaping the fish). Using a large spoon, remove about ⅓ cup of the fish mixture (for small croquettes, use about ¼ cup; for large ones, use ½ cup) and shape into a ball. Gently drop the balls, one at a time, into the stock.
4. Return the stock to a boil, cover, reduce the heat to low, and simmer for at least 1 hour and up to 2 hours. Add more water if the level threatens to fall below the fish.
5. Remove the gefilte fish and carrots and place in a glass container. For a more gelatinous fish sauce, boil the stock until reduced by half. Strain the stock and pour enough over the fish to cover. Let cool, then store in the refrigerator. Serve with horseradish.

Pâté-Stuffed Veal Breast
8 SERVINGS

*V*eal, the meat of a calf 2½ to 3 months old, is the most delicate meat and generally the most expensive. The breast, however, tends to be less costly. Since its flavor is less pronounced than beef, veal lends itself to flavorful stuffings and sauces.

PÂTÉ
1½ pounds finely ground veal or chicken
2 large eggs, lightly beaten
2 to 3 tablespoons brandy
About 2 teaspoons salt
1 teaspoon chopped fresh basil, marjoram, rosemary, or thyme
½ teaspoon ground black pepper
½ cup coarsely chopped pistachios or almonds (optional)

VEAL
1 (5½- to 6-pound) veal breast with pocket
Salt to taste
Ground black pepper to taste
Vegetable or olive oil
1 cup dry white wine or chicken broth (or ½ cup of each)

1. Preheat the oven to 400 degrees. (For even cooking, the veal should be at room temperature; remove it from the refrigerator about 1 hour before cooking.)
2. To make the pâté: Combine all the pâté ingredients. To test the pâté for seasoning, sauté a small amount until cooked, then taste.
3. Wash the veal and pat dry. Sprinkle inside and out with salt and pepper. Spread the pâté in the pocket and secure with skewers or toothpicks or sew up.
4. Place the veal, bone side down, in a shallow baking pan. Rub with the oil. Roast for 30 minutes.
5. Reduce the heat to 325 degrees. Add the wine to the pan, cover, and continue cooking, basting occasionally, until the veal is fork-tender and registers 175 degrees in the thickest portion, about 2½ additional hours or about 30 minutes per pound. Let stand for at least 15 minutes before carving. Serve warm or at room temperature.

Apple Kugel
8 SERVINGS

This sweet pudding is a popular Passover side dish in many households.

½ cup granulated or packed brown sugar
½ cup matza cake meal
¼ cup ground almonds
½ teaspoon ground cinnamon
½ teaspoon salt
4 large eggs, separated
¼ cup vegetable oil or melted unsalted margarine
1 teaspoon vanilla extract or grated lemon zest
6 large (about 2 pounds) tart apples, peeled, cored, and thinly sliced or diced
½ cup raisins, chopped pitted dates, or chopped dried apricots
½ cup coarsely chopped almonds, hazelnuts, pecans, or walnuts (optional)

1. Preheat the oven to 350 degrees. Grease a 9-inch-square baking pan.
2. Combine the sugar, matza cake meal, almonds, cinnamon, and salt. Beat the egg yolks until thick and creamy. Blend in the oil and vanilla. Stir in the sugar mixture. Add the apples, tossing to coat. Add the raisins and, if desired, the nuts.
3. Beat the egg whites on low speed until foamy, about 30 seconds. Increase the speed to high and beat until stiff but not dry, about 5 minutes. Fold ¼ of the whites into the apple mixture, then fold in the remaining whites.
4. Spoon the mixture into the prepared pan. Bake until golden brown, about 45 minutes. Serve warm or at room temperature.

Lemon-Glazed Asparagus
8 SERVINGS

2½ pounds asparagus
½ cup chicken broth
1 tablespoon fresh lemon juice
½ teaspoon grated lemon zest
½ teaspoon grated fresh ginger
Pinch of ground black pepper

1. Cook the asparagus in boiling salted water until tender-crisp, about 5 minutes. Do not overcook. Drain and pat dry.
2. Combine the broth, lemon juice, zest, ginger, and pepper in a small saucepan. Bring to a boil and cook until reduced to about 3 tablespoons. Strain. Brush over the asparagus. Serve warm or at room temperature

Carrot Puree

8 SERVINGS

2½ pounds (about 15 medium) carrots, sliced
2 tablespoons unsalted margarine
About 3½ cups water
½ teaspoon grated nutmeg
About ¼ teaspoon salt
1 to 3 tablespoons orange juice or orange liqueur (optional)
2 tablespoons granulated or brown sugar (optional)

1. Bring the carrots, 1 tablespoon of the margarine, and enough water to cover to a boil. Cook, stirring occasionally, until the carrots are tender and the water evaporates, about 25 minutes. If the carrots are not tender, add a little more water and continue cooking.
2. In a food processor or blender, puree the carrots, the remaining 1 tablespoon margarine, nutmeg, and salt. If desired, add the orange juice and/or sugar.
3. Cook the puree over medium heat, stirring frequently, until heated through. Serve warm.

Nut Torte (Nusstorte)
8 TO 10 SERVINGS

This cake requires much less sugar than a classic sponge cake.

CAKE
8 large eggs, separated
½ cup sugar
¼ cup orange juice or sweet wine
¾ cup (3 ounces) ground blanched almonds, hazelnuts, pecans, or walnuts
¼ cup matza cake meal
Pinch of salt

BUTTERCREAM
4 large eggs
¾ cup sugar
Pinch of salt
1 cup plus 2 tablespoons (2¼ sticks) unsalted margarine, softened
1 cup (4 ounces) ground blanched almonds, hazelnuts, pecans, or walnuts
⅛ teaspoon almond extract (optional)

1. Preheat the oven to 350 degrees. Grease a 9-inch springform pan.
2. To make the cake: Beat the egg yolks and sugar until thick and creamy, 5 to 10 minutes. Gently stir in the orange juice, nuts, and cake meal.
3. Beat the egg whites on low speed until foamy, about 30 seconds. Add the salt, increase the speed to high, and beat until the whites are stiff but not dry. Fold ¼ of the whites into the nut mixture, then gently fold in the remaining whites.
4. Pour into the prepared pan. Bake until the cake springs back when lightly touched, about 35 minutes. Invert and let cool completely in the pan.
5. To make the buttercream: In the top of a double boiler, beat the eggs, sugar, and salt until thick and very warm. Remove from the heat and beat until cool.
6. Meanwhile, beat the margarine until light and fluffy, 5 to 10 minutes. Gradually beat in the egg mixture. Stir in the nuts and, if desired, the almond extract.
7. To assemble: Cut the cake horizontally into 2 or 3 layers and frost the layers and sides with the buttercream.

A Sephardic Seder

*A*s with many other customs, differences developed between Ashkenazim and Sephardim regarding Passover practices and food. Most Sephardim carry the ritual items in and out of the dining room on small, low tables or trays in the Eastern fashion instead of placing them on a metal or ceramic Seder plate, as Ashkenazim do. Unlike the Ashkenazic Haggadahs, which commonly contain decorations around the text, Sephardic versions traditionally restrict illustrations to full-page biblical miniatures. Many Sephardim conduct the Seder using Ladino or Arabic.

In the time the Temple stood, the first night of Passover centered around the paschal sacrifice, and in most Sephardic households, lamb remains the main course for the Seder. Sephardim generally use romaine lettuce or chicory for *maror* (the bitter herb) and celery or parsley for *karpas* (the green vegetable), which they dip in vinegar. Dates always serve as the primary component of *charoset.* The Sephardic dinner usually features spring vegetables such as artichokes and peas, and because fava beans were purportedly the staple of the Jews' diet while they were in bondage in Egypt, fava beans or green beans are included. On the other hand, Ashkenazim rarely serve lamb, frequently substitute horseradish for the bitter herb and sometimes radishes or potatoes for the green vegetable, use salt water for dipping, make *charoset* from apples, and eschew all legumes (called *kitniyot*).

In addition to the dishes in this section, a typical Sephardic Seder might feature *huevos haminados* (brown eggs), *sopa de prasa* (leek soup), *apio* (sweet-and-sour celery or celeriac), and okra. Traditional desserts include *pan d'Espagna* (sponge cake), *torta de muez* (nut cake), *tishpishti* (a syrup-drenched nut cake), and *mustachudos* (macaroon crescents).

MATZA
FISH CROQUETTES IN TOMATO SAUCE
MOROCCAN LAMB STEW WITH PRUNES
TURKISH LEEK PATTIES
SEPHARDIC BRAISED STUFFED ARTICHOKES
PASSOVER GREEN SALAD
SEPHARDIC WINE COOKIES
FRESH FRUIT PLATTER (PAGE 217)
TEA AND COFFEE
AFIKOMEN

Fish Croquettes in Tomato Sauce
(Keftes de Pescado)
8 SERVINGS

You can omit the sauce and serve the fish croquettes with lemon wedges.

1 pound cod, haddock, or salmon fillets
1½ cups mashed cooked potatoes or 1 cup matza meal
2 large eggs
1 medium onion, minced (about ½ cup)
2 to 3 tablespoons chopped fresh parsley
2 tablespoons fresh lemon juice (optional)
About 1½ teaspoons salt
About ½ teaspoon ground black pepper

SAUCE
2 tablespoons olive or vegetable oil
1 medium onion, chopped (about ½ cup)
2 pounds tomatoes, peeled, seeded, and chopped (about 4 cups)
¼ cup chopped fresh parsley
About 1 teaspoon salt
Ground black pepper to taste

2 large eggs, lightly beaten (optional)
Matza meal for dredging (optional)
Vegetable oil for frying

1. Place the fish in boiling water to cover. Reduce the heat to low, cover the pan, and simmer until tender, about 5 minutes. Remove the fish from the poaching liquid, pat dry, and flake.
2. Combine the fish, potatoes, eggs, onion, parsley, lemon juice if desired, salt, and pepper. Chill for at least 2 hours.
3. To make the sauce: Heat the oil in a medium saucepan over medium heat. Add the onion and sauté until soft and translucent, 5 to 10 minutes. Add the tomatoes, parsley, salt, and pepper. Bring to a boil, cover, reduce the heat to low, and simmer until the tomatoes break down into a sauce, about 20 minutes.

4. Shape the fish mixture into croquettes 3 inches long and 1 inch wide (you will have 8 croquettes). If desired, dip in the beaten eggs, then dredge in the matza meal.
5. Heat the oil in a large skillet over medium-high heat. Fry the croquettes, turning, until golden brown on both sides. Drain on paper towels.
6. Add the patties to the sauce, cover, and simmer, occasionally basting with the sauce, for about 10 minutes. Serve warm or at room temperature.

Moroccan Lamb Stew with Prunes
(L'Haam bi Khokh f'Tagine)
8 SERVINGS

*L*amb, reminiscent of the paschal lamb sacrificed in the Temple for the Seder, is the most popular Sephardic Passover entrée.

1 pound pitted prunes
⅓ cup olive oil
⅓ cup vegetable oil
4 medium onions, chopped (about 2 cups)
½ cup chopped fresh cilantro or parsley (or ¼ cup each)
1 tablespoon salt
1 teaspoon ground black pepper
1 teaspoon sweet paprika
½ to 1 teaspoon ground cumin or 2 teaspoons ground cinnamon
½ teaspoon ground ginger
¼ teaspoon crushed saffron or ½ teaspoon turmeric
3 pounds boneless lamb shoulder, cut into 1-inch cubes
About 2 cups water
2 to 3 tablespoons honey or sugar (optional)

1. Soak the prunes in water overnight. Drain.
2. Combine the oils, onions, herbs, salt, and spices. Add the lamb, tossing to coat.

3. Place in a large pot, cover, and cook over medium-high heat, stirring occasionally, until the meat has absorbed most of the oil, about 15 minutes. Uncover and brown the meat on all sides.
4. Add the water, cover, and simmer over low heat (or bake in a 350-degree oven) until the lamb is tender, about 1¼ hours. The sauce will be very thick; if necessary, add a little more water during cooking to prevent burning.
5. Add the prunes and, if desired, the honey and simmer for 15 minutes.

Turkish Leek Patties *(Keftes de Prasa)*
ABOUT 30 PATTIES

*T*hese delicate patties can be made more substantial by adding ground beef.

10 medium (about 2 pounds) leeks, white and light green parts only
1 cup matza meal plus extra for dredging
3 large eggs, lightly beaten
About 1 teaspoon salt
Ground black pepper to taste
½ teaspoon grated nutmeg or cayenne (optional)
Vegetable oil for frying

1. Slice the leeks crosswise and wash well. Add the leeks to a large pot of lightly salted boiling water, cover, reduce the heat to low, and simmer until tender, about 30 minutes. Drain. When the leeks are cool enough to handle, squeeze out the excess liquid.
2. Combine the leeks, 1 cup of matza meal, eggs, salt, pepper, and if desired, the nutmeg. Shape the leek mixture into 2-inch patties ½ inch thick. Dredge in matza meal.
3. Heat a thin layer of oil in a large skillet over medium heat. In batches, fry the patties until golden brown on both sides. Drain on paper towels. (Keep the *keftes* warm in a 300-degree oven.) Serve with lemon wedges. (The *keftes* can be stored in the refrigerator, then reheated in a 250-degree oven.)

VARIATION
Reduce the leeks to 7 (1½ pounds) and add 8 ounces ground beef.

Sephardic Braised Stuffed Artichokes
(Medias de Inginaras)

8 SERVINGS

*M*aking use of the early artichokes of the season, many Sephardim serve them at the Seder.

8 small or medium artichokes, trimmed
½ lemon

STUFFING
10 ounces ground beef or veal
1 large egg
3 tablespoons matza meal
1 tablespoon vegetable oil
1 tablespoon chopped fresh parsley
About ½ teaspoon salt
Dash of ground black pepper

3 large eggs, lightly beaten
About ½ cup matza meal
Vegetable oil for frying
1½ cups chicken broth or water
Juice of 1 lemon
Salt to taste

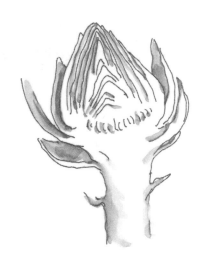

1. Preheat the oven to 350 degrees.
2. Cut about 1 inch off the tops of the artichokes, then cut in half vertically. Scrape out the chokes. Rub the cut edges with the lemon.
3. Combine all the stuffing ingredients and spoon into the artichokes. Dip the artichokes in the eggs, then roll in the matza meal.
4. Heat ¼ inch oil in a large skillet over medium heat. Fry the artichokes, stuffing side first, until lightly browned on both sides.
5. Arrange the artichokes, stuffing side up, in a single layer in a large baking dish. Add the broth, lemon juice, and salt.
6. Bake, uncovered, until tender, about 1 hour. Serve warm or at room temperature.

VARIATIONS

Balkan Fried Stuffed Artichokes (**Artichos Fritos**): Add 1 tablespoon chopped fresh dill to the stuffing.

Syrian Braised Stuffed Artichokes: Add ½ teaspoon ground allspice and, if desired, ½ teaspoon ground cumin to the stuffing. Substitute 1 cup tomato sauce for the broth and add 1 teaspoon temerhindi and 1 teaspoon sugar to the sauce.

Passover Green Salad *(Salata Verde de Pesach)*
8 SERVINGS

This salad, also called *salata de maror* (salad of bitter herbs), incorporates several types of greens that can represent the bitter herb at the beginning of the Seder. Greek and Turkish Jews frequently serve it as part of the Seder meal.

1 large head romaine lettuce, torn into bite-size pieces (about 6 cups)
2 to 3 cups torn curly endive (also called chicory or frisée)
2 cups arugula or watercress
6 to 8 scallions, chopped
½ cup chopped fresh parsley
¼ cup chopped fresh dill
6 tablespoons olive oil
6 tablespoons wine vinegar or fresh lemon juice
About 1 teaspoon salt
Ground black pepper to taste

Combine the greens, scallions, and herbs in a large bowl. Drizzle with the oil and vinegar. Sprinkle with the salt and pepper and toss to mix well.

Sephardic Wine Cookies *(Masas de Vino)*
ABOUT 2 DOZEN 2-INCH COOKIES

1½ cups matza cake meal
¾ cup ground almonds
¼ teaspoon ground cinnamon (or ⅛ teaspoon ground cinnamon
and ⅛ teaspoon ground cloves)
¼ teaspoon salt
1 cup (2 sticks) unsalted margarine, softened
½ cup sugar
½ cup sweet red wine

1. Preheat the oven to 350 degrees.
2. Combine the cake meal, almonds, cinnamon, and salt. Beat the margarine until smooth. Gradually add the sugar and beat until light and fluffy, about 5 minutes. Stir in the wine and matza mixture.
3. Form the dough into 1-inch balls. Place on an ungreased baking sheet and flatten.
4. Bake until the cookies are golden around the edges, about 15 minutes. Let stand until firm, about 1 minute, then transfer to a rack and let cool completely. Store in an airtight container at room temperature or in the freezer.

Passover Desserts of All Sorts

*M*y family is a bit spoiled when it comes to Passover desserts. During the years that I edited *Kosher Gourmet* magazine, I generally prepared two or three different desserts for each Yom Tov (holiday) meal in order to test them for the following year's Passover issue under actual battlefield conditions. Although I no longer prepare as many desserts, the family still expects an appropriate grand finale to the Passover meal. And friends still drop by during the afternoon for a sample.

A familiar witticism is that "good Passover dessert" is an oxymoron. Unfortunately, there is some truth to this. Store-bought cakes and macaroons leave much to be desired in the taste department and are inexcusably expensive. Yet there is no reason to serve a dessert on Passover that you would abstain from eating during the rest of the year. Consider any of the following to end your Passover or any other meal.

FLOURLESS CHOCOLATE TORTE
CHOCOLATE MOUSSE PIE
AMARETTI (ITALIAN MACAROONS)
MERINGUE NUT BARS
PASSOVER FRUIT STRUDEL
FRUIT BALLS
FRUIT LEATHER
ORANGES IN CARAMEL
ORANGES IN FUDGE
WINE-POACHED PEARS
BANANAS FLAMBÉ
CHOCOLATE SORBET

Flourless Chocolate Torte
10 TO 12 SERVINGS

*T*his is a dense, moist treat. Unrefrigerated, the texture is soufflé-like; after chilling, it becomes firmer.

Cocoa powder
8 ounces semisweet or bittersweet chocolate, chopped
1 cup (2 sticks) unsalted butter or margarine
2 teaspoons vanilla extract
2 tablespoons nut liqueur, orange liqueur, or cherry liqueur,
 or 2 teaspoons instant coffee powder (optional)
5 large eggs
1 cup sugar

1. Preheat the oven to 350 degrees. Grease a 9-inch springform pan, line with wax paper, grease the paper, and dust with cocoa powder. Wrap the outside of the pan with a large piece of foil.
2. In the top of a double boiler over barely simmering water, melt the chocolate and butter, stirring until smooth. Remove from the heat and add the vanilla and, if desired, the liqueur.
3. Beat the eggs and sugar until the sugar dissolves and the volume doubles, about 5 minutes. Fold into the chocolate mixture.
4. Pour the batter into the prepared pan. For a creamier texture, put the pan in a larger pan and add water to come halfway up the sides of the torte pan. Bake until a knife inserted in the center of the torte comes out clean, about 50 minutes.
5. Let cool in the pan. Invert onto a serving plate. (The torte can be stored at room temperature for 1 day or in the refrigerator for up to 3 days. Let stand at room temperature for at least 1 hour before serving.)

VARIATION

Flourless Chocolate Fudge Torte: Increase the chocolate to 1 pound and the eggs to 8.

Chocolate Mousse Pie
8 TO 10 SERVINGS

This versatile recipe can also be used to make a mousse cake or cake roll.

8 ounces semisweet or bittersweet chocolate, chopped
¼ cup water
8 large eggs, separated
1 teaspoon vanilla extract
Pinch of salt
1 teaspoon almond extract, ½ teaspoon peppermint extract, 2 tablespoons
*   crème de menthe, 3 tablespoons orange liqueur, 3 to 4 tablespoons*
*   coffee liqueur, or 1 tablespoon instant coffee powder (optional)*
⅔ cup sugar

1. Preheat the oven to 350 degrees. Grease a 9-inch pie pan and dust with sugar.
2. In the top of a double boiler over barely simmering water, melt the chocolate in the water, stirring until smooth. Remove from the heat and beat in the egg yolks, one at a time. Stir in the vanilla, salt, and if desired, the almond extract.
3. Beat the egg whites on low speed until foamy, about 30 seconds. Increase the speed to high and beat until soft peaks form. Gradually add the sugar, 1 tablespoon at a time, beating until the whites are stiff and glossy, about 5 minutes. Fold ¼ of the whites into the chocolate mixture, then gently fold in the remaining whites.
4. Pour 4 cups of the mousse into the prepared pan, reserving the remaining mousse in the refrigerator. Bake until set, about 25 minutes. Let cool for 30 minutes, then chill. (The center will fall.)
5. Pour the reserved mousse into the baked mousse shell. Refrigerate overnight or up to 2 days.

Amaretti (Italian Macaroons)
ABOUT 3 DOZEN COOKIES

*T*he word *macaroon* comes from the Italian *maccarone,* for "paste," referring to the cookie's main ingredient, almond paste. These chewy, flavorful macaroons are nothing like the insipid store-bought type.

1 cup (about 9 ounces) almond paste (page 361)
1 cup sugar
⅛ teaspoon salt
1 teaspoon almond extract (optional)
⅓ cup (about 3 large) egg whites
About 36 whole almonds (optional)

1. Preheat the oven to 350 degrees. Line a large baking sheet with parchment paper or lightly grease.
2. Using your hands, work together the almond paste, sugar, and salt until well blended. If desired, add the extract. Gradually beat in enough egg whites to make a soft dough with the consistency of cooked oatmeal.
3. Drop the batter by tablespoonfuls, 1 inch apart, onto the prepared baking sheet. If desired, press a whole almond into the center of each mound. Bake until the macaroons are lightly browned, about 15 minutes. Let sit on the sheet until firm, about 5 minutes, then transfer to a rack and let cool. (The amaretti can be stored in an airtight container at room temperature for up to 1 week.)

VARIATIONS

Iraqi Macaroons (**Hadgi Badam**): Add ¾ teaspoon ground cardamom.

Almond-Orange Macaroons: Add 2 teaspoons grated orange zest.

Meringue Nut Bars
12 TO 14 SERVINGS

10 large eggs, separated
Pinch of salt
2 cups sugar
2½ cups ground hazelnuts, pecans, or walnuts
8 ounces semisweet or bittersweet chocolate, chopped
¾ cup vegetable oil
1 teaspoon vanilla extract

1. Preheat the oven to 350 degrees. Grease a 13- by 9-inch baking pan.
2. Beat the egg whites on low speed until foamy, about 30 seconds. Add the salt, increase the speed to high, and beat until soft peaks form. Gradually add 1 cup of the sugar and beat the whites until stiff and glossy. Fold in the nuts.
3. Spread the meringue evenly in the prepared pan. Bake until lightly browned, about 30 minutes.
4. Meanwhile, in the top of a double boiler over barely simmering water, melt the chocolate with the oil, stirring until smooth. Let cool.
5. Beat the egg yolks and remaining 1 cup sugar until thick and creamy, 5 to 10 minutes. Stir in the cooled chocolate and the vanilla.
6. Pour the chocolate mixture over the warm meringue and bake for 10 minutes. Let cool. If the chocolate is too soft, chill until set. Cut into bars.

Passover Fruit Strudel
ABOUT 3 DOZEN PIECES

*A*lthough not as flaky as phyllo, this dough is easy to make and less fragile to handle.

DOUGH
2 cups matza cake meal
1 cup potato starch
½ cup sugar

⅛ teaspoon salt
4 large eggs, lightly beaten
½ cup vegetable oil
¼ cup water

FILLING

2½ cups (12½ ounces) golden raisins
2 medium oranges, seeded but not peeled
½ cup sugar
¼ cup apricot preserves or ⅓ cup brandy
3 tablespoons matza meal or cookie crumbs
1 tablespoon fresh lemon juice
1 tablespoon grated lemon zest
1½ cups chopped nuts or 1 cup grated coconut (optional)

Egg wash (1 large egg beaten with 1 tablespoon water)

1. Preheat the oven to 350 degrees. Grease a large baking sheet.
2. To make the dough: Sift together the cake meal, potato starch, sugar, and salt. Combine the eggs, oil, and water. Stir into the dry ingredients to make a stiff dough. Divide the dough in half or thirds and shape into balls.
3. To make the filling: In a food grinder or food processor, grind together the raisins, oranges, sugar, preserves, matza meal, lemon juice, and zest.
4. On a piece of wax paper or plastic wrap, roll out each dough ball into a thin rectangle. Spread the filling over the dough and, if desired, sprinkle with the nuts. From a long edge, roll up jelly-roll style.
5. Place, seam side down, on the prepared baking sheet and brush with the egg wash. Bake until golden brown, about 1 hour. Using a serrated knife, cut into slices.

VARIATIONS

Mixed Fruit Filling: Reduce the raisins to 1 cup and add ¾ cup chopped pitted dates and ¾ cup pitted prunes.

Jam Filling: Substitute 2 cups apricot preserves, strawberry jam, or orange marmalade for the filling and sprinkle with 1 cup dried currants or raisins, 1 cup chopped nuts, and if desired, 1 cup grated coconut.

Fruit Balls

ABOUT 3 DOZEN BALLS

2 cups (about 12 ounces) dried apricots
2 cups (about 12 ounces) pitted dates
2 cups (about 12 ounces) pitted prunes
About 3 tablespoons honey
About 1 cup sugar (optional)

1. In a food grinder or food processor, coarsely grind the fruit. Add enough honey to make a workable mixture.
2. Lightly oil your hands and form the fruit mixture into ¾-inch balls. If desired, roll in the sugar to coat. Let stand at room temperature overnight before serving. (The fruit balls can be stored in an airtight container at room temperature for up to 2 weeks.)

Fruit Leather

ABOUT 1 POUND

*K*ids love this treat. Fruit leather has to sit in the oven for a long time, so it's best to make this recipe when the oven will be free for a while. Any fruit puree or mixture of fruit may be substituted for the apricots or plums.

2½ pounds ripe fresh apricots or purple plums, peeled and pitted,
  or 1 pound dried apricots or pitted prunes
Sugar or honey
Lemon juice

1. Preheat the oven to 175 degrees. Line baking sheets with parchment paper or lightly oil the sheets.
2. In a food processor, puree the fruit. Add sugar and lemon juice to taste and process until smooth. Spread in a thin layer over the prepared baking sheets.

3. Place in the oven, leaving the door slightly ajar, until the fruit is dried, about 3 hours. Let cool.
4. Cut the fruit leather into strips and roll up in plastic wrap.

Oranges in Caramel

8 SERVINGS

*C*aramel sauce transforms a simple fruit into a fancy dessert.

1 cup sugar
½ cup cold water
½ cup warm water
8 large navel oranges

1. Bring the sugar and cold water to a boil in a heavy saucepan, occasionally swirling the pan but not stirring, and cook until browned. Remove from the heat, place the base of the pan in a bowl of warm water, and let stand for 1 minute to stop the cooking.
2. Pour the ½ cup warm water into the saucepan. Return to the heat and bring to a boil, stirring to dissolve the caramel. Pour into a heatproof bowl and let cool.
3. Meanwhile, peel the oranges, removing all of the white membrane. Cut each orange crosswise into ¼- to ½-inch-thick slices. Reshape the oranges and secure with toothpicks.
4. Arrange the oranges in a single layer in a baking dish and drizzle with the caramel. Refrigerate until chilled

Oranges in Fudge
EIGHTEEN ½-INCH SLICES

Slices of orange in rich chocolate taste as good as they look.

4 small navel oranges
4 cups sugar
1 quart water

FUDGE
1½ cups sugar
½ cup water
1½ cups (3 sticks) unsalted butter or margarine, softened
2¾ cups unsweetened cocoa powder
3 large egg yolks
2 large eggs
12 ounces semisweet chocolate, melted and cooled
¼ cup orange liqueur, other fruit liqueur, or brandy

1. Grease a 9- by 5-inch loaf pan, line the bottom and sides with wax paper, and grease the wax paper.
2. Bring a large pot of water to a boil. Add the oranges and parboil for 5 minutes. Remove the oranges from the water and poke all over with an ice pick or skewer.
3. Bring the sugar and water to a boil, stirring occasionally, over high heat. When the sugar is dissolved, add the oranges. Reduce the heat to low and simmer for 3 hours, stirring occasionally. Remove the oranges from the liquid and let cool. (Save the poaching liquid and use to flavor tea, seltzer, and desserts.)
4. To make the fudge: Bring the sugar and water to a boil over high heat, stirring until the sugar is dissolved. Let the sugar syrup cool.
5. Beat the butter until smooth, about 1 minute. Add the cocoa powder and beat until smooth. Beat in the egg yolks and eggs, one at a time. Blend in the chocolate, sugar syrup, and liqueur.
6. To assemble: Pour about 2 cups of the fudge into the prepared loaf pan and place in the refrigerator until firm, about 30 minutes.

7. Arrange the oranges down the center of the pan, stem end to end, and carefully pour in the remaining fudge. Refrigerate overnight.

8. Run a knife around the sides of the pan. Invert onto a platter, remove the wax paper, and cut into ½-inch-thick slices.

Wine-Poached Pears
8 SERVINGS

*U*sing red wine gives the pears an attractive red color.

8 firm pears with stems attached
Juice of 1 lemon
2 cups sweet red or white wine
½ cup sugar or honey
1 (3-inch) cinnamon stick or 1 split vanilla bean
2 or 3 large strips of lemon or orange peel or 4 whole cloves

1. Cut off a small slice from the bottom of each pear. Leaving the pears whole and the stems intact, scoop out the core (a melon baller works well). Peel the pears and rub with some of the lemon juice to prevent discoloration.

2. Combine the wine, 2 tablespoons of the lemon juice, the sugar, cinnamon stick, and lemon peel in a large nonreactive saucepan. Stand the pears in the wine mixture.

3. Bring to a boil, cover, reduce the heat to low, and simmer until the pears are tender but not mushy, 15 to 30 minutes, depending on the size and variety of the pears.

4. Remove from the heat, uncover, tip the pears over, and let cool, occasionally turning the pears for even coloring. Cover and refrigerate. Serve the pears in the cooking liquid or drizzle with melted chocolate.

Bananas Flambé

6 TO 8 SERVINGS

*T*o make serving this dessert an impressive event, light it at the table in front of your guests. But be careful.

5 tablespoons sugar
¼ cup (½ stick) unsalted butter or margarine
½ cup fresh orange juice
2 tablespoons orange or banana liqueur
4 medium bananas, split and halved
2 tablespoons brandy

1. Cook the sugar in a large skillet over medium heat until melted and lightly browned. Add the butter, orange juice, and liqueur and simmer until creamy.
2. Add the bananas and simmer until heated through, 2 to 3 minutes.
3. Warm the brandy in a small saucepan. Pour over the bananas, ignite, and serve.

Chocolate Sorbet

ABOUT 1½ QUARTS

½ cup boiling water
3 tablespoons unsweetened cocoa powder, preferably alkalized (Dutch process)
½ teaspoon ground cinnamon (optional)
8 large eggs, separated
2 teaspoons vanilla extract
1 cup sugar
Pinch of salt

1. Pour the boiling water over the cocoa and, if desired, the cinnamon and stir until dissolved. Let cool. Beat in the egg yolks and vanilla.
2. Beat the egg whites on low speed until foamy, about 30 seconds. Add the salt, increase the speed to high, and beat until soft peaks form. Gradually add the sugar, 1 table-

spoon at a time, and beat until the whites are stiff and glossy. Fold into the chocolate mixture.

3. Cover and place in the freezer until firm.

YOM HA'ATZMAUT

On the fifth day of the Hebrew month of Iyar (May 14, 1948), Israel declared its independence, ending more than two thousand years of foreign domination. On the anniversary of that historic occasion, Jews celebrate Yom Ha'atzmaut (Israel Independence Day). The day before is observed as Yom Ha'zikkaron (Remembrance Day), a time to memorialize the soldiers who died in defense of Israel. At sunset a siren blasts throughout the country, signaling the end of solemnity and the commencement of Yom Ha'atzmaut. The streets fill with people—laughing, conversing, and singing. The following day is celebrated with parades, fireworks, picnics, and an international Bible quiz. In America it is customary to serve foods associated with Israel: pita, falafel, hummus, cucumber-and-tomato salad, eggplant spread, and any of the dishes in the *meze* section: (pages 195–209), many of which are perfect for outdoor dining. The decor follows the colors of the Israeli flag: blue and white.

A Children's Lag b'Omer Picnic

SERVES 10

During the time when the Temple in Jerusalem stood, an offering was made on the second day of Passover of an *omer* (sheaf) of the newly harvested barley. Jews would then count forty-nine days, corresponding to the amount of time from the Exodus until the revelation on Mount Sinai. On the fiftieth day they celebrated Shavuot and made an offering of two loaves of bread produced from the first of the spring wheat crop. Although these grain offerings are no longer made, Jews continue the practice of "counting the *omer*."

The months following Passover were once a time of great happiness, when the pantry was stocked with the abundance of the early crop and expectations ran high for the next harvest. Then a series of national tragedies transformed this span into a very somber one. The Talmud relates that during one of the rebellions against Rome, twenty-four thousand students of Rabbi Akiva died from a plague—some scholars speculate that this plague was actually the Roman army—during the Omer period. Much later, beginning in 1095, most of the devastation on the Ashkenazic communities wrought by the Crusades occurred in the spring. Thus the Omer became a time of prolonged mourning.

There is an exception to the melancholy nature of the Omer, the thirty-third (*lag*) day. The Talmud records that on this day the plague abated. Also, according to tradition, this was the day on which the manna, which fed the Jews during their forty-year stay in the wilderness, first fell. Lag b'Omer is also purported to be the anniversary of the death of the talmudic sage Shimon ben Yochai, a central figure in Jewish mysticism, who spent much of his career in hiding from the Roman authorities. Thus Lag b'Omer became a minor holiday, primarily one for children, customarily celebrated with bonfires and picnics to commemorate how the students of Shimon ben Yochai disguised clandestine visits to their teacher as outings and hunting expeditions. Bows and arrows became the symbol of the holiday. In Israel thousands make an annual pilgrimage to Rabbi Shimon's grave in Meron, where they honor his memory with song and dance.

Carob is a traditional food for this day, as legend has it that Rabbi Shimon and his son were sustained during hiding by a carob tree. Hard-boiled eggs are another traditional food, associated with mourning and rebirth but also convenient to shlep on picnics. Many American Jews eat Middle Eastern fare on this holiday.

WRAPS
MIDDLE EASTERN ROAST LAMB OR TURKEY
MIDDLE EASTERN MEAT PATTIES ON SKEWERS
POTATO STARS
SEPHARDIC SWEETENED BARLEY
FEATHER-FROSTED CAROB BROWNIES
CUPCAKES
COOKIE ASSORTMENT (PAGES 346–362)

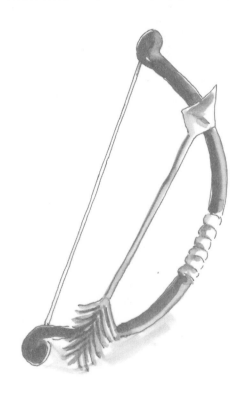

Wraps

10 SERVINGS

*W*rapped foods are among the most ancient of dishes, as they provide an easy way to make handheld meals. Yet today wraps are suddenly in style, found in chic restaurants as well as greasy spoon cafés. One of the favorite breads for wrapping is lavash, a very thin loaf from the Caucacus Mountain region. You can also use a flour tortilla or stuff fillings into pita bread. The simple technique for wrapping can be mastered by anyone, so your guests can choose a filling and roll their own. Or you can prepare the wraps ahead of time.

Almost any food lends itself to wrapping, including Barbecue Beef Brisket (page 246), hot dogs, hamburgers, and salads. For an Israeli touch, use falafel, Israeli salad, and tahini. Or try a combination of cream cheese, lox, chopped cucumber or capers, and chopped dill. For a Tex-Mex theme, offer refried beans, salsa or guacamole, and shredded lettuce. The possibilities are limited only by your imagination.

10 lavash (Caucasian flat bread), flour tortillas, or pitas
Middle Eastern Meat Patties (page 168), Shawarma (page 167), or other desired fillings

For each wrap, place a lavash on a flat surface. (The bread can be served warm or at room temperature.) Spread about 1¼ cups filling onto a 5- by 2-inch rectangle on the bottom half of the bread. Fold the right and left edges of the bread toward the center, partially covering the filling. (For an open-end roll, fold over only one edge.) Fold the bottom edge over the filling, then gently roll up. Serve or cover in plastic wrap and store in the refrigerator for 1 day or in the freezer for up to 1 week. (To reheat, bake the wraps in a 350-degree oven for about 15 minutes; 45 minutes if frozen.)

Middle Eastern Roast Lamb or Turkey (Shawarma)

10 SERVINGS

Visitors to Israel will recognize the aroma of shawarma that wafts through the streets.

2 cloves garlic, crushed
1 tablespoon salt
½ teaspoon ground black pepper
½ teaspoon ground cinnamon or cumin
⅛ teaspoon grated nutmeg
⅛ teaspoon ground cloves
Pinch of cayenne pepper
¼ cup water
2 tablespoons fresh lemon juice
1 tablespoon white vinegar
1 tablespoon olive oil
1 small onion, chopped (about ¼ cup)
½ lemon, sliced
5 pounds lamb shoulder or turkey, cut into ¼-inch-thick slices

1. Combine the garlic, salt, black pepper, cinnamon, nutmeg, cloves, and cayenne. Stir in the water, lemon juice, vinegar, oil, onion, and lemon slices. Rub the marinade over the meat, place in the refrigerator, and let stand overnight.
2. Remove the meat from the refrigerator and let come to room temperature.
3. Preheat an outdoor grill, preferably with a rotisserie, or an electric rotisserie.
4. Stack the slices of meat, placing the larger pieces on the bottom, on a spit. Place the spit on the rotisserie or grill and roast.
5. As the exterior of the meat browns, slice it off across the outside, cutting through all the layers to create shreds. Return the spit to the grill and continue browning and slicing the cooked meat. Wrap the strips of meat in lavash or stuff into a pita, adding, if desired, any combination of shredded lettuce, chopped tomatoes, chopped onions, and pitted olives.

Middle Eastern Meat Patties on Skewers (Kefta Kebab)
8 OR 16 SERVINGS

*K*ids love these hamburgers on a stick. The meat is commonly flavored with herbs and spices, including mint, cinnamon, and allspice.

2 pounds ground lamb or beef chuck (or 1 pound each)
1 cup chopped fresh parsley
6 scallions, white and light green parts only,
    or 1 medium onion, chopped (about ½ cup)
Salt to taste
Ground black pepper to taste
3 tablespoons finely chopped fresh mint or 2 teaspoons dried,
    3 tablespoons finely chopped fresh dill, ½ to 1 teaspoon
    ground allspice, ½ to 1 teaspoon ground cumin,
    ½ teaspoon ground cinnamon, or ½ teaspoon
    ground cardamom (optional)
Vegetable or olive oil

1. Preheat an outdoor grill or the broiler.
2. Combine the meat, parsley, scallions, salt, pepper, and herbs or spices.
3. Divide the meat mixture into 8 equal portions and shape each portion around a skewer into 1½-inch-thick ovals about 4 to 6 inches long. Or divide the meat mixture into 16 or 24 portions and shape each portion into 2-inch ovals, placing 2 or 3 ovals on each skewer. Brush with the oil.
4. Grill or broil about 4 inches from heat source (or bake in a 375-degree oven), turning occasionally, until browned on all sides, about 15 minutes for large or 10 minutes for small kebabs.

Potato Stars
IO SERVINGS

3 large baking potatoes
Melted unsalted margarine or oil
Salt to taste

1. Preheat the oven to 450 degrees.
2. Cut the potatoes crosswise into ½-inch-thick slices. Using a metal cookie cutter or a knife, cut the slices into Stars of David. Place in cold water until ready to bake.
3. Pat the potatoes dry and brush with melted margarine. Place on baking sheets.
4. Bake, turning, until the stars are golden brown on both sides, about 20 minutes. Or deep-fry them in several inches of 375-degree oil until golden, 3 to 5 minutes. Sprinkle lightly with salt.

Sephardic Sweetened Barley *(Belilah)*
ABOUT IO CUPS

Since the Omer traditionally began with an offering of newly harvested barley, this dish is particularly appropriate for celebration of Lag b'Omer. When made with cooked wheat berries, it is called *ashoora* in north Africa, *kofyas* in Turkey, *sleehah* in Syria, and *assuré* or *kolliva* in Greece. Sweetened barley or wheat mixed with fruits and nuts is also popular in the Middle East on Tu b'Shevat and at parties honoring a baby's first tooth.

Pinch of salt
2 cups pearl barley, rinsed and drained
2½ cups water
1¾ cups sugar
1 teaspoon fresh lemon juice
2 to 4 tablespoons orange blossom water or rose water
1½ teaspoons ground cinnamon (optional)
1 to 2 cups dried currants or raisins (or 1 cup raisins and 1 cup chopped pitted dates)
½ cup slivered or chopped almonds
½ cup pine nuts
½ cup coarsely chopped pistachios
½ cup coarsely chopped walnuts
Pomegranate seeds for garnish (optional)

1. Bring a large pot of water to a boil. Add the salt and barley, cover, reduce the heat to low, and simmer until tender, about 40 minutes. Remove from the heat and let stand for 15 minutes. Drain.
2. Meanwhile, make a syrup. Stir the water, sugar, and lemon juice over medium-low heat until the sugar dissolves. Add the orange blossom water and simmer for 2 minutes.
3. Pour the syrup over the barley. If desired, stir in the cinnamon. Add the raisins and nuts. Serve warm or at room temperature. If desired, sprinkle with the pomegranate seeds.

Feather-Frosted Carob Brownies
SIXTEEN 2-INCH BARS

*W*hen fresh, the pulp of the 6- to 10-inch-long, crescent-shaped, brownish black carob pod is soft and sweet. When dried and ground into a powder, it imparts a sweet flavor, brown color, and velvety texture to baked goods. Carob powder, available in health food stores, can be substituted for cocoa powder, although to be honest, the flavors are not the same. It is available both raw (actually, it is cooked for a short time) and roasted; the roasted type possesses more of a chocolate flavor. Health food stores also carry carob chips, which serve as a substitute for chocolate chips.

1 cup all-purpose flour
3 tablespoons carob powder
1 teaspoon baking powder or ½ teaspoon baking soda
¼ teaspoon salt
½ cup (1 stick) unsalted margarine, softened
¾ cup packed light brown sugar (or 6 tablespoons packed brown sugar
    and 6 tablespoons granulated sugar)
1 teaspoon vanilla extract
1 large egg
½ to 1 cup coarsely chopped walnuts, pecans, almonds, or peanuts
½ to 1 cup carob chips or raisins (optional)

FROSTING
1 cup sifted confectioners' sugar
¼ teaspoon vanilla extract
About 1½ tablespoons boiling water
1 teaspoon carob powder

1. Preheat the oven to 350 degrees. Line an 8-inch-square baking pan with aluminum foil and grease the foil.
2. Sift together the flour, carob powder, baking powder, and salt. Beat the margarine until smooth, about 1 minute. Gradually add the sugar and beat until light and fluffy, about 4 minutes. Beat in the vanilla and egg. Stir in the flour mixture, nuts, and if desired, the carob chips.
3. Spread the mixture evenly in the prepared pan. Bake until a wooden tester comes out clean, about 30 minutes. Let cool completely.
4. To make the frosting: Beat the sugar, vanilla, and water until smooth. Remove 3 tablespoons of the frosting and combine with the carob. Spread the white frosting over the brownies. Put the carob frosting in a pastry bag fitted with a small tip and pipe narrow lines at ½-inch intervals over the white frosting. Using a toothpick or skewer, draw across the carob lines at ½-inch intervals, reversing the direction every other time. Refrigerate until set.
5. Using the overlapping ends of the foil, remove the cake from the pan. Place on a flat surface and cut into 2-inch squares.

VARIATION

Double the recipe and bake in a 13- by 9-inch baking dish or 10-inch round cake pan.

Basic Cupcakes
12 MEDIUM CUPCAKES

1¼ cups all-purpose flour
1½ teaspoons baking powder
¼ teaspoon salt
½ cup (1 stick) unsalted margarine, softened
¾ cup sugar
2 large eggs
1 teaspoon vanilla extract
½ cup nondairy creamer or water
About 1 cup Basic Buttercream (page 370)

1. Preheat the oven to 350 degrees. Grease 12 standard-size muffin-tin cups or line with cupcake papers.
2. Sift together the flour, baking powder, and salt. Beat the margarine until smooth, about 1 minute. Gradually add the sugar and beat until light and fluffy, about 5 minutes. Beat in the eggs, one at a time, then the vanilla. Stir in the flour mixture, then the creamer.
3. Fill the prepared muffin cups ¾ full with the batter. Bake until the cakes spring back when lightly touched and a tester inserted in the center comes out clean, 15 to 20 minutes. Let cool in the pan for 5 minutes, then transfer to a rack and let cool completely. (The cupcakes can be wrapped in plastic, then in foil, and stored at room temperature for up to 3 days or in the freezer for several months.) Spread the buttercream over the tops of the cupcakes. (To make frosting easy, dip the top of the cupcakes into the frosting and twirl.)

VARIATIONS

Chocolate Fudge Cupcakes: Substitute 1 cup light brown sugar for the granulated sugar. Reduce the margarine to 6 tablespoons (¾ stick). Add 2 ounces melted unsweetened chocolate.

LAG B'OMER CUPCAKES

1 cup Basic Buttercream (page 370)
Several drops blue food coloring
12 Basic Cupcakes

Tint ⅓ cup of the buttercream with the food coloring. Spread the tops of the cupcakes with the remaining white buttercream. Fit a pastry bag with a ¹/₁₆-inch writing tip and fill with the tinted buttercream. Pipe a bow and arrow (or a Star of David) on each cupcake.

CLOWN CUPCAKES

12 Basic Cupcakes
1 cup Basic Buttercream (page 370)
Candies for garnishing (such as gumdrops, licorice strips, candy-coated licorice)

Spread the tops of the cupcakes with the buttercream. Garnish with the candies (or additional tinted buttercream) to form the eyes, nose, mouth, ears, and hair of a clown.

BASEBALL CUPCAKES

1⅓ cups Basic Buttercream (page 370)
Several drops red, black, or brown food coloring
12 Basic Cupcakes

Tint ⅓ cup of the buttercream with the food coloring. Spread the tops of the cupcakes with the remaining white buttercream. Fit a pastry bag with a ¹/₁₆-inch writing tip and fill with the tinted buttercream. Pipe 2 parallel half circles with arcs pointed toward the center on each cupcake, then pipe small perpendicular lines over each half circle to form stitches.

BASKETBALL CUPCAKES

1⅓ cups Basic Buttercream (page 370)
Several drops black food coloring
Several drops red food coloring
Several drops yellow food coloring
12 Basic Cupcakes

Tint ⅓ cup of the buttercream with the black coloring. Tint the remaining frosting with the red and yellow colorings to produce an orange color. Spread the cupcakes with the orange-colored frosting. Fit a pastry bag with a ¹/₁₆-inch writing tip and fill with the black frosting. Pipe a line down the center of the cupcakes, then pipe a perpendicular line. Pipe a semicircle with arcs pointed toward the center on both sides of one line.

CHILDREN'S PARTIES

Children can be very picky when it comes to food, but they also tend to be less discerning than adults, a vital point to keep in mind when planning a child's party. Serving fancy or sophisticated food to most kids proves a waste. Instead, concentrate on the activities and decorations and serve simple and beloved items such as pizza, burgers, sandwiches, chips, and cookies. Children do appreciate a sense of whimsy, which you can express in out-of-the-ordinary cakes and cookies. If you want the youngsters to eat something healthful, offer fresh fruit, especially strawberries, grapes, and cut-up melon. Food should be appropriate for a child's hands and not too messy. Serve small portions to young children; plan on a lot more for teenage boys.

Other things to keep in mind in planning a child's party:

- Keep it simple.

- The party should be 2 hours long at the most.

- Don't invite more children than you can handle.

- Pick an appropriate theme—such as sports, ballet, dinosaurs, cowboys, or Hawaii—and use it for the invitations, decorations, games, and food.

- Let the kids help design and construct the invitations and decorations.

- The decorations should be age appropriate. Balloons are always a favorite. If you find someone like my brother Arthur, who is a master at making balloon animals, you can turn the decorations into part of the entertainment.

- Some decorations can be gifts for every child to take home. For example, cut out animal shapes from sheets of plastic, glue on joggly eyes, and use as place mats.

- Use a roll of white paper for the tablecloth and supply crayons for the young artists.

- Since children tend to be hard on a house, hold the party in the family room or an outdoor location, most notably the backyard (have a backup plan in case of inclement weather). A trip with box lunches is an interesting and practical alternative.

- Children have short attention spans and tend to run through games quickly. So plan on having more age-appropriate activities than you might think necessary.

- Plan entertainment in which everyone can get involved. Consider a number of noncompetitive activities in which no one will feel like a loser. Crafts and kitchen activities, such as make-your-own pizza or decorate-your-own cookies, will be well received. (To make edible play dough, combine 2 cups smooth peanut butter, 3 tablespoons honey, and about 2 cups powdered milk for a mixture that is not too sticky.)

- Make sure every child is involved in the goings-on, but don't force anyone to participate.

Something Different for Shavuot

SERVES 8

The festival of Shavuot (Hebrew for "weeks") is a two-day Pilgrim Festival (one day in Israel) commemorating the giving of the Torah at Mount Sinai seven weeks after the Israelites departed Egypt. Also known as Chag ha'Katzir (Festival of the Harvest), Shavuot marks the end of the barley harvest and the beginning of the spring wheat harvest. During the time when the Temple stood, two loaves of wheat bread—symbolizing the bounty of the season—were "waved before the Lord" (Leviticus 23:17–20) on Shavuot, this being the only occasion during the year when leavened bread was used in the Temple. Since the bread offering is one of the few biblical rites for this holiday, a special emphasis is placed on the holiday challah. Saffron, the most expensive of spices, is sometimes added to the dough. Ukrainian Jews follow the custom of shaping a Shavuot challah into a five- or seven-rung ladder symbolizing Moses' ascent of Mount Sinai to receive the Torah. Many Sephardim prepare round seven-layered breads called *siete cielos* (seven heavens).

The preeminent Shavuot custom is to eat dairy food. It is partially based upon the legend that, after receiving the Torah and the laws of *kashrut,* the Jews could no longer eat the meat foods they had prepared beforehand or use any of their cooking utensils, which were now unkosher. Therefore they had to eat dairy dishes on the first Shavuot. Another legend relates that when the Jews returned to camp after receiving the Torah, they found that their milk had soured and turned into cheese. Numerologists add that the value of *chalav,* the Hebrew word for "milk," is forty, the number of days that Moses was on Mount Sinai. Shavuot also corresponds to the time of the year when young ruminants are still being suckled; the abundance of milk makes dairy dishes an obvious choice for the holiday. In addition, dairy products and other white foods such as rice are considered symbols of purity.

CHALLAH

RASPBERRY WINE SOUP

POACHED SALMON STEAKS WITH CUCUMBER RAITA

BLINTZ CASSEROLE WITH STRAWBERRY SAUCE

SPINACH LASAGNA ROLLS

ENGLISH FLOATING ISLANDS

CHOCOLATE KREPLACH

TEA AND COFFEE

 Wine Suggestions: Riesling, Chenin Blanc, Sauvignon Blanc, or Chardonnay

Raspberry Wine Soup
8 SERVINGS

*A*shkenazim traditionally start Shavuot meals with a chilled soup, especially a fruit soup, alluding to the first fruits of the harvest.

2 pints fresh or 40 ounces frozen unsweetened raspberries
4 cups dry red or rosé wine (or 2½ cups fruity dry white
*   such as Riesling and 1½ cups dry red wine)*
1½ cups fresh orange juice or water
½ cup fresh lemon juice
½ to ¾ cup sugar or honey
¼ cup quick-cooking tapioca
1 (3-inch) stick cinnamon (optional)

1. If using frozen raspberries, drain and reserve any juice. In a 3-quart saucepan, combine the raspberry juice, wine, orange juice, lemon juice, sugar, tapioca, and if desired, the cinnamon stick. Bring to a gentle boil, stirring occasionally, over medium-high heat. Reduce the heat to low and simmer for 10 minutes.
2. Remove from the heat and let cool for 10 minutes. Discard the cinnamon stick. Add the raspberries. Refrigerate overnight and up to 3 days. Serve in chilled bowls.

Poached Salmon Steaks with Cucumber Raita
8 SERVINGS

*I*f desired, substitute another firm-fleshed fish steak, such as halibut, sea trout, or grouper, for the salmon.

4 cups water
About 2 tablespoons salt
8 (6-ounce) salmon steaks, about ½ inch thick

1. In a large skillet over high heat, bring the water and salt to a boil.
2. Add 4 of the fish steaks, reduce the heat to low, cover, and simmer until the fish is tender, 6 to 8 minutes. Remove the steaks with a wide spatula. Repeat with the remaining steaks. Refrigerate until chilled. Serve accompanied by cucumber raita (below) or herb mayonnaise.

CUCUMBER RAITA
ABOUT 6 CUPS

*I*ndian yogurt salads, called *raita*s (pronounced RAY-tas), are cool concoctions meant to contrast with the spiciness of Indian curries. They usually contain raw or partially cooked vegetables.

3 cups (24 ounces) plain yogurt
About 1 teaspoon ground cumin
About ½ teaspoon salt
Ground white pepper
3 medium cucumbers, peeled, seeded, and diced

Combine the yogurt, cumin, salt, and pepper. Stir in the cucumbers. Cover and chill for at least 1 hour.

Blintz Casserole with Strawberry Sauce

8 SERVINGS

*T*his variation raises an old eastern European favorite to new heights. Baked in a custard, these blintzes are so tasty you may want to double the recipe and bake in a 13- by 9-inch pan. Or you can simply fry the blintzes in a little butter or margarine and serve with a little sour cream.

CREPES

¾ cup milk
½ cup water
3 large eggs, lightly beaten
2 tablespoons unsalted butter or margarine, melted and cooled
About ½ teaspoon salt
¾ cup all-purpose flour
Butter or vegetable oil for frying

CHEESE FILLING

1 pound farmer, pot, or small-curd cottage cheese
1 large egg
2 to 4 tablespoons sugar
1 tablespoon melted unsalted butter, sour cream, or cream cheese
1 teaspoon vanilla extract
¼ teaspoon salt

CUSTARD

1 cup sour cream
3 large eggs
2 to 4 tablespoons sugar
1 teaspoon vanilla extract
⅛ teaspoon salt
2 tablespoons fresh orange or lemon juice (optional)

1. To make the crepes: Whisk together the milk, water, eggs, butter, and salt. Gradually whisk in the flour to make a smooth, thin batter with the consistency of heavy cream.

Strain if there are any lumps. (The easiest way to prepare the batter is to process all of the ingredients in a blender until smooth.) Cover and refrigerate for at least 2 hours or up to 2 days.

2. Heat a 6-inch skillet (cast iron or nonstick is best) over medium heat. Brush lightly with butter or oil. (You do not have to rebrush the pan before every crepe.)

3. Pour in about 2 tablespoons of the batter and tilt the pan until the batter just coats the bottom. Cook until the edges begin to brown and come away from the sides of the pan, about 1 minute. Flip onto a dry towel or piece of wax paper. Repeat to make 8 crepes. (The crepes can be stacked between pieces of parchment or wax paper and stored in the refrigerator for up to 3 days or in the freezer for up to 2 months.)

4. To make the filling: Combine all the filling ingredients.

5. Place about 2 tablespoons filling just below the center of each crepe. Fold the bottom of the crepe over the filling. Fold the sides over and roll up the crepe, enclosing the filling completely. Repeat until you have 8 filled blintzes. (The blintzes can be refrigerated overnight or stored in the freezer for up to 1 month.)

6. Preheat the oven to 350 degrees. Grease a 9-inch-square baking pan.

7. To make the custard: Beat the sour cream and eggs until fluffy. Blend in the sugar, vanilla, salt, and if desired, the juice.

8. Arrange the blintzes in the prepared pan and pour the custard over them. (The casserole can be prepared up to 8 hours ahead and stored in the refrigerator.) Bake until the custard is puffed and golden brown, about 50 minutes. Serve with strawberry sauce (below), sour cream, or fresh fruit.

STRAWBERRY SAUCE
ABOUT 2 CUPS

3 cups fresh or 20 ounces unsweetened frozen strawberries
⅔ to 1 cup sugar
¾ cup water
2 tablespoons orange liqueur, brandy, or lemon juice

Bring the berries, sugar, and water to a boil in a medium saucepan over medium-high heat. Reduce the heat to low and simmer, stirring occasionally, until syrupy, about 10 minutes. Stir in the liqueur.

Spinach Lasagna Rolls
12 ROLLS

*T*here is no need to cut this lasagna, as it comes in individual serving portions.

12 lasagna noodles
About 2 cups tomato pasta sauce
3 cups (1½ pounds) ricotta or small-curd cottage cheese
2 (10-ounce) boxes frozen chopped spinach, thawed and squeezed
½ cup (about 2 ounces) grated Parmesan cheese
2 large eggs or 4 large egg whites
¼ teaspoon grated nutmeg
Ground black pepper to taste
1 cup (8 ounces) shredded mozzarella cheese (optional)

1. Cook the lasagna noodles in a large stockpot of lightly salted boiling water, stirring occasionally, until tender but not mushy, 12 to 15 minutes. Drain and place in cold water for 1 minute. Drain and place on a kitchen towel for up to 1 hour.
2. Preheat the oven to 375 degrees.
3. Spread a thin layer of pasta sauce in a 13- by 9-inch baking dish. Combine the ricotta cheese, spinach, Parmesan, eggs, nutmeg, and pepper. Place the noodles on a flat surface, spread about ⅓ cup of the cheese mixture over each noodle, and roll up. Arrange, seam side down, in the prepared dish. Cover with the remaining sauce and, if desired, sprinkle with the mozzarella. (The lasagna can be covered with plastic wrap and refrigerated for 1 day or covered with foil and frozen for up to 1 month. Thaw before baking.)
4. Bake until bubbly, about 35 minutes. Serve warm.

English Floating Islands *(Oeufs à la Neige)*
8 SERVINGS

*Y*ou can substitute 3 cups of berry sauce for the custard sauce (crème anglaise).

MERINGUES
4 large egg whites, at room temperature
⅛ teaspoon salt
½ cup plus 2 tablespoons sugar
2 teaspoons potato starch (optional)

CRÈME ANGLAISE
2 cups heavy cream or milk (or 1 cup heavy cream and 1 cup milk)
⅔ cup sugar
1 vanilla bean, split lengthwise, or 1 teaspoon vanilla extract
Pinch of salt
6 large egg yolks
1 teaspoon cornstarch (optional)
2 to 4 tablespoons brandy, bourbon, rum, orange liqueur, Irish cream liqueur, or kirsch (optional)

CARAMEL
¼ cup sugar
2 tablespoons water
Dash of fresh lemon juice

1. Bring a large pot of water to a simmer (about 170 degrees) over medium heat.
2. To make the meringues: Beat the egg whites on low speed until foamy, about 30 seconds. Add the salt, increase the speed to medium-high, and beat until soft peaks just begin to form, about 1 minute. Gradually add the sugar, about 1 tablespoon at a time, beating about 1 minute between additions. Increase the speed to high and continue beating until the whites are stiff and glossy, 5 to 8 minutes. If desired, fold in the potato starch (it will help hold the meringues together).
3. Using a large spoon or ½-cup ice cream scoop, slide mounds of the egg whites into the simmering water to form egg shapes. Poach, turning once, until the meringues are firm, 1 to 2 minutes per side. Repeat until all the egg whites are used.

4. Using a slotted spoon, remove the meringues from the water and let drain on paper towels. To store the meringues, place in a large bowl, cover (be careful that the plastic wrap does not touch the meringues), and refrigerate overnight.

5. To make the crème anglaise: In a heavy-bottomed medium saucepan, heat the cream or milk (cream produces a thicker sauce), ⅓ cup of the sugar, the vanilla bean, and salt over medium heat until small bubbles appear around the edges. (If using vanilla extract, stir it into the cooked custard, after step 7.) Reduce the heat, cover, and simmer until the vanilla infuses the cream, about 10 minutes.

6. Meanwhile, beat the egg yolks and remaining ⅓ cup sugar until thick and creamy, about 5 minutes. If desired, beat in the cornstarch. Gradually beat the hot cream into the egg mixture.

7. Return the mixture to the saucepan and cook over medium-low heat, stirring constantly with a wooden spoon, until it registers 175 degrees on a candy thermometer and is thick enough to coat a spoon, about 5 minutes. (If you run a finger down the back of the spoon, a path will remain for several seconds.) Do not boil or the egg yolks will curdle. Remove the vanilla bean and reserve for another use.

8. Strain the custard into a nonreactive bowl, such as stainless steel. If desired, stir in the brandy. To cool quickly, place the bowl in a larger bowl filled with ice water. When the custard is cooled, cover the surface with plastic wrap and chill. (Crème anglaise keeps in the refrigerator for up to 4 days.)

9. To make the caramel: Combine all the ingredients for the caramel in a small saucepan and cook, stirring, over medium-low heat until the sugar dissolves. Stop stirring, increase the heat to medium, and cook, shaking the pan occasionally, until the syrup turns an amber color, about 10 minutes. Remove from the heat and stop cooking by placing the pan in ice water, but do not leave long enough to set the caramel.

10. Spread a generous amount of custard sauce over the bottom of each serving plate and top with the meringues. Using a fork, drizzle threads of caramel over the meringues. (Final assembly can be done 2 to 3 hours before serving and the floating islands can then be chilled.)

HINTS: If the sauce separates, puree it in food processor or blender until smooth. Poach the meringues in milk and use the leftover milk for making the custard sauce. Substitute shaved chocolate for the caramel.

Chocolate Kreplach

ABOUT 21 CANDIES

*K*replach are a traditional Ashkenazic meat-stuffed pasta served in soup or fried to a golden brown. To mystics, the wrapping of a filling in dough represents the divine envelopment of mercy and kindness, and the triangular shape represents the three Patriarchs: Abraham, Isaac, and Jacob. Cheese kreplach: are a popular Shavuot treat. In this recipe I have adapted the concept by creating a kreplach consisting of a luscious chocolate filling enclosed in white chocolate. The white chocolate "dough" can also be formed into shapes such as roses and ribbons and used to decorate cakes.

12 ounces white chocolate, chopped
½ cup light corn syrup
Confectioners' sugar
1½ cups chocolate mousse (page 369) or ganache (page 132)

1. In the top of a double boiler over barely simmering water, melt the white chocolate, stirring until smooth. Remove the top part of the double boiler, add the corn syrup, and stir until the mixture forms a ball. Wrap in plastic and let stand at room temperature overnight.

2. On a flat surface dusted with confectioners' sugar, knead the white chocolate mixture until it is smooth and pliable (it will be greasy).

3. Lightly dust the surface again with confectioners' sugar and roll out the chocolate to a ⅛-inch thickness (a rectangle about 27 by 9 inches). Trim the edges. Cut into 3-inch squares.

4. Place about 1 tablespoon chocolate mousse in the center of each white chocolate square and fold 2 opposite corners together to form a triangle. Seal the edges with the tines of a fork. Store in the refrigerator. Return to room temperature before serving.

VARIATION

Quick White Chocolate Kreplach: Place a 3-ounce white chocolate bar in an oven with a pilot light or in a microwave on the lowest setting until it is pliable but not mushy. (The secret is not to melt the chocolate but only to soften it until pliable. Since the chocolate hardens quickly, it is advisable to work with one bar at a time. Each 3-ounce bar yields 3 candies, so you will need 7 bars for this recipe.) On a flat surface, roll out the white chocolate with a rolling pin or put it through a pasta machine until it is ⅛ inch thick. Cut into 3-inch squares and proceed with step 4.

An International Sabbath Dinner

SERVES 8

*F*rom twilight Friday until the appearance of the first three stars on Saturday night, Jews pray, study, reflect, and in fulfillment of the commandment of *oneg Shabbat* (enjoyment of the Sabbath), also socialize, sing, and partake of three meals. The first meal is on Friday night, the second on Saturday following morning prayer services, and the last, *shalosh seudot* (third meal), late on Saturday afternoon. A 1995 study conducted by an Israeli foundation discovered that 54 percent of Israelis regularly have a special meal on the Sabbath, while 26 percent do so occasionally. That 80 percent of all Israelis appreciate the warmth and inspiration of a home-centered observance demonstrates the deep-seated position the Sabbath meal continues to maintain in Jewish life.

Sabbath dinner possesses a singular ambience. The table is set with the family's finery. Candlesticks sprout dancing flames, casting a genial glow over the surroundings. Lively *zemirot* (traditional songs) are sung intermittently throughout the meal. (To tell the truth, my immediate family does little singing, as we are so off-key the neighbors think we are strangling chickens. Fortunately, all the nieces and nephews appear to have inherited musical genes from the in-laws and are a joy to hear.) Thus, a profoundly religious activity and enjoyable gastronomic experience become one and the same.

PERSIAN MEATBALL SOUP
MOROCCAN YELLOW OR RED FISH
SYRIAN CHICKEN WITH PASTA
ITALIAN COOKED VEGETABLE SALAD
INDIAN TOMATO SALAD
HUNGARIAN COFFEE CAKE
TEA AND COFFEE

 Wine Suggestions: Dry Riesling, Sauvignon Blanc, or Soave

Persian Meatball Soup (Morgh-Gushe Ghondi)
8 SERVINGS

*P*ersians commonly serve *ghondi* (meatballs) on Friday and holiday nights, sometimes as the entrée, sometimes as the opener, followed by a main course of chicken and always rice.

MEATBALLS
1½ pounds ground beef or chicken
2 medium onions, minced or grated (about 1 cup)
1 large egg, lightly beaten
⅓ cup chopped fresh parsley
About 1 teaspoon salt
½ teaspoon ground cardamom or cinnamon
¼ teaspoon turmeric
⅛ teaspoon ground black pepper

SOUP
2 quarts Chicken Soup (page 137)
3 medium carrots, sliced
3 medium boiling potatoes, peeled and quartered
1 teaspoon ground cumin
½ teaspoon turmeric
Pinch of cayenne pepper or red pepper flakes
About 4 cups cooked rice
About 1½ cups cooked chickpeas (optional)

1. To make the meatballs: Combine all the meatball ingredients and refrigerate until easy to handle, at least 1 hour.
2. Meanwhile, place the soup, carrots, and potatoes in a large pot and bring to a boil. Cover, reduce the heat to low, and simmer for 30 minutes. Add the cumin, turmeric, and cayenne.
3. Using wet hands, form the meatball mixture into 1-inch balls. (There will be about 24 meatballs.)
4. Bring the soup to a boil, add the meatballs, cover, reduce the heat to low, and simmer until tender, about 30 minutes. (The soup with the *ghondi* can be stored in the refrigerator for up to 3 days and reheated.)

5. Place a heaping spoonful of rice in the bottom of each serving bowl and ladle some soup and meatballs on top. If desired, garnish with the chickpeas.

VARIATIONS

Persian Prune Meatball Soup (**Kiufta Bozbash**): Press a pitted prune in the center of each meatball, pinching the edges of the meat to enclose.

Azerbaijani Meatball Soup (**Kololik**): Add ⅓ cup chopped fresh mint or cilantro to the meatballs.

Moroccan Yellow Fish *(Hout Metbuch)*
8 SERVINGS

*M*oroccan seasoning differs from that in the rest of Africa, relying on character and a combination of ingredients for flavor. The liberal use of seasonings produces delightful nuances of flavor, aroma, and color. Moroccans have a particular fondness for fish, frequently serving it at Sabbath meals. Thus the popular saying "Whoever eats fish will be saved from the judgment of Gehenna."

About 4 cups water
¼ cup olive or vegetable oil
3 tablespoons fresh lemon juice
1 large onion, chopped (about ¾ cup)
½ cup chopped fresh parsley
2 stalks celery
6 to 8 whole cloves garlic
2 tablespoons capers
½ teaspoon turmeric or pinch of saffron
About 1 teaspoon salt
1 teaspoon ground cumin (optional)
4 pounds fillets or 8 (1-inch-thick) steaks firm-fleshed fish, such as cod,
    haddock, halibut, grouper, sea bass, or whitefish

1. Combine all the ingredients except the fish in a large saucepan. Bring to a boil, reduce the heat to medium-low, and simmer for 30 minutes.
2. Add the fish and return to a boil. Cover, reduce the heat to low, and simmer until the fish is tender, about 20 minutes for fillets, about 40 minutes for steaks.
3. Remove the fish and arrange on a serving platter. Strain the cooking liquid and arrange the solids over the fish. Return the liquid to the pot and boil over high heat until reduced by half, about 15 minutes. Pour the liquid over the fish. Serve at room temperature or chilled.

VARIATION

Moroccan Red Fish: Omit the capers and add 2 tablespoons paprika and about ½ teaspoon cayenne.

Syrian Chicken with Pasta *(Dajaaj al Macaruna)*
8 SERVINGS

This dish was designed to slow-cook for several hours, providing a warm and flavorful entrée for Friday night dinner. It is also a popular choice on Rosh Hashanah and Hanukkah.

About 5 pounds chicken pieces
1 large onion, chopped (about ¾ cup)
3 to 4 cloves garlic, minced
1 cup water
2 pounds spaghetti, broken into 3-inch pieces, or macaroni or ziti
2 tablespoons olive or vegetable oil
2 cups (1 pound) tomato sauce or 6 ounces tomato paste
About 2½ teaspoons salt
1 teaspoon ground cinnamon
½ to 1 teaspoon ground allspice

1. Preheat the oven to 350 degrees.

2. Place the chicken, onion, and garlic in a large roasting pan. Add the water, cover, and bake until the chicken is tender, about 1¼ hours.
3. Meanwhile, cook the pasta in a large pot of lightly salted boiling water until *al dente* (tender yet firm to the bite). Drain and rinse under cold water. Toss with 1 tablespoon of the oil.
4. Remove the chicken from the pan. Stir the tomato sauce, remaining 1 tablespoon oil, salt, cinnamon, and allspice into the pan juices. Stir in the pasta. If desired, bone and shred the meat. Bury the chicken in the pasta.
5. Cover and bake at 350 degrees for about 30 minutes or at 250 degrees for 2 to 4 hours. Serve warm.

Italian Cooked Vegetable Salad *(Insalata Russa)*
8 SERVINGS

*N*amed for Russia, this simple salad was once a ubiquitous Sabbath dish in Italy.

4 medium (about 1 pound) boiling potatoes
4 medium carrots, sliced
½ pound cauliflower, cut into florets
½ pound green beans, cut into ½-inch pieces
1 cup green peas
1 large onion, chopped (about ¾ cup)
½ cup black olives
2 tablespoons drained capers
4 scallions, chopped
½ cup mayonnaise
2 tablespoons olive oil
1 tablespoon wine vinegar or cider vinegar
Salt to taste
Ground black pepper to taste
Anchovy fillets for garnish
Sliced hard-boiled eggs for garnish

1. Cook the potatoes in lightly salted boiling water until tender but not mushy, about 1 hour. Peel and cut into ½-inch cubes.
2. Steam or boil the carrots, cauliflower, green beans, peas, and onion until tender-crisp, about 3 minutes. Combine the cooked vegetables, olives, capers, and scallions in a large bowl.
3. Stir together the mayonnaise, oil, vinegar, salt, and pepper. Pour over the vegetables, tossing to coat. Cover and refrigerate for at least 30 minutes. Garnish with anchovies and egg slices.

Indian Tomato Salad *(Puccha)*
ABOUT 6 CUPS

Since the tomatoes require extra effort to prepare, this salad is reserved for special occasions such as Sabbath dinner and holidays.

2 pounds ripe tomatoes, peeled, seeded, and crushed (about 6 cups)
5 to 6 scallions (including most of the green part), chopped
¼ cup chopped fresh cilantro or parsley
1 to 2 fresh hot green chilies, such as jalapeño or serrano,
    seeded and minced (optional)
⅓ cup lemon juice
About ¾ teaspoon salt
Ground black pepper to taste

Combine all the ingredients.

Hungarian Coffee Cake *(Arany Galuska)*
8 TO 10 SERVINGS

*B*alls of dough are placed next to and on top of each other, so that everyone can pull off pieces of the sweet bread.

1 (¼-ounce) package (2½ teaspoons) active dry yeast or 1 (0.6-ounce) cake fresh yeast
1 cup warm water (105 to 115 degrees for dry yeast; 80 to 85 degrees for fresh yeast)
1 cup sugar
⅓ cup unsalted margarine, softened
1 large egg
1 teaspoon table salt or 2 teaspoons kosher salt
About 4 cups bread or unbleached all-purpose flour
1½ teaspoons ground cinnamon
½ cup (1 stick) unsalted margarine, melted

1. Dissolve the yeast in ¼ cup of the warm water. Stir in 1 teaspoon of the sugar and let stand until foamy, about 5 minutes.
2. Add the remaining water, ¼ cup of the sugar, the margarine, egg, and salt. Blend in 1½ cups of the flour. Add enough of the remaining flour, ½ cup at a time, to make a workable dough.
3. On a lightly floured surface or in a mixer with a dough hook, knead the dough, adding more flour as needed, until smooth and elastic, about 5 minutes. Place in a greased bowl, turning to coat. Cover loosely with a towel or plastic wrap and let rise in a warm, draft-free place until nearly double in bulk, about 1½ hours, or in the refrigerator overnight. Punch down the dough.
4. Grease a 9- or 10-inch tube pan. (In place of a tube pan, set a custard cup or foil-covered 1½-inch tube in the center of a springform pan or deep casserole.)
5. Combine the remaining sugar and the cinnamon. Shape the dough into 1-inch balls. Dip into the melted margarine, then roll in the cinnamon sugar to coat. Arrange in layers in the pan. Cover loosely with a towel or plastic wrap and let rise until nearly double in bulk, about 45 minutes.
6. Preheat the oven to 375 degrees.
7. Bake until the coffee cake is golden brown, about 40 minutes. Loosen from the sides of the pan and invert onto a serving platter.

VARIATION

Basic Coffee Cake: Press the dough into a greased 13- by 9-inch baking pan, dot with the margarine, and sprinkle with the cinnamon sugar. Reduce the baking time to about 25 minutes.

A Sabbath *Meze*— Perfect for Any Occasion

SERVES 12

*G*rowing up, I always thought of an appetizer as one large dish served at the beginning of a meal, the standard European-American custom. So I experienced major culture shock the first time I was fortunate enough to attend a *meze* during a trip to Israel. Spread out before me were dozens of interesting tidbits. And they were all served in small portions, which better suited my style of enjoying a buffet or even a dessert selection—sample one or two bites, then move on to the next gastronomical adventure. At a *meze* you can literally get a taste of the Middle East.

A *meze* may start any Middle Eastern meal or serve as the meal itself, providing more variety than set courses. The usual definition of a *meze* as an appetizer assortment fails to do it justice, for even a modest *meze* table is a medley of tastes, textures, aromas, and colors, featuring at least a half-dozen dishes, both cooked and uncooked, simple and elaborate, hot and cold. A typical *meze* includes a variety of spreads, salads, olives, pickles, and small pastries. A more elaborate affair may contain meat dishes, such as *kibbe* (meat patties) and *mortadel* (filled meatballs). There is also a sweet table called *meze allegre.*

Middle Eastern Jews enjoy a *meze* upon returning home from Sabbath and festival morning services, as well as on other special occasions. The multitude of items allows diners to recite the appropriate blessing over each of them. At times a community *meze* is served at a synagogue, providing a Sabbath meal for the poor.

The following recipes are not the be-all and end-all of *meze* but merely an introduction. Add any of your favorite Middle Eastern dishes, such as Tabbouleh (page 64) and Phyllo Cigars (page 306). For that matter, any dish can be incorporated in a *meze* as long as it projects a vivid personality of its own and is served in small portions.

PITA BREAD

MIDDLE EASTERN STUFFED GRAPE LEAVES

MIDDLE EASTERN PHYLLO TRIANGLES

MIDDLE EASTERN FILLED MEATBALLS

SYRIAN MEAT TORPEDOES

ISRAELI MARINATED EGGPLANT FINGERS

VEGETABLE OMELET

TURKISH WHITE BEAN SALAD

MIDDLE EASTERN ARTICHOKE SALAD

NORTHWEST AFRICAN GRILLED VEGETABLE SALAD

SYRIAN PAREVE *KIBBE NAYE*

RED PEPPER AND WALNUT SPREAD

MIDDLE EASTERN CHILI OLIVES

TEA AND COFFEE

 Liquor Suggestions: Arak or beer

Middle Eastern Stuffed Grape Leaves (Yaprak Dolmas)

ABOUT 40 LARGE OR 60 SMALL ROLLS

*S*tuffed grape leaves, which originated as a way to utilize these otherwise inedible greens, are popular in much of the Middle East and Mediterranean region. Although rice is the most common filling, other popular possibilities include meat, bulgur, and chickpeas. Meat-stuffed *yaprak dolmas* are generally served warm; rice-stuffed *dolmas,* cold.

FILLING

3 tablespoons olive or vegetable oil
3 medium onions, chopped (about 1½ cups)
2 to 3 cloves garlic, minced
1½ cups long-grain white rice
½ cup pine nuts or coarsely chopped pistachios
½ cup dried currants or raisins
¼ cup chopped fresh mint or parsley
About 1¼ teaspoons salt
½ teaspoon ground black pepper
½ teaspoon ground allspice
½ teaspoon ground cinnamon
2½ cups chicken broth or water

40 large or 60 small (1-pound jar) grape leaves
About 2 cups chicken broth or water
¼ cup fresh lemon juice
3 whole cloves garlic
¼ cup olive oil (optional)
2 to 3 teaspoons sugar (optional)

1. To make the filling: Heat the oil in a large saucepan over medium heat. Add the onions and sauté until soft and translucent, 5 to 10 minutes. Add the garlic and sauté for 1 minute. Add the rice and sauté until opaque, 3 to 5 minutes. Stir in the pine nuts, currants, mint, salt, pepper, allspice, and cinnamon. Add the broth and bring

the mixture to a boil. Cover, reduce the heat to low, and simmer until the liquid is absorbed, about 15 minutes. Let cool.

2. To assemble: Unroll the grape leaves, rinse under cold water, and soak in water to cover for 5 minutes. Drain and pat dry. Carefully cut off the stems. Place the leaves, shiny side down and vein side up, on a flat surface.

3. Place 1 tablespoon filling on each large leaf and a heaping teaspoon filling on each smaller leaf. Carefully fold each leaf from the stem end to cover the filling. Fold the sides over and, starting from the filling end, roll up the leaf to make a neat package.

4. Cover the bottom of a heavy pot or baking dish with any extra leaves. Arrange the rolled leaves, seam side down, in layers in the pot.

5. Mix the broth, lemon juice, garlic, and if desired, the oil and/or sugar and pour over the stuffed grape leaves to cover. Weight down with a heavy plate.

6. Cover the pot and bring to a boil. Reduce the heat to low and simmer over low heat (or place in 350-degree oven and bake) until the leaves are tender, about 1 hour. Drain. Serve warm or at room temperature.

Middle Eastern Phyllo Triangles (Ojaldres)
ABOUT 48 SMALL APPETIZERS

*T*hese phyllo turnovers—also known as *samsada* in Turkey, *briates* in Morocco, *shamiziko* in the Balkans, and *tyropita* in Greece—are found throughout the Middle East and Mediterranean region. Small triangular-shaped phyllo pastries make an attractive appetizer, while large triangles make a tempting main course or side dish. Substitute pumpkin filling (see Sephardic Pumpkin Turnovers, page 257), cheese filling (see Phyllo Cigars, page 306), or Mock Chopped Liver (page 52) for the spinach filling.

SPINACH FILLING
2 pounds fresh spinach, washed but not dried, or 2 (10-ounce) boxes
  frozen chopped spinach, thawed and squeezed dry
3 tablespoons olive or vegetable oil
1 medium onion, chopped (about ½ cup)
1 clove garlic, minced

¼ cup chopped fresh parsley
¼ cup chopped fresh cilantro or dill
½ cup mashed cooked potatoes or finely chopped walnuts
2 large eggs, lightly beaten
About ½ teaspoon salt
About ½ teaspoon ground black pepper
⅛ teaspoon ground cumin or ¼ teaspoon grated nutmeg (optional)

1 pound (about 24 sheets) phyllo dough
About 1 cup (2 sticks) unsalted margarine, melted

1. To make the filling: If using fresh spinach, place with the water clinging to the leaves in a heavy pot over medium heat, cover, and cook until wilted, about 5 minutes. Drain, then chop.
2. Heat the oil in a large skillet over medium heat. Add the onion and garlic and sauté until soft and translucent, 5 to 10 minutes. Add the spinach, parsley, and cilantro and stir until the liquid evaporates. Let cool. Stir in the remaining ingredients for the filling.
3. Preheat the oven to 350 degrees. Lightly brush a large baking sheet with margarine.
4. To assemble: Cut the phyllo sheets lengthwise into 3½-inch-wide strips. (When not in use, cover the strips with a damp towel.) Working with 1 piece at a time, place a phyllo strip on a flat surface, lightly brush with the melted margarine, top with a second strip, and brush with margarine.
5. About 1 inch from a short end, place 1½ teaspoons of the filling in the center of the strip. Fold a corner diagonally over the filling, forming a triangle. Continue folding, maintaining a triangular shape, until the end of the strip. (The triangles can be refrigerated for up to 1 day or frozen for several months. Do not thaw frozen pastries; increase the baking time by about 10 minutes.)
6. Place the triangles on the prepared baking sheets and brush with margarine. Bake until crisp and golden brown, about 25 minutes. Serve warm or at room temperature.

VARIATIONS

Large Phyllo Triangles: Cut the phyllo into 6-inch-wide strips and fill with 2 tablespoons filling.

Mini Phyllo Triangles: Cut the phyllo into 2-inch-wide strips and fill with 1 teaspoon filling.

Middle Eastern Filled Meatballs (Mortadel)
12 LARGE MEATBALLS

4 pounds ground beef or lamb
2 to 4 cloves garlic, minced
2 teaspoons ground cinnamon
About 1½ teaspoons salt
1 teaspoon ground allspice
About ½ teaspoon cayenne pepper
Ground black pepper to taste
12 hard-boiled eggs, peeled
About ¼ cup vegetable oil
1 cup red wine vinegar

1. Combine the meat, garlic, cinnamon, salt, allspice, cayenne, and pepper. Divide the meat mixture into 12 pieces and form each piece into a ball around an egg, enclosing it in the center.
2. Heat the oil in a large saucepan over medium heat. In batches, add the meatballs and brown on all sides, about 15 minutes.
3. Add the vinegar, then return all of the meatballs to the pan. Cover, reduce the heat to low, and simmer until cooked through, about 25 minutes. Let cool, then cut each meatball into slices.

VARIATION
Omit the hard-boiled eggs and mix in ¾ cup coarsely chopped pistachios.

Syrian Meat Torpedoes (Kuasattes)
ABOUT 24 MEATBALLS

The Farsi word *kebab* (ball) and several variations refer throughout the Middle East and Central Asia to various meat patties and free-form sausages. Fried stuffed torpedoes, usually encased in a bulgur shell, are called *kubeh* and *kibbe mi'leeye*. *Kuasatte*s are large *kibbe*.

FILLING

¼ cup vegetable oil
1 medium onion, minced (about ½ cup)
1 pound ground beef or lamb
About ¾ teaspoon salt
½ teaspoon ground allspice
½ teaspoon ground cinnamon or cumin
Ground black pepper to taste
¼ cup pine nuts, chopped pistachios, or chopped walnuts (optional)

SHELLS

2¼ pounds lean ground beef
¾ cup finely ground raw rice or cream of rice
1½ teaspoons salt

¼ cup vegetable oil
6 tablespoons tomato paste
About 4 cups water
Salt to taste

1. To make the filling: Heat the oil in a large skillet over medium heat. Add the onion and sauté until soft and translucent, 5 to 10 minutes. Add the meat and sauté until it loses its pink color, about 5 minutes. Remove from the heat and stir in the salt, allspice, cinnamon, pepper, and if desired, the nuts. Let cool.

2. To make the shells: In a meat grinder or food processor, grind together the beef, rice, and salt until smooth. (Some butchers will do this for you.)

3. To assemble: Moisten your hands with cold water (do this often while shaping the torpedoes) and shape the shell mixture into 2-inch balls. Push a forefinger into the middle of each ball and work with your finger to form a hollow cone shape about 5 inches long. Stuff the cone with filling and close the open end. Pinch the ends of the *kuasatte*s to form tapered points.

4. Heat the oil in a large skillet over medium heat. In batches, fry the *kuasatte*s until golden brown on all sides. Remove from the pan.

5. Stir in tomato paste, 3 cups of the water, and the salt into the skillet. Return the *kuasatte*s, add enough water to cover, bring to a boil, and cook, uncovered, until the liquid is reduced by half. Let cool. Serve whole or sliced with the tomato sauce.

Israeli Marinated Eggplant Fingers (Hatzilim)
IO TO I2 SERVINGS

*N*o *meze* would be complete without eggplant. I discovered this zesty version in Israel.

2 medium (about 1¼ pounds each) eggplants,
*   cut into ½-inch-thick sticks*
About 2 tablespoons kosher salt
About ½ cup olive or vegetable oil for frying

MARINADE
3 tablespoons olive or vegetable oil
2 to 4 serrano, jalapeño, or other fresh green
*   or red chilies, seeded and minced*
2 cloves garlic, minced
¼ cup chopped fresh parsley
2 cups cider vinegar or wine vinegar
½ cup water
1 tablespoon ground cumin
1 tablespoon paprika

1. Place the eggplant in a colander, sprinkle with the salt, and let stand for 1 hour. Rinse the eggplant under cold water, then press between several layers of paper towels. Repeat pressing several times until the eggplant feels firm. (The eggplant can be prepared ahead and stored in the refrigerator for up to 4 hours.)
2. Heat about 3 tablespoons of the oil in a large skillet over medium heat. In several batches (adding more oil between batches), fry the eggplant on both sides until lightly browned and fork-tender, about 3 minutes per side. Drain on paper towels.
3. To make the marinade: Heat the oil in a large skillet over medium heat. Add the chilies and garlic and sauté until soft. Sprinkle the chili mixture and parsley over the eggplant sticks, tossing to coat.
4. Bring the vinegar and water to a boil. Reduce the heat to low and simmer for 5 minutes. Add the cumin and paprika. Drizzle over the eggplant. Refrigerate for at least 1 day.

Vegetable Omelet *(Fritada)*

ABOUT 48 SMALL SERVINGS

This flat, thick baked omelet is similar to the Persian *kuku* and the southern European *frittata*. Many *fritada* recipes call for spinach, but this omelet offers a great way to use up any leftover vegetable, cheese, or meat.

3 tablespoons olive or vegetable oil
8 large eggs, lightly beaten
About 4 cups coarsely chopped cooked artichoke hearts, asparagus,
    cauliflower, or potatoes, or raw bell peppers, spinach,
    zucchini, or any combination
½ cup bread crumbs, matza meal, or mashed potatoes (optional)
2 tablespoons chopped fresh parsley
About 1 teaspoon salt
½ teaspoon ground black pepper

1. Preheat the oven to 375 degrees. Spread the oil in a 13- by 9-inch baking pan and place in the oven to heat.
2. Combine the remaining ingredients.
3. Pour into the prepared pan. Bake until the *fritada* is golden and firm, about 40 minutes. Serve warm or at room temperature. Cut into 1½-inch squares.

Turkish White Bean Salad (Salata di Fijon Blanco)
ABOUT 10 CUPS

*This dish, also called *piyaziko,* is popular in the Balkans as well as Turkey.*

6 cups cooked (1 pound dried) white beans
4 to 6 (1 pound) large plum tomatoes, seeded and chopped
10 brine-cured black olives
1 large red onion or 4 to 5 scallions, chopped
3 to 4 tablespoons chopped fresh parsley, cilantro, dill, or mint
1 bulb fresh fennel, trimmed and sliced (optional)
¼ cup lemon juice or wine vinegar (or 2 tablespoons each)
About 1 teaspoon salt
About ¼ teaspoon ground black pepper
½ cup olive or vegetable oil
3 hard-boiled eggs, cut into wedges

1. Combine the beans, tomatoes, olives, onion, parsley, and if desired, the fennel. Combine the lemon juice, salt, and pepper. Whisk in the oil. Drizzle over the salad. Refrigerate for several hours.
2. Arrange the eggs on top of the salad. Serve at room temperature.

Middle Eastern Artichoke Salad (Salatat Carchof)
ABOUT 8 CUPS

2 (10-ounce) boxes frozen artichoke hearts, cooked and quartered (about 4 cups)
2 cups chopped celery
2 cups (about 12 ounces) chopped tomatoes
1 medium yellow or red onion, chopped (about ½ cup)

DRESSING

¾ cup olive or vegetable oil
½ cup fresh lemon juice or wine vinegar
1 to 2 cloves garlic, minced
2 tablespoons chopped fresh parsley
About 2 teaspoons salt
½ teaspoon ground black pepper
1 tablespoon sugar (optional)

Combine the artichoke hearts, celery, tomatoes, and onion. Combine all the dressing ingredients and pour over the mixture, tossing to coat. Refrigerate for at least 1 hour or up to 2 days.

VARIATION

Artichoke and Mushroom Salad:
Substitute 1 pound sliced mushrooms for the celery and tomatoes.

Northwest African Grilled Vegetable Salad (Salata Mechouiya)

ABOUT 4 CUPS

*T*his salad's name (pronounced mesh-WE-yah) means "roasted" or "grilled" in Arabic. The dish originated in the Maghreb, where it frequently accompanies lunch or dinner throughout the growing season. A combination of bell peppers and chilies creates an interesting contrast of sweet and pungent. Grilling the vegetables adds an intriguing smoky flavor to the salad. The large amount of garlic and addition of cumin mark this as a Jewish version.

6 to 8 fresh Anaheim or poblano chilies
6 plum tomatoes (about 2 pounds total)
2 medium (about 5 ounces each) green bell peppers
2 medium (about 5 ounces each) red bell peppers
6 to 8 cloves garlic, unpeeled

DRESSING
¼ cup olive oil
3 tablespoons fresh lemon juice
About ¾ teaspoon salt
½ teaspoon ground cumin
Pinch of ground coriander
Ground black pepper to taste
Pinch of ground anise (optional)
1 tablespoon tiny capers (optional)

1. Preheat an outdoor grill or the broiler.
2. Place the chilies, tomatoes, bell peppers, and garlic on an oiled rack about 5 inches from the heat and grill or broil, turning, until the skins crack and blacken. Place in a bag or covered bowl and let cool for 10 minutes.
3. Peel, stem, seed, and coarsely chop the chilies, tomatoes, and peppers. Peel and mash the garlic.
4. Combine the vegetables in a nonreactive bowl and let stand at least 1 hour to allow the flavors to meld. (The salad can be stored in the refrigerator for up to 1 day. Let stand at room temperature for at least 30 minutes before serving.)
5. Just before serving, combine the dressing ingredients, pour over the salad, and toss to coat.

Syrian Pareve *Kibbe Naye*

ABOUT 20 SERVINGS

*K*ibbe naye, the national appetizer of Syria and Lebanon, is the Middle Eastern version of steak tartare. This is a vegetarian version.

2 large tomatoes, peeled, seeded, and finely chopped
2 medium onions, minced (about 1 cup)
1 medium green bell pepper, seeded and minced
3 to 4 scallions, minced
3 tablespoons chopped fresh parsley
1 teaspoon ground cumin
Pinch of crushed red pepper flakes
1 cup red lentils
2 cups water
2 cups fine bulgur, unwashed
½ cup vegetable or olive oil
¼ cup tomato paste (optional)

1. Combine the tomatoes, onions, bell pepper, scallions, parsley, cumin, and red pepper flakes and let stand while preparing the lentils.
2. Bring the lentils and water to a boil, reduce the heat to medium-low, and simmer until tender, about 25 minutes. Stir in the tomato mixture.
3. Pour the lentil mixture over the bulgur. Stir in the oil and, if desired, the tomato paste. Cover and let stand for 30 minutes.
4. Shape into patties or torpedoes. Serve with *tahina* (page 250) or relishes.

Red Pepper and Walnut Spread (Mouhamara)
ABOUT 4 CUPS

*T*his unusual combination of ingredients, popular in Turkey and Lebanon, produces an intriguingly pungent and exotic spread.

2½ pounds (about 5 large) red bell peppers
2 cups ground walnuts
½ cup bread crumbs
1 small onion, chopped (about ¼ cup), and/or 2 to 3 cloves garlic, minced
2 tablespoons hamoud er rumman (see Note)
1 tablespoon fresh lemon juice
1 to 3 teaspoons ground cumin
½ teaspoon sugar
About ¾ teaspoon salt
Pinch of cayenne pepper, ½ teaspoon red pepper flakes, or 1 seeded and minced jalapeño
½ cup extra-virgin olive oil
Pine nuts or chopped fresh parsley (optional)

1. Place the peppers under a broiler 2 inches from the heat, turning about every 5 minutes, until charred, 15 to 25 minutes. Or hold the peppers over a gas burner using tongs or a long-handled barbecue fork, turning occasionally, until the skin blackens, about 3 minutes. Place in a paper bag or a covered bowl and let sit until the skin peels off easily, about 15 minutes. Peel but do not rinse. Remove and discard the caps and seeds. Mash the warm peppers.
2. In a food processor, puree the walnuts, bread crumbs, onion, *hamoud er rumman*, lemon juice, cumin, sugar, salt, and cayenne.
3. Add the peppers and puree. With the machine on, add the olive oil in a slow stream. Cover and refrigerate overnight or up to 5 days. Bring to room temperature before serving.
4. To serve, spread the *mouhamara* on a platter and, if desired, garnish with the pine nuts or parsley. Serve with crackers, pita bread, or crudités.

VARIATION

Reduce the walnuts to 1 cup and increase the bread crumbs to 1 cup.

NOTE: *Hamoud er rumman,* also called *dibs rumman* and pomegranate molasses, is a Middle Eastern pomegranate concentrate used to add a tart flavor to stews and savory fillings. It is not the same as *narshrab* (pomegranate syrup), which contains sugar and is not concentrated. It is available at Middle Eastern markets. To make your own, boil pomegranate juice until reduced by three-fourths (e.g., 2 cups reduced to ½ cup).

Middle Eastern Chili Olives *(Zeitoon)*
ABOUT 6 CUPS

These spicy olives are a popular part of many Middle Eastern meals.

2 pounds pitted green olives
⅔ cup vegetable oil
4 large tomatoes, peeled, seeded, and minced
8 to 10 cloves garlic, crushed
2 tablespoons tomato paste
6 slices lemon
2 teaspoons cayenne pepper
1 teaspoon ground cumin
Salt to taste
Ground black pepper to taste
About 6 tablespoons water

1. Place the olives in a large saucepan and add water to cover. Bring to a boil, then drain. Repeat boiling and draining one more time.
2. Heat the oil in a large skillet or saucepan over medium heat. Stir in the tomatoes and garlic, then the tomato paste, and sauté until the paste begins to darken, 2 to 3 minutes.
3. Add the olives, lemon slices, cayenne, cumin, salt, pepper, and water and simmer over low heat until the liquid evaporates. Discard the lemon slices and let cool.

An Unorthodox Sabbath or Holiday *Kiddush*

SERVES 10 OR 60

*F*ollowing Sabbath and festival morning synagogue services, Ashkenazim traditionally enjoy a buffet in the synagogue called a *kiddush,* named after the Hebrew word for the blessing over wine. A *kiddush* may be a simple affair consisting solely of wine or schnapps, a plate of pickled herring, and some *kichel* (egg cookies) or crackers, or it may be an elaborate sit-down spread. Occasionally bread rolls accompany the *kiddush* and it serves as the Sabbath morning *seudah* (meal).

ROLLS

CRUDITÉS WITH CURRY DIP AND AVOCADO MOUSSE

POACHED CHICKEN CUTLETS WITH TARRAGON MAYONNAISE

BROCCOLI TERRINE

COLD SESAME NOODLES

COUSCOUS SALAD

BLACK BEAN SALAD

HEALTH SALAD

FRESH FRUIT PLATTER

QUICK BREADS ASSORTMENT (PAGES 373–382)

COOKIE ASSORTMENT (PAGES 346–362)

TEA AND COFFEE

 Wine Suggestions: Chardonnay, Sauvignon Blanc, or Chenin Blanc

Crudités with Curry Dip and Avocado Mousse

*T*he following vegetables are basic, but you can use any of your favorites including green beans, cucumbers, zucchini, cooked asparagus, blanched snow peas, radishes, and cherry tomatoes. If you choose to use only one of the dips, double that amount.

8 servings	60 servings	
2 medium	2 pounds	carrots, cut into sticks
2 stalks	2 bunches	celery, cut into sticks
1 small	3 medium	green bell peppers, seeded and sliced
1 small	3 medium	red bell peppers, seeded and sliced
1 small	3 medium	yellow bell peppers, seeded and sliced
1 cup	2 heads	broccoli, cut into florets
1 cup	2 heads	cauliflower, cut into florets

Spoon the dips into separate serving cups and place in the center of a basket or platter. For an attractive presentation, serve the dips in a hollowed-out cabbage or bell pepper. (Afterwards, cut up the cabbage/peppers for coleslaw.) Arrange the vegetables in colorful groups around the cups.

CURRY DIP:

(About 1¼ cups)	(About 8 cups)	
1 cup	6 cups	mayonnaise
2 to 3 tablespoons	¾ to 1 cup	honey
2 teaspoons	3 tablespoons	curry powder
2 teaspoons	3 tablespoons	lemon juice
1 teaspoon	2 tablespoons	Worcestershire sauce
¼ teaspoon	1 teaspoon	salt
Dash	½ teaspoon	ground black pepper

Combine all of the ingredients. Store in the refrigerator.

AVOCADO MOUSSE:

(About 1½ cups)	(About 9 cups)	
1 small (12 ounces)	3 large (1 pound each)	ripe avocados, peeled and seeded
1 tablespoon	⅓ cup	lemon or lime juice

½ cup	3 cups	mayonnaise
¼ teaspoon	1 teaspoon	salt
Dash	½ teaspoon	ground white pepper

In a food processor or blender, process all of the ingredients until smooth. Store in the refrigerator.

Poached Chicken Cutlets with Tarragon Mayonnaise

10 servings	60 servings	
10	60	chicken cutlets
1 small	4 medium	onions, chopped
1½ cups	8 cups	dry white wine
1½ cups	8 cups	water
1 tablespoon	½ cup	fresh lemon juice
½ teaspoon	2 teaspoons	salt
Pinch	1 teaspoon	ground white pepper
1½ cups	8 cups	chopped liver or Mock Chopped Liver (page 52) (optional)

TOPPING

| 3 cups | 4 quarts | mayonnaise |
| 5 teaspoons | ½ cup | tarragon vinegar |

1. Arrange the cutlets in a single layer in a baking dish or large skillet, leaving a little room between each piece. Sprinkle with the onion. Mix together the wine, water, lemon juice, salt, and pepper and pour over the cutlets.
2. Cover with aluminum foil and bake in a 350-degree oven until tender, about 20 minutes. Or bring to a boil, reduce the heat to low, cover, and simmer until tender, about 7 minutes. Remove from the liquid and let cool. If desired, cut each cutlet in half horizontally, spread the bottom half with 2 to 3 tablespoons chopped liver, and replace the top half.
3. To make the topping: Combine the mayonnaise and vinegar. Spread over the cutlets. If desired, decorate with vegetable pieces such as carrot slices and scallion strips arranged as flowers. Chill.

Broccoli Terrine

10 servings	60 servings	
¼ cup	*1 cup*	*unsalted margarine*
1 cup	*6 cups*	*thinly sliced scallions (about 1 or 6 bunches)*
2 large	*12 large*	*carrots, coarsely shredded (optional)*
2 (10-ounce) boxes	*7½ pounds*	*frozen broccoli, thawed and pureed (about 3 or 18 cups)*
1 cup	*6 cups*	*chicken broth*
About 1¾ teaspoons	*3 tablespoons*	*salt*
1 teaspoon	*2 tablespoons*	*dried basil OR*
⅛ teaspoon	*2 teaspoons*	*grated nutmeg*
4 large	*24 large*	*eggs, lightly beaten*

1. Preheat the oven to 350 degrees. Grease an 8- by 4-inch loaf pan (or 6 loaf pans), line with wax paper, and grease the wax paper.
2. Melt the margarine in a saucepan over medium heat. Add the scallions and, if desired, the carrots and sauté until softened, about 10 minutes.
3. Stir in the broccoli, broth, salt, and basil or nutmeg and bring to a boil. Remove from the heat and stir in the eggs.
4. Pour into the prepared pan (or pans) and cover with a piece of greased wax paper. Place in a larger pan and add hot water to reach halfway up the sides of the loaf pan. Bake until the terrine is set and a knife inserted in the center comes out clean, about 1¼ hours.
5. Remove from the water and let cool on a rack. Refrigerate overnight. Invert the terrine onto a flat surface, remove the wax paper, and cut into slices.

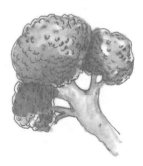

Cold Sesame Noodles

10 servings	60 servings	
DRESSING		
½ cup	3 cups	tahini (sesame paste) or creamy peanut butter
¼ cup	1½ cups	soy sauce
3 tablespoons	1 cup	toasted sesame oil
3 tablespoons	1 cup	rice vinegar or red wine vinegar
2 tablespoons	¾ cup	vegetable oil
¼ teaspoon	1½ teaspoons	crushed red pepper flakes or Asian chili paste
1 teaspoon	2 tablespoons	sugar
2 teaspoons	4 tablespoons	minced fresh ginger (optional)
2 teaspoons	4 tablespoons	minced garlic (optional)
SALAD		
1 pound	6 pounds	vermicelli, spaghetti, or linguine
3 to 4	20 to 24	scallions, chopped
3 tablespoons	1 cup	sesame seeds (optional)

1. To make the dressing: In a food processor or blender, combine all the dressing ingredients. If the mixture is too thick, add a little water.
2. In a large pot (or pots) of lightly salted boiling water, cook the pasta until *al dente* (tender yet firm to the bite), about 12 minutes. Rinse under cold water and drain.
3. Drizzle the dressing over the noodles, tossing to coat. Stir in the scallions. Chill. If desired, sprinkle with the sesame seeds.

Couscous Salad

10 servings	60 servings	
2¼ cups	*13½ cups*	*water*
½ teaspoon	*2 teaspoons*	*salt*
1½ cups	*9 cups*	*couscous (10 ounces or 3¾ pounds)*
5 tablespoons	*½ cup*	*fresh lemon juice, fresh lime juice, or wine vinegar*
¼ teaspoon	*1½ teaspoons*	*ground black pepper*
6 tablespoons	*⅔ cup*	*extra-virgin olive oil*
½ cup	*3 cups*	*chopped fresh parsley*
4 to 6	*32 to 36*	*scallions, thinly sliced*
¾ cup	*4 cups*	*chopped green bell peppers*
¾ cup	*4 cups*	*cooked chickpeas*
¾ cup	*4 cups*	*chopped tomatoes*

1. In a medium saucepan (or large stockpot), bring the water and salt to a boil. Stir in the couscous, cover, remove the pan from the heat, and let stand for 5 minutes. Fluff with a fork.
2. Combine the lemon juice and pepper. In a slow, steady stream, whisk in the oil. Pour over the couscous, tossing to coat. Stir in the remaining ingredients. (The salad can be stored in the refrigerator for up to 2 days.)

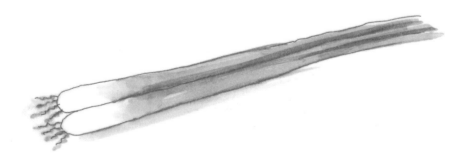

Black Bean Salad

10 servings	60 servings	
4 cups	20 cups	cooked black beans
4 to 5	24 to 30	scallions, chopped
¼ cup	1¼ cups	chopped fresh parsley or cilantro
⅔ cup	3½ cups	corn kernels
⅔ cup	3½ cups	chopped green bell peppers
⅔ cup	3½ cups	chopped red bell peppers
⅔ cup	3 cups	sliced papaya or fresh fennel (optional)

DRESSING

¼ cup	1¼ cups	wine vinegar or lemon juice
To taste		Salt and ground black pepper
½ cup	2½ cups	olive or vegetable oil

Combine the beans, scallions, parsley, corn, peppers, and papaya. Combine the vinegar, salt, and pepper. Whisk in the oil. Drizzle over the bean salad, tossing to coat. Refrigerate for at least 2 hours or up to 3 days. Serve at room temperature.

VARIATION

Mixed Bean Salad: Use any combination of cooked black beans, white beans, red kidney beans, chickpeas, and green beans.

Health Salad

A variation on coleslaw, health salad is marinated in vinegar instead of mayonnaise.

10 servings	60 servings	
1 small	4 medium	heads green cabbage, cored and shredded
1 tablespoon	¼ cup	kosher salt

1 medium	6 medium	green bell peppers, seeded and chopped
1 medium	6 medium	red bell peppers, seeded and chopped
1 medium	6 medium	yellow bell peppers, seeded and chopped
2 medium	12 medium	carrots, shredded
6 to 8	40 to 48	scallions, chopped
1 cup	6 cups	cider vinegar or white vinegar
2 tablespoons	¾ cup	sugar

1. Place the cabbage in a colander, sprinkle with the salt, and let stand for 30 minutes.
2. Combine the cabbage with the remaining ingredients and place in the refrigerator for at least 2 hours.

Fresh Fruit Platter

*U*se whatever fruit is ripe and plentiful.

10 servings	60 servings	
3	12	navel oranges, peeled and sliced
1	4	yellow grapefruit, peeled and sliced
1	4	pink grapefruit, peeled and sliced
1 pound	4 pounds	seedless grapes
2 cups	8 cups	Bing cherries
1 pint	5 pints	strawberries
1 cup	5 cups	blueberries
1 cup	5 cups	raspberries or blackberries
1	5	mangoes, peeled and sliced
3	10	kiwis, peeled and sliced

Arrange the fruit in attractive patterns to contrast colors and shapes. Chill until ready to serve.

Beyond *Cholent:* Something Different for Sabbath Lunch

SERVES 6 TO 8

*T*he Midrash relates the story of a Roman general by the name of Antoninus who frequently called upon the leader of the Jewish people, Rabbi Yehuda Hanasi. One of these visits fell on the Sabbath, and the rabbi invited his guest to join him for lunch. The general enjoyed a dish, probably an early form of *hamin/cholent,* so much that he asked for the recipe. Later Antoninus returned to complain that the dish was not the same, that some spice must be missing. "The name of the missing spice," Rabbi Yehuda answered, "is Shabbat."

During the course of history, there have been many of these Sabbath dishes. Some are long forgotten; others are still served on Jewish tables weekly. There are certain unadventurous sorts who insist on eating the same thing every week and will not tolerate any deviation from the standard *cholent.* But for those who appreciate the opportunity to sample something different, the following recipes are just the ticket.

PERSIAN SABBATH CHICKEN
CROCKERY CHICKEN COUSCOUS
CHICKEN WITH CHILI SAUCE
CROCKERY PAELLA
CROCKERY BEEF BOURGUIGNON
GEORGIAN POACHED POULTRY IN WALNUT SAUCE
BEEF, APPLE, AND JICAMA SALAD

Persian Sabbath Chicken *(Morg Tupor)*
6 TO 8 SERVINGS

*I*raqis and Syrians prepare a similar dish called both *tabyeet* (shelter) and *hamin* (hot), flavoring it with favorite spices.

8 ounces (1 cup) dried chickpeas or fava beans
3 tablespoons vegetable oil
1 (3- to 4-pound) whole chicken
2 medium onions, chopped (about 1 cup)
½ teaspoon turmeric
2 cups long-grain white rice
½ cup yellow split peas
1 teaspoon ground cumin
4 cups peeled, seeded, and chopped tomatoes
½ cup chopped fresh dill
About 1½ teaspoons salt
About ¼ teaspoon ground black pepper
8 cups water

1. Cover the chickpeas or fava beans with water and let soak overnight. Drain.
2. Heat the oil in an 8-quart pot over medium-high heat. Add the chicken and brown on all sides. Remove the chicken.
3. Reduce the heat to medium, add the onions to the pot, and sauté until soft and translucent, 5 to 10 minutes. Stir in the turmeric, then the rice and split peas, and sauté until the rice is opaque, about 3 minutes.
4. Stir in the cumin. Add the tomatoes, dill, salt, pepper, and 6 cups of the water. Cover, bring to a boil, reduce the heat to low, and simmer for 15 minutes.
5. Spoon 1 cup of the rice mixture into the chicken's cavity. Place the chicken, breast side up, in the pot on top of the remaining rice. Add the chickpeas or fava beans and remaining 2 cups water.
6. Tightly cover and simmer over very low heat or in a 225-degree oven overnight. Remove and debone the chicken. Scrape the crispy rice from the bottom of the pot and serve with the chicken.

VARIATIONS

Indian Sabbath Chicken (**Hameen**): With the turmeric, add 1 to 2 teaspoons curry powder and 1 teaspoon grated fresh ginger.

Iraqi Sabbath Chicken (**Tabyeet**): Omit the split peas, dill, and cumin. Increase the rice to 2½ cups. Add ¾ to 1 teaspoon ground allspice or cardamom and ¼ teaspoon ground cinnamon.

Crockery Chicken Couscous
6 TO 8 SERVINGS

*T*he following version of the classic northwest African dish is prepared in a crockery slow cooker to be served warm for Sabbath lunch. Other old favorites—stuffed cabbage, stuffed peppers, beef goulash, brisket, and of course, *cholent*—can also be simmered overnight in a slow cooker.

3 pounds chicken thighs or legs, skinned
1¾ cups chicken broth
1 pound acorn or butternut squash, peeled and seeded
3 medium boiling potatoes, peeled and quartered
3 medium carrots, cut into ½-inch pieces
2 stalks celery, cut into ½-inch pieces
1 medium onion, sliced
3 medium turnips, cut into ½-inch pieces (optional)
2 cups cooked chickpeas
2 to 4 cloves garlic, minced
1 tablespoon chopped fresh parsley
1 (3-inch) stick cinnamon or 1 teaspoon ground cinnamon
½ teaspoon turmeric
About 1 teaspoon salt
About ¼ teaspoon ground black pepper
3 cups water
3 tablespoons unsalted margarine
2 cups (about 12 ounces) instant couscous

1. Combine the chicken, broth, squash, potatoes, carrots, celery, onion, turnips if desired, chickpeas, garlic, parsley, cinnamon, turmeric, ½ teaspoon of the salt, and the pepper in a 5-quart slow cooker. Cover and cook on a high setting for 30 minutes.
2. Reduce the setting to low and cook for 9 to 10 hours or on high for 2 to 3 hours.
3. To make the couscous: Bring the water, remaining salt, and margarine to a boil. Remove from the heat, stir in the couscous, cover, and let stand for 5 minutes. Fluff with a fork. Store the couscous in the refrigerator and return to room temperature about 1 hour before serving.
4. To serve: Pile some of the couscous onto each plate and spoon some of the stew and cooking liquid on top.

Chicken with Chili Sauce *(Mole Poblano)*
6 TO 8 SERVINGS

*A*lthough the combination of chilies and chocolate might seem strange to the northern palate, Mexicans have been enjoying it for centuries.

SAUCE
1 pound tomatoes, peeled, seeded, and chopped (about 2½ cups)
¾ cup chicken broth or water
1 medium onion, chopped (about ½ cup)
½ cup blanched almonds
¼ cup pumpkin seeds or sesame seeds
¼ cup raisins
1 to 2 fresh red chilies or jalapeños and/or 1 to 3 tablespoons chili powder
1 to 2 cloves garlic, minced
1 ounce grated unsweetened chocolate or ¼ cup unsweetened cocoa powder
1 teaspoon sugar
About 1 teaspoon salt
½ teaspoon ground cinnamon
½ teaspoon ground coriander
⅛ teaspoon ground cloves or nutmeg

2 (3-pound) chickens or 1 (6-pound) turkey, cut up

1. In a food processor or blender, puree all the sauce ingredients.
2. Place in a 5- to 6-quart slow cooker. Add the chicken or turkey, cover, and cook on a high setting for 30 minutes.
3. Reduce the setting to low and cook for 10 to 11 hours or on high for about 5 hours. Serve with rice or noodles.

Crockery Paella (Spanish Rice Pilaf)

6 TO 8 SERVINGS

*P*aella, a form of pilaf and one of Spain's foremost culinary contributions, is a meal in one dish. Its ingredients vary from region to region—seafood in coastal areas and meat and game inland. Spaniards prefer a special variety of medium-grain rice from Valencia called *arroz bomba* or *calasparra*. Paella is traditionally made in a special shallow pan of the same name, but a crockery slow cooker makes a handy substitute.

8 chicken thighs or drumsticks or a combination
2 teaspoons dried oregano or mild chili powder
½ teaspoon ground black pepper
¼ cup olive or vegetable oil
½ to 1 pound chorizo or other spicy sausage (optional)
2 medium onions, chopped (about 1 cup)
2 green bell peppers, cut into strips
2 red bell peppers, cut into strips
2 to 3 cloves garlic, minced
1 tablespoon paprika or 1 teaspoon cayenne pepper
1 bay leaf
1½ cups arborio or long-grain rice
½ teaspoon saffron threads or 1 teaspoon turmeric
3 cups chicken broth or water
1 pound tomatoes, peeled, seeded, and chopped (about 2½ cups)
½ cup dry white wine
¼ cup chopped fresh cilantro or parsley
About 1½ teaspoons salt

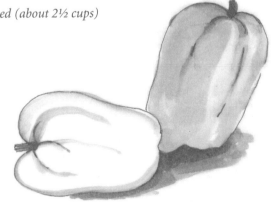

1. Pat the chicken pieces dry. Rub with the oregano and pepper. Let stand for 15 minutes.
2. Heat the oil in a large skillet over medium-high heat. In batches, add the chicken and brown on all sides, about 10 minutes per batch. Remove the chicken. If desired, add the chorizo and sauté until browned and cooked through, about 5 minutes. Remove the chorizo and cut into thin slices or chunks.
3. Reduce the heat to medium, add the onions, bell peppers, and garlic, and sauté until softened, about 10 minutes. Stir in the paprika and bay leaf. Add the rice and stir until lightly browned, about 10 minutes. If using saffron, dissolve it in the broth; if using turmeric, stir it into the rice.
4. Transfer the rice mixture, chicken, and chorizo to a 5-quart slow cooker. Add the broth, tomatoes, wine, cilantro, and salt. Cover and cook on a low setting for 8 to 10 hours or on high for about 2½ hours

Crockery Beef Bourguignon
6 TO 8 SERVINGS

*T*his famous French dish is actually beef stewed in red wine. When done properly, it is simply delicious. For the harried cook, beef bourguignon offers a special advantage: it is every bit as good reheated.

3 pounds boneless beef chuck, cut into 1-inch pieces
3 tablespoons vegetable oil
¾ cup dry red wine
¾ cup chicken or beef broth
¼ cup quick-cooking tapioca
1 pound mushrooms
1 medium onion, chopped (about ½ cup)
2 cloves garlic, minced
1 medium carrot, chopped
1 tablespoon tomato paste

1 sprig fresh or ½ teaspoon dried thyme
1 bay leaf
About 1 teaspoon salt
About ½ teaspoon ground black pepper

1. Pat the beef dry with paper towels and toss with 1 tablespoon of the oil. Heat the remaining 2 tablespoons oil in a large pot over medium-high heat. In several batches, add the beef and brown on all sides. Drain off the fat.
2. Transfer the beef to a 5-quart crockery slow cooker and add the remaining ingredients. Cover and cook on a low setting for 10 to 12 hours or on high for 5 to 6 hours. Serve with noodles or rice.

Georgian Poached Poultry in Walnut Sauce (Satsivi)

8 TO 10 SERVINGS

*S*atsivi means "eaten cold," an appropriate name for this dish, which requires lengthy chilling to allow the multifarious flavors to meld. One of the most popular party dishes throughout the former Soviet Union, *satsivi* typifies Georgian cooking. The pungent sauce is made with walnuts, fresh herbs, garlic, and a subtle blend of spices and, being rich, is served primarily on special occasions. Although poached poultry is the most common base, the sauce can also be served on poached fish. *Satsivi* is perfect for entertaining because it not only is delicious but is prepared the day before. Leftover sauce can be used as a dip for flat bread (*lavash* or *puri*) or corn bread (*mchadi*).

4 pounds chicken or turkey breasts and thighs
2 medium onions, quartered
2 medium carrots, cut into chunks
About 7 cups water

WALNUT SAUCE

1 pound walnuts (about 3¾ cups)
8 to 10 large cloves garlic, chopped
½ cup chopped fresh cilantro
1 small fresh hot red chili, seeded and chopped (optional)
3 tablespoons sunflower or vegetable oil
5 medium onions, chopped (about 2½ cups)
5 large egg yolks, lightly beaten
1 to 2 teaspoons ground coriander
¾ teaspoon sweet paprika
¾ teaspoon turmeric or 2 teaspoons ground marigold petals
½ teaspoon ground fenugreek
¼ to ½ teaspoon cayenne
⅛ teaspoon ground cinnamon
Salt to taste
¼ cup wine vinegar (or 2 tablespoons vinegar and 2 tablespoons
*   pomegranate concentrate or juice)*

1. Put the chicken, onions, and carrots in a large pot and add enough water to cover. Bring to a boil, reduce the heat to low, cover, and simmer until the chicken is tender, about 50 minutes. Remove the chicken, reserving the broth. When the chicken is cool enough to handle, remove and discard the skin and bones. Shred the chicken into finger-size pieces.

2. To make the sauce: Using a mortar and pestle or a food processor, finely grind the walnuts, garlic, cilantro, and if desired, the chili. Let stand at room temperature for at least 30 minutes.

3. Heat the oil in a large saucepan over medium heat. Add the onions and sauté until soft and translucent, about 10 minutes. Gradually stir in 6 cups of the reserved broth and bring to a simmer. Add the walnut mixture and return to a simmer.

4. Gradually stir about 1 cup of the walnut sauce into the beaten egg yolks, then stir the yolk mixture back into the saucepan. Simmer over low heat—do not boil or the yolks will curdle—stirring constantly, until the sauce begins to thicken.

5. Add the spices and salt and simmer, stirring frequently, for about 10 minutes. Remove from the heat and stir in the vinegar.

6. Arrange the poultry pieces in a deep serving platter, pour the sauce on top, and refrigerate overnight. Serve cold or at room temperature. If desired, garnish with additional cilantro, walnut pieces, and/or pomegranate seeds.

Beef, Apple, and Jicama Salad
6 TO 8 SERVINGS

*B*eef salad is a tasty way to use up a leftover roast, but it is also good enough to merit preparing a roast for the salad alone.

4 to 5 cups (about 2 pounds) cubed or thinly sliced rare
    cooked beef rib-eye or shoulder chuck
2 medium apples, cored and thinly sliced
1 pound jicama, peeled and julienned
2 scallions or 1 small red onion, chopped (about ¼ cup)

DRESSING
⅓ cup red wine vinegar
2 to 3 teaspoons prepared mustard
2 cloves garlic, mashed
About 1 teaspoon salt
About ⅛ teaspoon ground black pepper
1 to 3 teaspoons sugar (optional)
1 cup vegetable oil

In a large bowl, combine the beef, apples, jicama, and scallions. Combine the vinegar, mustard, garlic, salt, pepper, and if desired, the sugar. In a slow steady stream, whisk in the oil. Drizzle the dressing over the salad, tossing to coat. Store in the refrigerator.

SEUDAT SHLISHIT

The atmosphere at Seudat Shlishit (the third Sabbath meal), the participants saddened by the imminent departure of the day, contrasts with that of the others. The songs are slow and almost mournful. The fare is simpler than that served at the other Sabbath meals, consisting primarily of challah, cold fish, and perhaps a few salads and some dessert. This meal is frequently held in the synagogue between the afternoon and evening services.

MELAVEH MALKEH

According to legend, King David asked God when he would die and was informed that his demise would occur on the Sabbath. From then on, when the Sabbath was over, David and his subjects celebrated his surviving another week. The Sabbath is also viewed metaphorically as a queen. A party, therefore, is a symbolic way to escort the queen and in the process prolong the special feelings of the Sabbath. Whatever its source, following the Havdalah ceremony on Saturday night, there is a custom of holding a party called a Melaveh Malkeh (literally, Escorting the Queen) by Ashkenazim, Noche de Alhad by Sephardim, and Seudat David Hamelek (Feast of King David) by Moroccans. Cold dishes prepared before the Sabbath, often dairy, are integral parts of the event.

Family Celebrations

I have, at the time of this book's completion, twenty-four nephews and nieces as well as a great-nephew and either another great-nephew or a great-niece on the way. I long ago gave up trying to count the growing number of cousins. Among the benefits of being part of such a prolific clan are the numerous opportunities to mark personal transitions. In this year alone, my immediate family witnessed a baby naming, a brit, a bar mitzvah, a bat mitzvah, several weddings, and my parents' fiftieth wedding anniversary. Accompanying each of these milestones were a ceremony and a celebration consisting of a host of customs and foods. Some of the fare served at these gatherings consisted of contemporary trends or personal favorites. On the other hand, many of the associated rituals and foods date to the beginnings of the Jewish people or to various locales in Europe, and their enduring practice links generations together in an unbroken chain. Thus participation in these gatherings not only bonds and strengthens the family but enhances the prospects of the transmission of our heritage to future generations.

Life-cycle events are communal functions and therefore tend to be rather large. Participation in the accompanying *seudah* (celebratory meal) is considered not merely a matter of enjoyment but also a *mitzvah* (religious obligation). Wine, a symbol of joy and plenty, and bread initiate most of the meals. A *seudat mitzvah* can be held anytime during the day; those held earlier tend to be dairy, while later meals are frequently meat.

BABY NAMING

A name, in Jewish lore, is not simply an appellation, but also reflects a person's inner being. In biblical times a baby might have been named for a concept, an event, an animal, or even an inanimate object, each one indicative of the child's perceived characteristics, destiny, or strength. (In my case, "celebration" is literally my middle name, Simcha.) Thus the seemingly incessant listing of names in Genesis is not merely an exercise in genealogy but a commentary on the personality of the individuals and the nations they founded. Eventually the custom arose of naming children after a relative or famous person in the hopes that the child would follow in the namesake's footsteps.

Girls are named at a ceremony called *zebed habat* or *las fadas* (destiny) by Sephardim and *me shebarach* (who blesses) by Ashkenazim. It is generally performed in the synagogue at the Torah reading on the Sabbath, Monday, Thursday, or Rosh Chodesh (new moon) nearest to her birth. Sometimes the naming is postponed until the mother is able to attend and recite *birkat hagomel* (prayer for rescue from a life-threatening situation). After the father is called to the Torah reading, the rabbi recites *me shebarach*, a prayer for

the baby's health in which the girl's name is given. Following services, families generally sponsor a *kiddush/sabt* in honor of the occasion. Among Sephardim, stuffed vegetables, symbolizing a full life, and sweets are traditional fare.

Some communities, especially in Morocco and the Balkans, hold the baby naming at home within forty days following the birth. Relatives and friends gather at the parents' residence to recite prayers and enjoy some favorite treats. This setting turns the ceremony into more of a family affair, as the mother and other close relatives are present. In recent years home ceremonies have gained in popularity among Ashkenazim as well.

SHALOM ZAKHAR/BEN ZAKHAR

On the first Friday night following the birth of a son, relatives and friends gather in the house of the new parents for a party variously called Ben Zakhar (male son) by some Sephardim, Shasha by Yemenites, and most commonly Shalom Zakhar (welcome [or peace] to the male child). The Shalom Zakhar provides an opportunity to offer congratulations on the birth and also fulfill the commandment of *bikour cholim* (visiting the sick) to the baby in regard to his upcoming brit, similar to the Lord and three angels visiting Abraham following his circumcision (Genesis 18:1). Another possible source derives from the Talmud (Nidah 30:B): "While in the womb, an angel comes and teaches a child the entire Torah . . . and just before birth, the angel hits him on the mouth [thus, the source of the indentation on the top lip] and he forgets all the Torah"; the Shalom Zakhar is held in consolation for this lost knowledge. There are no set rituals for this occasion, although it is common to recite Jacob's blessing to Ephraim and Manasseh (Genesis 48:16), as well as assorted psalms. Light food is served, including pastries, fruit, drinks, and chickpeas. The reason for the latter is that chickpeas are a symbol of mourning, in this case a lament for the baby's lost knowledge of the Torah.

SIMCHAT HA'BAT

In an attempt to match the attention displayed to newborn boys, some families hold a ceremony to honor a female baby. This affair, which has of yet not developed any definitive customs, is variously called *simchat ha'bat* (joy in the daughter), *shalom bat* (welcome to the daughter), *shalom nekeva* (welcome to the female), and *brit bat* (covenant of the daughter). It is typically held on a Friday night after the baby has passed her first month, the age at which Jewish law considers a person to be viable.

VAKHNACHT/YESHUA HABEN

Many communities hold a gathering called *vakhnacht* (watch night) by Ashkenazim, *veula* in Salonika, or *yeshua haben* (protect the boy) by other Sephardim on the night preceding the brit. Some believe that this custom developed from a practice of the *mohel,* accompanied by anxious family and friends, of examining the baby before his brit. Eventually it became customary to surround the baby's crib to recite various psalms and study the Torah. Folklore later ascribed this vigil as a way to protect the uncircumcised baby from Lilith, the legendary first wife of Adam, or other demons. Ashkenazim light candles, ask schoolchildren to visit the baby to recite the Shema, and serve honey cakes, poppy seed cakes, and sometimes a meal featuring bean dishes, a symbol of fertility.

Syrians hold a gathering called a Shadd-il-Asse (Arabic for "pulling of the branches") in accordance with the Zohar, using myrtle branches and a *limud* (learning session) to protect the baby. Following the *limud,* the assembly chants *pizmonim* (liturgical poems) and partakes of special foods.

Moroccans hold a Tachdid ceremony each night until the brit to protect the baby. Amulets—including Psalms 121 and 126, the names of three angels, and the phrase *Adam, Chava, chutz Lilit* (Adam and Eve, get out Lilith)—are dispersed throughout the baby's room, and *piyutim* (liturgical poems) are sung. On the evening prior to the brit, female relatives and friends spend the night, offering the wisdom of their experience and protecting the mother and child from harm.

BRIT MILAH

The Hebrew word *brit* means "covenant," referring originally to God's pledge to Abraham that his descendants would inherit the Land of Canaan (Genesis 17:2), which was sealed by the act of *milah* (circumcision). Thus, *brit milah* endures as one of the integral symbols of Judaism. Historically, prohibitions against it by Antiochus Epiphanes and later the Roman emperor Hadrian helped lead, respectively, to the Maccabean and Bar Kochba rebellions.

The brit is held on the baby's eighth day and is of such importance that it takes place even if the day falls on the Sabbath or Yom Kippur. Indeed, tradition recounts that Abraham's brit occurred on Yom Kippur. If the baby suffers from any ill health, however, it is postponed until there is no longer any threat of danger to the child. That day is considered his new birthday and the brit is performed seven days later, but in this instance, not on the Sabbath or Yom Kippur.

It is the father's obligation to circumcise his son, a duty usually fulfilled through a specially trained agent known as a *mohel*. In the tenth century the custom arose of honoring a relative or friend with the role of *sandek* (from the Greek *synteknos,* meaning "with the child" but assuming the sense of "godfather"). The *sandek* is seated in a special chair and holds the child on his lap during the ceremony. In addition, Ashkenazim created the roles of *kvater* (from the German for "godfather," *gottvater*) and *kvaterin* (godmother), usually a wife-and-husband team who relay the child from the mother to the *sandek* and back. Among Sephardim the *madrino* (godmother) and *padrino* (godfather) fulfill this role. It is customary to place another chair next to that of the *sandek,* which is called the Chair of Elijah in honor of the prophet considered to be the protector of children, "the angel of the covenant" (Malachi 3:1), and "the herald of the covenant" (I Kings 19:14).

There is a long-standing custom not to directly invite people to a brit, since refusing such an honor would be improper. Therefore desired attendees are simply informed of the time and place of the ceremony.

In the Middle Ages the custom arose among Ashkenazim and some Sephardim of performing the circumcision in the synagogue. Today many have reverted to the earlier practice of holding the ceremony at home. Following the actual circumcision, the *mohel* recites a blessing over a glass of wine, then a prayer praising God for establishing his covenant. The *mohel* then names the baby and proceeds to give him a few drops of wine to drink.

A Baby-Naming or Brit Breakfast

SERVES 10 OR 80

*T*he brit or baby naming is usually performed in the morning, emulating Abraham, who arose early in his eagerness to perform the divine command. The accompanying *seudat mitzvah,* usually a sit-down brunch, tends to be dairy and relatively simple. Sephardim typically serve filled foods, including *borekas* (small turnovers), *bulemas* (pastry coils), and stuffed vegetables, symbolizing a rich and full life. Traditional Ashkenazic fare includes herring, honey cake, and *branfen* (whiskey or brandy).

TEDDY BEAR BREAD SCULPTURES

ROLLS OR BAGELS

CREAM CHEESE AND BUTTER

LOX PINWHEELS

STUFFED EGGS WITH CAVIAR

APPLE SOUFFLÉ PANCAKE

GEORGIAN BAKED VEGETABLE OMELET

WHITEFISH SALAD

CHICKPEA SALAD

GREEK SALAD

BABY BOOTIE CUPCAKES

MUFFIN ASSORTMENT (PAGES 383–393)

FRESH FRUIT PLATTER (PAGE 217) OR FRUIT SALAD

TEA, COFFEE, ORANGE JUICE, AND MILK

Teddy Bear Bread Sculptures

*Y*ou can use this dough to create bread sculptures that are symbolic of a particular occasion or to make fanciful figures to delight young and old alike; you are limited only by your imagination. Edible decorations make the holiday table festive: a shofar for Rosh Hashanah; an etrog and a lulav or sheaf of grain for Sukkot; a menorah or dreidel for Hanukkah; a megillah (scroll) for Purim; and a Torah scroll, tablets, ladders, or sheaf of grain for Shavuot. A friend once asked me to make one of these bread sculptures in the shape of an open Torah scroll for her brother's bar mitzvah, and she shlepped it, surrounded by foam peanuts, on a plane to her home in Melbourne, Australia. From reports I understand that it arrived in one piece and was still quite tasty.

I made teddy bear breads for a niece's baby naming held at the day school in San Diego where my brother Jeff teaches. He invited the entire student body and faculty to the brunch, and when the kids saw these centerpieces (surrounded by pink and white chocolates formed into pacifiers, bottles, booties, rattles, and such), their faces lit up. One young girl was so smitten that she partially devoured a hapless bear before her tablemates had a chance to share. Fortunately, there were plenty of others to go around.

The directions yield medium-size teddy bears, but you can increase or decrease the size to make large or small bears. One or two loaves are more than enough for ten people. You will need at least ten breads for a crowd of eighty, placing one bear on each table seating eight guests each.

3 medium bears	*10 medium bears*	
1	*3*	*(¼-ounce) packages active dry yeast*
½ cup	*1⅔ cups*	*warm water*
5 large	*16 large*	*eggs*
¾ cup	*2¼ cups*	*unsalted margarine, softened*
½ cup	*1⅔ cups*	*sugar*
½ teaspoon	*1½ teaspoons*	*salt*
About 5 cups	*5 pounds*	*unbleached all-purpose flour*

Egg wash (1 or 3 large eggs beaten with 1 or 3 tablespoons water)

1. To make the dough: In a large bowl, dissolve the yeast in half of the warm water. Blend in the remaining water, eggs, margarine, sugar, salt, and 2 cups (6½ cups) of

the flour. Beat in enough of the remaining flour, ½ cup (1 cup) at a time, to make a stiff dough. Do not knead. Cover loosely with plastic wrap or a towel and let rise in a warm, draft-free place until double in bulk, about 1½ hours.

2. Punch down the dough. Knead on a lightly floured surface until smooth and elastic, 10 to 15 minutes.

3. To form the bread sculptures: It is best to start with a large base and create details with smaller pieces. No piece should be thicker than 1 inch, or the bread might crack. To join pieces, simply place them touching each other. Use small pieces of dough or scissors to add fine details. If making separate sculptures, leave 2 inches between them. For very large sculptures, place 2 baking sheets together, cover with foil, and grease.

4. For 3 medium bears: Divide the dough into 3 equal pieces, then divide into smaller pieces to fit the following instructions. For each bear, form a 5-inch piece of dough into a ball, place on a greased baking sheet, and flatten slightly to form the body. Insert a very small dough ball in the center of the round to form a belly button.

5. Roll 2 pieces of dough into 5-inch-long ropes 1 inch thick. Arrange 1 rope on top of the dough round and the other on the bottom, bending the ropes slightly to form the arms and legs.

6. Form a 3-inch piece of dough into a ball, place above the arms, and flatten slightly to form the head. Place two ½- to ¾-inch dough balls on the sides of the head to form ears. Place 1 small ball in the center of the head to form a nose, then place 2 very small pieces of dough above the nose to form the eyes. Roll a small piece of dough into a thin strip, bend slightly, and arrange under the nose to form the mouth.

7. Cover loosely with plastic wrap or a towel and let rise until puffed, about 30 minutes.

8. Preheat the oven to 350 degrees.

9. Brush the dough with the egg wash. Bake until the bread is golden brown and sounds hollow when tapped on the bottom, about 30 minutes. Let cool on the baking sheet for 10 minutes, then carefully transfer to a rack and let cool completely.

Lox Pinwheels

4 DOZEN 1-INCH WHEELS

This is an attractive way to present two old favorites. Multiply the recipe for the desired yield.

8 ounces cream cheese, at room temperature
1 tablespoon fresh lemon juice
¼ teaspoon chopped fresh dill
8 ounces (fifteen 3-inch-square pieces) lox or smoked salmon

Beat the cream cheese, lemon juice, and dill together until smooth. Spread about 2 teaspoons of the cheese mixture over each piece of lox. Roll up the lox and cut each roll into 3 pieces. Cover and chill.

Stuffed Eggs with Caviar

10 servings	80 servings	
5 large	40 large	eggs
3 tablespoons	1½ cups	mayonnaise
1 tablespoon	½ cup	unsalted butter, softened (optional)
2 tablespoons	1 cup	chopped fresh dill
2 teaspoons	⅓ cup	prepared mustard
¼ teaspoon	1½ teaspoons	salt
Pinch	1 teaspoon	ground black pepper
1 ounce	8 ounces	whitefish or salmon caviar

1. Bring a large pot of water to a boil. Gently place the eggs, no more than 25 at a time (more will tend to cook unevenly), in the pot, immediately reduce the heat to low, and simmer for 15 minutes. Drain and place under cold running water.
2. Peel the eggs and slice in half lengthwise. Carefully remove the yolks and mash them. (For large amounts, this can be done in a food processor.) Stir in the mayonnaise, butter if desired, dill, mustard, salt, and pepper.
3. Pipe the yolk mixture through a pastry bag fitted with a large star tip or spoon it into the cavity of the egg whites. Cover and refrigerate until ready to serve.
4. Spoon a dab of caviar on top of each egg. If desired, serve the eggs on a bed of greens. (This not only is attractive but keeps the eggs from sliding around.)

VARIATION

Lox-Stuffed Eggs (10 servings): Omit the caviar and stir 1 ½ ounces chopped lox into the yolk mixture.

Apple Soufflé Pancake *(Apfel Schmarren)*

This pancake is a popular breakfast and dessert treat in Alsace, Austria, and southern Germany. The large amount of eggs in the pancake causes it to puff up during baking like a soufflé.

10 servings	*80 servings*	
6 large	48 large	eggs
1½ cups	3 quarts	milk
1 cup	8 cups	all-purpose flour
¼ cup	2 cups	sugar
1½ teaspoons	¼ cup	vanilla extract
½ teaspoon	1 tablespoon	salt
¼ teaspoon	2 teaspoons	ground cinnamon
½ cup	2 cups	unsalted butter
2 large	12 large	apples, peeled, cored, and thinly sliced
		confectioners' sugar

1. Preheat the oven to 400 degrees.
2. In a blender or food processor, blend the eggs, milk, flour, sugar, vanilla, salt, and cinnamon until smooth.
3. Place the butter in a 13- by 9-inch baking dish or 12-inch round quiche dish and melt in the oven. Add the apples, toss to coat well, and bake for about 5 minutes. Do not let the butter burn.
4. Pour the batter over the apples and bake until the pancake is puffed and golden brown, about 20 minutes. Sprinkle with confectioners' sugar and cut into squares or wedges. Serve hot.

Georgian Baked Vegetable Omelet (Chizhipizhi)

*T*his popular breakfast dish is native to the Caucasian country that was formerly part of the Soviet Union, not my father's southern American birthplace.

10 servings	80 servings	
½ cup	3 cups	vegetable oil
4 medium	24 medium	onions, chopped
2½ pounds	15 pounds	tomatoes, peeled, seeded, and chopped (about 4 or 24 cups)
3 medium	24 medium	green bell peppers, seeded and chopped
2 medium	18 medium	red bell peppers, seeded and chopped
1 cup	6 cups	chopped fresh cilantro
½ cup	3 cups	chopped fresh parsley
About 1½ teaspoons	About 2 tablespoons	salt
½ teaspoon	1 tablespoon	ground black pepper
10 large	60 large	eggs
⅓ cup	2 cups	grated feta, mozzarella, Muenster, or Swiss cheese (optional)

1. Preheat the oven to 350 degrees.
2. Heat half of the oil in a large skillet (or skillets) over medium heat. Add the onions and sauté until lightly golden, about 20 minutes. Add the tomatoes and cook until softened, about 5 minutes. Stir in the bell peppers, cilantro, parsley, salt, and pepper. Add the eggs and, if desired, the cheese.
3. Heat the remaining oil in a 13- by 9-inch baking pan (for 10 servings).
4. Pour the egg mixture into the prepared pan. Bake until set and golden, about 45 minutes. Cut into squares or diamonds and serve warm, accompanied by yogurt if desired.

VARIATION

Miniature Omelets: Spoon about 2 tablespoons of the egg mixture into miniature muffin cups (about 100 total for 10 servings) and bake for about 20 minutes.

Whitefish Salad (Fischesalat)

This classic eastern European salad maintains its popularity in America. Whitefish is a high-fat freshwater fish and member of the salmon family. It is commonly found smoked in delicatessens.

10 servings	80 servings	
3 pounds (about 2)	18 pounds (about 16)	smoked whitefish, skinned, boned, and flaked
¾ cup	4½ cups	mayonnaise
1 cup	6 cups	chopped celery
3 tablespoons	1 cup	lemon juice
2 tablespoons	¾ cup	prepared white horseradish or snipped fresh dill (optional)
		ground black pepper to taste

Combine all the ingredients. Cover and store in the refrigerator. Serve with crackers, dark bread, or Belgian endive leaves.

VARIATION

Creamy Whitefish Salad (10 servings): Reduce the mayonnaise to 2 tablespoons and add about 1¼ cups sour cream.

Chickpea Salad (Salata de Garvonsos)

Chickpeas, customarily served on the Friday night following the birth of a child, make a tasty salad.

10 servings	80 servings	
6 cups	4 quarts	cooked chickpeas
1 medium	6 medium	red onions, chopped
1 medium	6 medium	green bell peppers, seeded and coarsely chopped
1 medium	5 medium	red bell peppers, seeded and coarsely chopped

DRESSING

10 servings	80 servings	
½ cup	3 cups	olive or vegetable oil
⅓ cup	2 cups	fresh lemon juice or wine vinegar
½ cup	3 cups	chopped fresh parsley or cilantro
2 to 3	12 to 15	cloves garlic, minced
1½ teaspoons	1 tablespoon	salt
¼ teaspoon	1½ teaspoons	ground black pepper
2 tablespoons	¾ cup	chopped fresh mint
1 teaspoon	2 tablespoons	ground cumin

Combine the chickpeas, onions, and bell peppers. Combine all the dressing ingredients, pour over the chickpeas, and toss to coat. Refrigerate for at least 1 hour or up to 2 days.

Greek Salad *(Horiataki)*

*H*oriataki is the Greek word for "village," referring to this peasant salad's origins. Called *michoteta* in the Middle East, Greek Salad has become a favorite in both America and Israel.

10 servings	80 servings	
1 large	8 large	heads romaine or Boston lettuce, torn into pieces
3 large	16 large	tomatoes, cut into eighths
2 medium	16 medium	cucumbers, peeled and sliced
1 medium	8 medium	green bell peppers, seeded and thinly sliced
1 medium	8 medium	red bell peppers, seeded and thinly sliced
1 medium	8 medium	yellow bell peppers, seeded and thinly sliced
1 medium	8 medium	red onions, thinly sliced
¼ cup	2 cups	chopped fresh parsley
8 ounces	4 pounds	feta cheese, crumbled (1½ or 12 cups)
6 ounces	3 pounds	brine-cured olives, such as kalamata, pitted (1 or 8 cups)
3 tablespoons	1 cup	drained capers (optional)
8	50	anchovy fillets (optional)

DRESSING

¾ cup	6 cups	olive oil
¼ cup	2 cups	fresh lemon juice or wine vinegar
1 to 2	8 to 12	cloves garlic, minced
2 teaspoons	⅓ cup	dried oregano
½ teaspoon	1 tablespoon	salt
⅛ teaspoon	2 teaspoons	ground black pepper

1. Toss together the vegetables, parsley, feta, olives, and if desired, the capers and/or anchovies.
2. Place all the dressing ingredients in a jar with a tight-fitting lid and shake well. Just before serving, shake again, drizzle over the salad, and toss to coat. If desired, serve with garlic croutons or garlic bread.

VARIATION

Swiss Salad (10 servings): Omit the tomatoes and olives. Substitute 1 ½ cups julienned Swiss cheese for the feta. If desired, add 1 peeled, pitted, and sliced avocado and 1 peeled and segmented navel orange.

Baby Bootie Cupcakes
1 PAIR OF BOOTIES

*T*hese cute little cakes can be served as individual portions or used to garnish a large cake.

3 Basic Cupcakes (page 172)
Basic Buttercream (page 370)
Several drops red or blue food coloring
2 gumdrops or 2 pieces shoestring licorice

1. Stir several drops of the food coloring into the buttercream to create a pink or light blue shade.
2. Cut a small slice off the side of 1 cupcake, discarding the slice. Cut the remaining part of the cupcake horizontally in half.
3. Place the 2 whole cupcakes upside down. Spread a little buttercream over the cut vertical side of one of the cake halves and place the frosted side adjacent to a whole cupcake so that the cut piece adheres. Repeat with the remaining cake half and second whole cupcake. Frost the tops and sides of the cakes.
4. Roll the gumdrops into a long strip and tie into a bow, or tie the licorice into bows and arrange on the booties.

A *Pidyon Haben* Luncheon

SERVES 10 OR 80

*B*ecause the Jews were spared from the plague that killed the firstborn Egyptian males, the Torah instructed that firstborn sons were to be devoted to the service of God. After the incident of the golden calf, however, the tribe of Levi was substituted for the firstborn, who henceforth must be redeemed through a ceremony called *pidyon haben* (literally, "redemption of the son"). A redemption is not required if the father or the mother is a Cohain or Levi. In addition, since the text explicitly states *pehter rechem* (opens the womb), no *pidyon haben* is required if the firstborn is delivered through cesarean section or if the mother previously suffered a miscarriage. Thus, only once have I had the opportunity to cater a family *pidyon haben*. And since my two oldest nieces have married a Levi and a Cohain, it will be quite a while before I have another chance.

A *pidyon haben* is held on the thirty-first day after the birth, even if a *brit milah* has not yet been performed. Since a money transaction is at the heart of this ceremony, it is not held on the Sabbath or a holiday, when such transactions are forbidden, but postponed until the following weekday. Sephardim traditionally hold the *pidyon haben* on the evening of the thirty-first day, while Ashkenazim prefer the following morning. Some Moroccans hold the ceremony at the same time of day that the child was born.

At the ceremony the father presents his son on a silver tray accompanied by a payment of five *shekalim* or the equivalent in silver coins (the custom in America is to use silver dollars, while the Bank of Israel mints special *pidyon haben* coins) to a Cohain. In the tenth century a symbolic dialogue was established in which the Cohain asks the father whether he wants to give up his son for priestly service. Of course, the father responds that he would prefer to keep him. At this point the father pays the Cohain, who announces three times, "*Bencha pahdoy*" (Your son is redeemed). The money is commonly returned to the father, who donates it or its equivalent to charity. Following the *pidyon haben,* the Cohain recites a blessing over a cup of wine and blesses the child, then joins the relatives and friends in a *seudat mitzvah.*

Kaiser Rolls and Sliced Rye Bread
Prepared Mustard
Dill Pickles and Olives
Deli Platters
Barbecue Beef Brisket
Sweet Potato Salad
Curried Pasta Salad
Yemenite Red Cabbage Salad in *Tahina*
Broccoli and Red Pepper Salad
Quick Breads Assortment (pages 373–382)
Cookie Assortment (pages 346–362)
Fresh Fruit Platter (page 217) or Fruit Salad
Coffee, Tea, and Orange Juice

Deli Platters

*T*he word *delicatessen* derives from the German for "delicacies," indicating an evaluation of the products sold as well as the originators of the concept. Early American delis primarily offered a line of German and Alsatian *wurst*s (sausages) and sauerkraut. Then as eastern European Jews flocked to America at the beginning of the twentieth century, they usurped the delicatessen business, expanding its repertoire with smoked and cured fish, corned beef, Romanian pastrami, dill pickles (both sours and half-sours), pickled green tomatoes, kugels, knishes, and Jewish rye bread. These items soon became a common sight at Jewish life-cycle events, particularly for lunch.

The following suggested amounts allow about 3 ounces of meat per person. When serving Barbecue Beef Brisket (below), you will need less deli.

10 servings (2½ pounds total)	80 servings (15 pounds total)	
14 ounces	5½ pounds	corned beef, sliced
12 ounces	4 pounds	turkey, sliced
9 ounces	3½ pounds	pastrami, sliced
5 ounces	2 pounds	salami, sliced

Arrange the meat on large serving platters.

Barbecue Beef Brisket

*I*n this recipe, brisket, a longtime Ashkenazic staple, meets Tex-Mex. Let each guest fill a roll with slices of brisket, or provide French or Italian bread—twenty loaves should amply supply a crowd of eighty. This barbecue sauce is also tasty with chuck roast or grilled chicken.

10 servings	80 servings	
1 (4-pound)	3 (5-pound)	first-cut beef briskets
		salt to taste
		ground black pepper to taste

BARBECUE SAUCE

3 tablespoons	½ cup	vegetable oil
1 large	3 large	onions, chopped
1 to 2	4 to 5	cloves garlic, minced
3 cups	9 cups	tomato sauce or puree
½ cup	1½ cups	water
⅓ cup	1 cup	packed brown sugar (light or dark)
¼ cup	¾ cup	cider vinegar or red wine vinegar
2 tablespoons	6 tablespoons	lemon juice
2 tablespoons	6 tablespoons	honey or molasses
2 tablespoons	6 tablespoons	Worcestershire sauce OR
½ teaspoon	1½ teaspoons	liquid smoke
1½ teaspoons	4 teaspoons	chili powder
1½ teaspoons	4 teaspoons	dry mustard
½ teaspoon	1½ teaspoons	ground cumin
About 1 teaspoon	2½ teaspoons	salt
About 1 teaspoon	1 tablespoon	ground black pepper

1. Preheat the oven to 325 degrees.
2. Rub both sides of the meat with salt and pepper. Wrap in several layers of heavy-duty aluminum foil and cook until the meat is fork-tender and the thickest part of the brisket registers 175 degrees on a meat thermometer, about 4 hours. Let cool.
3. To make the sauce: Heat the oil in a large saucepan (or stockpot) over medium heat. Add the onions and garlic and sauté until soft and translucent, 5 to 10 minutes. Add the remaining ingredients, bring to a boil, reduce the heat to low, and simmer, stirring occasionally, until slightly thickened, about 30 minutes. (The sauce can be refrigerated or frozen until ready to use.)
4. Slice the brisket diagonally against the grain about ⅛ inch thick. Arrange a layer of meat in a large baking dish and spread with some sauce. Repeat until all of the meat and sauce is used. Cover with foil. (The brisket can be prepared ahead to this point and refrigerated for up to 3 days or frozen for up to 3 months. Return to room temperature.)
5. Preheat the oven to 350 degrees.
6. Bake the brisket, covered, until heated through, about 1 hour. Serve warm.

Sweet Potato Salad

*S*weet potatoes provide a break from the standard white potato salad.

10 servings	*80 servings*	
3 pounds	20 pounds	sweet potatoes, peeled
1 tablespoon	½ cup	sugar
1	7	(2-inch) sticks cinnamon
3 stalks	20 stalks	celery, sliced
2	16	scallions, chopped
¾ cup	6 cups	chopped walnuts, almonds, or roasted peanuts (optional)

VINAIGRETTE

6 tablespoons	2¼ cups	vegetable oil
6 tablespoons	2¼ cups	orange juice
3 tablespoons	1 cup	red wine vinegar
		salt to taste
		ground black pepper to taste

1. Place the potatoes, sugar, and cinnamon sticks in a large pot (or pots) and add water to cover. Bring to a boil, cover, reduce the heat to low, and simmer until the potatoes are tender but not mushy, 30 to 45 minutes. Drain and cube.
2. Combine the potatoes, celery, scallions, and if desired, the nuts. Combine all the vinaigrette ingredients, drizzle over the salad, and toss to coat. Serve chilled or at room temperature.

Curried Pasta Salad

*T*he pasta turns bright yellow and the curry mellows as it stands.

10 servings	60 servings	
1 pound	4 pounds	fusilli or rotini pasta
1 cup	4 cups	white vinegar
½ cup	2 cups	sugar
¼ cup	1 cup	curry powder
½ teaspoon	1½ teaspoons	salt
⅛ teaspoon	1 teaspoon	ground black pepper
½ cup	2 cups	vegetable oil
2 pounds	8 pounds	carrots, sliced
4 cups	16 cups	broccoli florets
4 cups	16 cups	cauliflower florets
1 cup	4 cups	raisins
1 cup	4 cups	unsalted roasted peanuts

1. In a large pot (or pots) of lightly salted boiling water, cook the pasta, uncovered, until *al dente* (tender yet firm to the bite). Drain.
2. In a jar with a tight-fitting lid, shake the vinegar, sugar, curry powder, salt, and pepper until the sugar dissolves. Add the oil and shake well.
3. Pour the vinaigrette over the pasta and toss to coat. Add the vegetables, raisins, and peanuts. Refrigerate for several hours or up to 2 days. Serve at room temperature.

Yemenite Red Cabbage Salad in *Tahina*

*T*he boiled vinegar preserves the cabbage's bright red color.

10 servings	80 servings	
1½ pounds	9 pounds	red cabbage, shredded (about 1 medium or 4 large heads)
½ cup	3 cups	white wine vinegar
½ cup	3 cups	tahina *(recipe follows)*
¼ cup	1½ cups	fresh lemon juice
1 teaspoon	1½ tablespoons	salt
1 teaspoon	1½ tablespoons	ground black pepper
½ cup	2 cups	chopped scallions *(optional)*

1. Place the cabbage in a large bowl (or bowls). Bring the vinegar to a boil, pour it over the cabbage, and toss to coat. Let cool.
2. Combine the *tahina,* lemon juice, salt, and pepper. Pour over the cabbage and toss to coat. Let stand at least 30 minutes before serving. If desired, garnish with the scallions.

VARIATION

Substitute ¾ cup vegetable oil for the *tahina.* If desired, add 1 tablespoon sugar and 2 teaspoons anise extract.

TAHINA (MIDDLE EASTERN SESAME SAUCE)
ABOUT 1⅓ CUPS

*T*oasted sesame seeds are ground into a paste called tahini. It is available in most grocery stores. Tahini separates during storage, so stir in the oil to make a smooth paste before using. Loosening the paste with water and a little lemon juice produces a *tarator bi tahina* (sesame sauce), popular in the Middle East as a dip, as a salad dressing, and with falafel.

1 cup tahini (sesame seed paste)
3 tablespoons fresh lemon juice
1 to 2 cloves garlic, minced
¾ teaspoon salt
About ½ cup water

With a fork or in a food processor, blend together the tahini, lemon juice, garlic, and salt until smooth. Add enough water to make a sauce of pouring consistency.

Broccoli and Red Pepper Salad

*F*or a colorful presentation, arrange alternate rows of broccoli and peppers in a 1½-quart bowl, drizzle the dressing over the vegetables, and let marinate in the refrigerator. Just before serving, invert onto a serving plate.

10 servings	80 servings	
2 large	6 large	heads broccoli, cut into florets (6 or 18 cups)
3 medium	9 medium	red bell peppers, sliced
1 small	3 small	onions, halved and sliced

DRESSING

½ cup	1½ cups	olive or vegetable oil
¼ cup	¾ cup	wine vinegar or tarragon vinegar
2 to 3	5 to 6	cloves garlic, crushed
1 teaspoon	1 tablespoon	sugar
½ teaspoon	1 teaspoon	salt
⅛ teaspoon	½ teaspoon	ground black pepper

1. Steam or parboil the broccoli until tender-crisp, about 2 minutes. Rinse under cold water and drain. Combine the broccoli, bell peppers, and onions.
2. Place all the dressing ingredients in a jar with a tight-fitting lid, shake well, and drizzle over the salad. Let marinate in the refrigerator, tossing occasionally, for at least 2 hours but no longer than 24 hours.

FIRST TOOTH CELEBRATION

The appearance of a baby's first tooth is a special moment among Sephardim, who hold a party in honor of this milestone. The most common foods at this meal are those that resemble teeth, including raisins, pine nuts, pomegranate seeds, wheat berries, and barley (see Sephardic Sweetened Barley, page 169).

UPSHEARIN

From the agricultural law that the fruit of trees is forbidden until after the tree's third year (Leviticus 19:23) emerged the custom in some circles of not cutting a boy's hair until the age of three. The great kabbalist Yitzchak Luria, known as the Ari (1534–1572), waited until the *hillula* festivities of Lag b'Omer (see page 164) held in Meron at the grave of Rabbi Shimon ben Yochai to give his son his first haircut, tossing the locks into a bonfire. Subsequently, some Sephardim emulated the custom of waiting until Lag b'Omer for *halaqa* (Arabic for "to cut hair"), as did Hasidim, who called the custom *upshearin* (Yiddish for "to cut"). A *kiddush* or *seudat mitzvah* (meal) commonly follows the haircut.

A Cold Bar or Bat Mitzvah Buffet

SERVES 10 OR 80

*I*n Judaism a child is not held personally responsible for his or her religious acts until the age of puberty, set at twelve years and one day for a female and thirteen years and one day for a male. This transition is automatic, with no ritual required. By the fourteenth century the child's change in status was formalized in Germany with a ceremony in which a young man is called up to the reading of the Torah to publicly demonstrate his new role in the community. If the bar mitzvah boy is capable, he reads from the Torah scroll, then recites the Haftorah; otherwise, he recites only the blessing. Afterward, it is customary in many congregations to shower the bar mitzvah boy with candy, frequently tied in small sacks. Some parents employ a little creativity in preparing for this custom by decorating the bags: they paint black lines on a white bag, then tie strings on the four corners to resemble a *tallit* (prayer shawl).

The concept of the bar mitzvah (meaning both "son of the commandment" and "subject to the law") ceremony eventually spread to other parts of the Ashkenazic community, as well as to various non-European Jewish communities. Today it is among the best known of all Jewish rituals. However, since women historically played no role in the synagogue, a girl's maturation was observed quietly or not at all. Eventually, however, recognition of the need for religious instruction for females as well as the value of a ceremony to mark the emergence of their religious obligations increased. Jacob Ettlinger (1798–1871), a German rabbi, countenanced such an observance for females in order to combat assimilation. The first mention of the term *bat mitzvah* was in the book *Ben Ish Chai* (1898) by Joseph Chaim ben Elijah of Baghdad. The actual observance of a bat mitzvah ceremony similar to one for males did not occur until 1922, when the oldest daughter of Reconstructionist founder Mordechai Kaplan, Judith, was called to the Torah at the Society for the Advancement for Judaism in New York City. Today traditionalists who observe a bat mitzvah generally do so after the synagogue service or at home or school, while egalitarian congregations encourage girls to perform the same rituals as boys.

In central Europe the bar mitzvah was generally held on a Saturday, followed by a buffet and sometimes a banquet. Eastern Europeans, on the other hand, historically downplayed what they considered a minor event, usually holding it on a Monday or Thursday (two other times when the Torah is publicly read) with little or no fanfare. However, as the bar mitzvah grew in importance in affluent post–World War II America, the accompanying meal did so as well, all too often turning into an excessive and pretentious affair, stereotyped in popular culture by chopped liver sculptures, exotic dancers, and marching bands.

Many parents, worried that these events have become "all bar and no mitzvah," are seeking ways of making the bar or bat mitzvah a more personal, expressive, and spiritual event. Guest lists are more frequently limited to those who are close to the family rather than assorted business acquaintances. Jewish music is increasingly replacing the all-too-common rock band. The inclusion of nonsectarian entertainment—ranging from psychic readings to video games—has declined. Instead of paying for an elaborate catered affair, more and more parents are using the money to take the immediate family to Israel. Others make a point of establishing a family program of performing traditional acts of kindness, such as visiting the elderly and helping the poor. Some celebrants donate part of their gift money to *tzedaka* (charity). A popular activity that parents and children can do together is to research and chart the family genealogy. A practical idea is to use religious books or ritual objects as table decorations and then to distribute them to the guests or donate them to the synagogue. The return to tradition, as well as the development of various spiritual innovations, makes for a more meaningful and long-remembered celebration.

CHALLAH ROLLS

CRUDITÉS WITH CURRY DIP AND AVOCADO MOUSSE (PAGE 211)

WHOLE POACHED SALMON

MEDITERRANEAN CHICKEN

SEPHARDIC PUMPKIN TURNOVERS

JERUSALEM ARTICHOKE AND EGG SALAD

ISRAELI FENNEL AND OLIVE SALAD

FRUITED WILD RICE SALAD

SALAD BAR

TEFILLIN CAKES

CHILLED FRUIT SOUP WITH POACHED PEARS AND ANISE

COOKIE CROUTONS

COOKIE ASSORTMENT (PAGES 346–362)

 Wine Suggestions: Chardonnay, Beaujolais, or Soave

Whole Poached Salmon
16 TO 20 SERVINGS PER SALMON

*N*o matter what the occasion, whole poached salmon makes any affair special. If salmon is too expensive for your budget, substitute another large fish such as a sea bass. If you do not own a fish poacher (a long, narrow pan with a removable rack and cover), substitute a foil-lined deep baking pan or a large foil pan. Allow about ½ pound salmon for each person. One small salmon will generously serve a small party, while four will be necessary for a large affair.

1 (8- to 12-pound) whole salmon
6 to 8 cups water
2 cups dry white wine
2 medium onions, sliced
2 medium carrots, sliced
10 whole peppercorns
4 teaspoons salt
1 bay leaf

1. Remove the scales, fins, gills, and guts from the fish; leave on the head and tail. To determine how much poaching liquid is needed, place the fish in the cooking pan, add water to cover by at least ¼ inch, then measure the amount of water. Rinse the fish under cold water and pat dry. For easy handling and retention of shape, wrap the fish in a double layer of cheesecloth.

2. Place the water, wine, onions, carrots, peppercorns, salt, and bay leaf in a fish poacher or large foil-lined pan set over 2 burners and bring to a simmer over medium heat. (The temperature for poaching should be about 180 degrees, which is below the boiling point, with small bubbles visible on the surface. Higher temperatures toughen the flesh, while lower temperatures require a longer cooking time, which destroys the fish's flavor.)

3. Lower the fish into the liquid, making sure it is completely covered. Cover the pan, reduce the heat to low, and simmer or bake in a 350-degree oven until the flesh is opaque, about 7 minutes per pound, or 40 minutes to 1 hour. The fish is done when a bone pulled from the area of the dorsal fin comes out clean and easily.

4. Using 2 large metal spatulas, remove the fish from the cooking liquid. Immediately cut away the cheesecloth. (Save the poaching liquid for another use, such as soups or sauces.)

5. Using a small sharp knife or kitchen shears, cut down the backbone of the fish and remove the skin from the top side. Let the fish cool before attempting to turn and remove the skin from the second side. Cover with plastic wrap and refrigerate for 4 hours or overnight. Garnish with lemon slices, sliced cucumbers, and parsley. If desired, serve the salmon with mayonnaise mixed with a little dill or tarragon.

Mediterranean Chicken

*M*arinated chicken turns out moist and tender, even when cold. This version incorporates food items prevalent in the Mediterranean region.

10 servings	*80 servings*	
MARINADE		
6 tablespoons	*1½ cups*	*cider vinegar or wine vinegar*
6 tablespoons	*1½ cups*	*olive or vegetable oil*
2 medium	*6 medium*	*red onions, sliced*
6 to 8	*35 to 40*	*cloves garlic, minced*
3 medium	*12 medium*	*pears, peeled, cored, and sliced (optional)*
¾ cup	*3 cups*	*pitted prunes*
½ cup	*2 cups*	*pitted green olives*
⅓ cup	*1½ cups*	*capers*
3 tablespoons	*¾ cup*	*dried oregano*
4	*16*	*bay leaves*
1¼ teaspoons	*4 teaspoons*	*salt*
½ teaspoon	*2 teaspoons*	*ground black pepper*

CHICKEN

3	12	(2½- to 3-pound) chickens, each cut into 8 pieces
¾ cup	3 cups	dry white wine
¾ cup	3 cups	packed brown sugar, granulated sugar, or honey

1. Combine the marinade ingredients. Add the chicken, cover, and let marinate in the refrigerator, turning occasionally, overnight. (For easy storage and cleanup, marinate the chicken in plastic bags.)
2. Preheat the oven to 350 degrees.
3. Spread the marinade in shallow roasting pans and arrange the chicken, skin side up, in a single layer on top. Drizzle with the wine and sprinkle with the sugar.
4. Bake, basting occasionally, until the chicken is golden brown and the juices run clear when a thigh is pierced with a fork, about 1 hour. Serve warm or at room temperature.

Sephardic Pumpkin Turnovers
(Empanadas de Calabaza)

*E*mpanadas, from the Spanish *empanar* (to cover with bread), are one of the most ancient of Sephardic dishes. The original filling appears to have been made with fish, but over the years variations emerged, including vegetable, cheese, and meat fillings. Sephardim who settled in Turkey merged the empanada with local pastries, further expanding the types of fillings. Pumpkin and squash are symbolic of plenty and fruitfulness.

Makes 20	Makes 120	3-inch turnovers
DOUGH		
About 2 cups	12 cups	all-purpose flour
½ teaspoon	1 tablespoon	salt
½ cup	3 cups	vegetable oil
⅓ cup	2 cups	warm water
FILLING		
1 cup	6 cups	pureed cooked pumpkin, winter squash, or sweet potatoes
½ large	3 large	eggs, lightly beaten
1 tablespoon	6 tablespoons	all-purpose flour or fine bread crumbs
5 tablespoons	1 cup	granulated or packed brown sugar
½ teaspoon	1 tablespoon	ground cinnamon
Pinch	1 teaspoon	salt

Egg wash (1 or 3 eggs beaten with 1 or 3 tablespoons water)

1. To make the dough: Place 1½ cups of the flour and the salt in a large bowl or bowls. Gradually stir in the oil and water. Add enough of the remaining flour to make a firm dough. Wrap and let stand at room temperature for 30 minutes.
2. To make the filling: Combine all the filling ingredients.
3. Preheat the oven to 375 degrees.
4. On a lightly floured surface, roll out the dough to a ⅛-inch thickness. Cut out 4-inch rounds.
5. Brush the dough edge with water or egg wash. Place a tablespoon of the filling in the center of each round. Fold one side over to create a half circle and press to seal the edges and evenly distribute the filling. Crimp the edges with your fingers or the tines of a fork. Curve the ends to form a crescent. (Empanadas can be covered and stored in the refrigerator for 1 day.)
6. Place the empanadas on baking sheets 1 inch apart and brush the tops with the egg wash. Bake until golden brown, about 20 minutes. Serve warm or at room temperature. (Cooked empanadas can be frozen for up to 4 months; reheat in a 350-degree oven for about 20 minutes.)

Jerusalem Artichoke and Egg Salad

Jerusalem artichokes, also called sunchokes, are not artichokes and are not native to the Holy Land, although they are popular in Israel now. There are two theories about how this tuber got its misleading name. Some claim it's a mistranslation of the Italian word for sunflower, *girasole*. According to others, the Italians originally gave the name Jerusalem to the globe artichoke because the Jews introduced it to Italy, and when the sunchoke appeared, it was identified with the globe artichoke and acquired its name. Raw Jerusalem artichokes have a slightly sweet-nutty flavor and crunchy texture; cooked, they have a firm texture and can be used like potatoes in salad.

10 servings	*80 servings*	
2 pounds	*12 pounds*	*Jerusalem artichokes*
4 large	*24 large*	*hard-boiled eggs, chopped*
4	*24*	*stalks celery, chopped*
1 small	*3 medium*	*onions, chopped*
⅔ cup	*4 cups*	*mayonnaise*
		salt to taste
		ground black pepper to taste

1. Scrub the Jerusalem artichokes well to remove any dirt. Place them whole in boiling water and cook until tender, about 20 minutes. Let cool. Cut into cubes.
2. Combine the artichokes, eggs, celery, and onions. Add the mayonnaise, salt, and pepper. Chill.

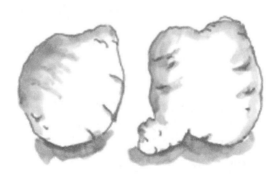

Israeli Fennel and Olive Salad

*F*ennel was common in ancient Israel, where it grew wild in the countryside, and is regaining its popularity in modern Israel. This anise-flavored relative of dill and parsley resembles celery with a bulbous base.

10 servings	*80 servings*	
2¾ pounds	*17 pounds*	*fresh fennel bulbs, trimmed (2 or 12 medium)*
6 ounces	*3 pounds*	*brine-cured black olives, pitted and coarsely chopped (1 or 8 cups)*
⅓ cup	*2 cups*	*olive or vegetable oil*
¼ cup	*1½ cups*	*fresh lemon juice or wine vinegar (or a combination)*
½ cup	*3 cups*	*chopped fresh parsley*
½ teaspoon	*2½ teaspoons*	*salt*
¼ teaspoon	*1½ teaspoons*	*ground black pepper*
1 tablespoon	*⅓ cup*	*Dijon mustard (optional)*
6 cups	*8 quarts*	*any combination of curly endive, romaine lettuce, watercress, Belgian endive, and radicchio*

1. Cut the fennel bulbs in half from the root end. Slice crosswise into thin crescents. Add the olives.
2. Combine the oil, lemon juice, parsley, salt, pepper, and if desired, the mustard. Drizzle over the fennel mixture and let marinate in the refrigerator for at least 30 minutes. Serve on a bed of the greens.

VARIATIONS (FOR 10 SERVINGS)

Fennel and Apple Salad: Substitute 2 cored and chopped or sliced tart green apples for the olives. If desired, add ¾ cup pomegranate seeds.

Fennel and Artichoke Salad: Substitute 28 ounces thinly sliced cooked and drained artichoke hearts for the olives.

Fennel and Grapefruit Salad: Substitute 3 peeled and sectioned grapefruit for the olives and 4 to 6 tablespoons grapefruit juice for the lemon juice.

Fruited Wild Rice Salad

*W*ild rice, indigenous to North America and not truly a rice, was not mentioned in the Bible. However, the addition of biblical fruits and nuts enhances this salad.

10 servings	*80 servings*	
1½ cups	8 cups	wild rice
9 cups	12 quarts	water
1½ cups	8 cups	coarsely chopped almonds or pistachios
¾ cup	4 cups	golden raisins
¾ cup	4 cups	chopped pitted dates
½ cup	3 cups	chopped figs or pomegranate seeds
6 tablespoons	2 cups	vegetable oil
¾ cup	4 cups	fresh orange juice
½ cup	2½ cups	chopped fresh mint or parsley
8 to 9	50	scallions, chopped
1 teaspoon	1½ tablespoons	salt
¼ teaspoon	1½ teaspoons	ground black pepper

1. Bring the wild rice and water to a rapid boil. Reduce the heat to medium-low and simmer, uncovered, until the rice is tender but not mushy, about 45 minutes. Drain.
2. Mix the remaining ingredients into the wild rice and let marinate in the refrigerator for at least 4 hours or up to 2 days. Serve at room temperature.

Salad Bar

*T*he following ingredients are suggestions only—substitute your favorite or available vegetables and toppings. For the mixed greens, try a combination of iceberg and leaf lettuces (such as romaine and Bibb). Estimate about ¼ cup dressing per person.

10 servings	*80 servings*	
12 cups	*12¼ quarts*	*mixed salad greens, torn into bite-size pieces (about 2 or 18 pounds)*
3 cups	*20 cups*	*shredded red cabbage (½ small or 2 large heads)*
8 ounces	*4 pounds*	*carrots, sliced or coarsely shredded*
1 medium	*8 medium*	*cucumbers, thinly sliced*
2 cups	*14 cups*	*marinated artichoke hearts, sliced*
1 medium	*7 medium*	*green bell peppers, seeded and sliced*
1 medium	*7 medium*	*red bell peppers, seeded and sliced*
1 medium	*7 medium*	*yellow bell peppers, seeded and sliced*
6 ounces	*3 pounds*	*mushrooms, sliced*
6 ounces	*3 pounds*	*cured black olives (1 or 8 cups)*
1 pint	*8 pints*	*cherry tomatoes*
1 medium	*5 medium*	*red onions, sliced*
2 cups	*12 cups*	*cooked chickpeas*
2 cups	*12 cups*	*alfalfa or bean sprouts*

TOPPINGS

2 cups	*14 cups*	*croutons*
½ cup	*4 cups*	*sunflower seeds*
4 large	*24 large*	*hard-boiled eggs, sliced or chopped*

Prepare the vegetables no more than 24 hours before serving and store in plastic bags in the refrigerator. Arrange the various salad ingredients and dressings in bowls and let the guests help themselves.

ORANGE VINAIGRETTE
ABOUT 4 CUPS

1 cup fresh orange juice
¾ cup fresh lemon juice, fresh lime juice, or red wine vinegar
4 teaspoons grated orange zest
½ cup chopped fresh cilantro or mint (optional)
3 to 4 tablespoons sugar or honey (optional)
About 1 teaspoon salt
1 cup olive oil
1 cup vegetable oil

Combine all the ingredients except the oils. Gradually whisk in the oils. Shake well before serving.

LEMON-HONEY DRESSING
ABOUT 4½ CUPS

½ cup fresh lemon juice
½ cup white vinegar
¼ cup honey
About 1¾ teaspoons salt
Ground black pepper to taste
3½ cups vegetable oil

Combine the lemon juice, vinegar, honey, salt, and pepper. In a slow, steady stream, whisk in the oil. Shake well before serving.

APPLE-WALNUT DRESSING
ABOUT 5 CUPS

1½ cups cider vinegar
⅓ cup apple cider
⅓ cup Dijon mustard (optional)
Salt to taste
2 cups olive oil
1 cup walnut oil
¾ cup (3 ounces) walnuts, toasted and chopped

Combine the vinegar, cider, mustard, and salt. In a slow, steady stream, whisk in the oils. Add the nuts. Shake well before serving.

GINGER DRESSING
ABOUT 4 CUPS

1 cup peanut or vegetable oil
2 medium onions, chopped (about 1 cup)
½ cup rice vinegar
½ cup water
About ⅓ cup soy sauce
¼ cup minced fresh ginger
¼ cup minced celery or carrot
2 tablespoons sugar
4 teaspoons fresh lemon juice
4 teaspoons tomato paste or 3 tablespoons ketchup
Salt to taste
Ground black pepper to taste

In a blender, process all the ingredients until smooth. Store in the refrigerator for up to 1 week. Shake well before serving.

Tefillin Cakes

9 SMALL CAKES

One of the rituals incumbent upon reaching religious maturity is the wearing of *tefillin* (phylacteries). These small leather boxes with straps contain parchment inscribed with portions of the Torah and are placed on the head and wound on the arm during weekday morning services. For this dessert, cake, buttercream, and marzipan are used to create replicas of *tefillin* boxes and straps.

1 (13- by 9-inch) chocolate cake (page 368), silver-white cake (page 332), or other favorite cake
About 6 cups chocolate or mocha buttercream (page 371)
1 recipe (about 1 pound) Marzipan (page 309)

1. Using a serrated knife, trim off the sides and top of the cake. Cut the cake crosswise into four 3-inch-wide rectangles, then cut 3 of the rectangles into thirds. (You will have nine 3-inch squares.) Cut nine 1½-inch squares from the remaining cake.
2. Spread the tops and sides of the cake squares with the buttercream. Using a metal spatula, carefully arrange a smaller square on the top of each larger square, centering it.
3. On a piece of parchment or wax paper, roll out the marzipan ⅛ inch thick. Cut into ½-inch-wide strips, then cut the strips into 5- or 6-inch lengths. Arrange 2 strips on opposite sides of each bottom cake layer. Tuck one end of each strip under the cake and drape the other end over the *tefillin*.

VARIATION

Large Tefillin Cake (about 50 servings): For a single large cake, use three 13- by 9-inch cakes and the same amount of buttercream and marzipan. Place one of the cakes on a foil-wrapped board or tray and spread the top with buttercream. Place a second cake on top and spread with buttercream. Cut the remaining cake in half crosswise and place one half in the center of the large cake. Spread the top with buttercream and place the remaining half on top. Cover the top and the sides of all the layers with buttercream. Roll out the marzipan and cut into 2 long strips about 2 inches wide. Place on the cake as described above. Use any remaining buttercream to pipe decorations on the cake if desired.

Chilled Fruit Soup with Poached Pears and Anise Cookie Croutons

10 servings	80 servings	
2 large	14 large	pears, peeled, cored, and chopped
2 medium	14 medium	Granny Smith or McIntosh apples, peeled, cored, and chopped
6 cups	10 quarts	any combination blueberries, raspberries, and halved strawberries
1 cup	7 cups	cranberry juice
About ½ cup	3½ cups	sugar
2 tablespoons	1 cup	lemon juice
10	80	Wine-Poached Pears (page 161)
60	480	Anise Cookie Croutons (recipe follows)
10	80	mint sprigs (optional)

1. Combine the raw fruit, cranberry juice, sugar, and lemon juice in a large nonreactive pot. Bring to a boil, reduce the heat to low, and simmer until the fruit is tender, about 30 minutes.
2. In a food processor or blender, puree the fruit and juice until smooth. Strain, then chill. (Store in the refrigerator for up to 1 week.)

3. To serve: Pour about ⅔ cup soup into a shallow soup bowl. Arrange a poached pear in the center and sprinkle about 6 croutons around it. If desired, garnish with a mint sprig.

ANISE COOKIE CROUTONS *(Anise Lebkuchen)*
150 CROUTONS

3 cups all-purpose flour
½ teaspoon baking powder
½ teaspoon baking soda
¼ teaspoon salt
1 teaspoon ground cinnamon
1 teaspoon ground coriander
½ teaspoon ground cloves
¼ teaspoon grated nutmeg or mace
1 cup sugar
½ cup honey
2 large eggs, lightly beaten
½ teaspoon anise extract
1½ cups finely chopped almonds or hazelnuts (optional)

1. Sift together the flour, baking powder, baking soda, salt, and spices. In a small saucepan, stir the sugar and honey over low heat until the sugar dissolves. Let cool. Stir in the eggs, anise extract, and if desired, the nuts.
2. Beat the honey mixture into the flour mixture to make a stiff dough. Cover and refrigerate for at least 1 hour or overnight.
3. Preheat the oven to 325 degrees. Line 2 or 3 baking sheets with parchment paper or foil.
4. On a lightly floured surface, roll out the dough to a ¼-inch thickness. Cut the dough into 1-inch squares (about 150) or Stars of David. Place on the baking sheets.
5. Bake until the cookies are firm and lightly colored, about 25 minutes. Transfer to a wire rack and let cool completely.

An All-Dessert Bar or Bat Mitzvah

SERVES 50

$\mathcal{D}$essert is more than the last course of a meal; it is a passion. You can see it in the excitement and anticipation of people as they spy a dessert cart or pass a bakery window, a reaction that rarely fades with age. You can see it in the renewed interest of diners, even at the end of a large meal, when the dessert arrives at the table.

The custom among many Sephardim has been to celebrate a bar or bat mitzvah with a *meze allegre* (sweet table), a symbolic way of wishing a sweet life. Serving only desserts is an interesting and attractive way to entertain a large crowd. An all-dessert menu is perfect for parties that start rather late or at a time when the attendees may have already eaten a regular meal. (If you are planning a dairy affair, be sure to inform your guests on the invitations so that no one eats meat immediately beforehand.) An added advantage of serving desserts is that most of the dishes can be prepared well in advance, making setup a snap. Preparations before the event primarily consist of cutting up fresh fruit and last-minute assembling. And once the tables are set, you do not need much staff except to clear away dirty plates.

The key to an all-dessert affair is to offer a mix of sophisticated treats and comfort foods, a combination of flavors, textures, and colors. Remember that guests take smaller portions when there are many choices. Therefore, the larger the selection of treats, the less you will need of each dish. Ten different desserts are ample for a group of fifty, yet more is an allowable extravagance. Here is a sample menu, which you can supplement with other desserts from this book and some store-bought treats as well. Although most people will throw caution to the wind and enjoy themselves, be sure to have a fruit salad or some fresh fruit available for the inevitable calorie-conscious guest.

Nut Horns with Fresh Berries
Hungarian Seven-Layer Cake
Sachertorte
Strawberry-Rhubarb Pie
Berry Glacé Pie
Pear Frangipane Tart
Italian Rice Tart
Figs in Phyllo Purses
Russian Cheesecake
Moroccan Almond Coils
Lemon Mousse in a Chocolate Bowl or Cups
Chocolate-Dipped Strawberries
Applesauce Spice Cake (page 367)
Chocolate Mousse Cake (page 368)
Cookie Assortment (pages 346–362)
Cheese Assortment
Fresh Fruit Platter (page 217)
Cream Dip for Fruit

 Wine Suggestions: Asti Spumante, Champagne, late-harvest Riesling, or muscat

Nut Horns with Fresh Berries
ABOUT 12 COOKIES

⅓ cup all-purpose flour
¼ teaspoon salt
3 large egg whites
½ cup confectioners' sugar
3 tablespoons unsalted butter or margarine, melted
1 teaspoon vanilla extract
1 teaspoon brandy or anise extract (optional)
⅔ cup chopped almonds, hazelnuts, pecans, or pine nuts
About 2½ pounds (about 10 cups) assorted blackberries, blueberries, raspberries, and strawberries

1. Preheat the oven to 350 degrees. Grease and flour the back side of 2 or 3 baking sheets.
2. Sift together the flour and salt. Beat the egg whites until soft peaks form. Gradually add the sugar, beating until the whites are stiff and glossy. Fold in the flour mixture, butter, vanilla, and if desired, the brandy. Fold in the nuts.
3. Drop 1 tablespoon of the batter onto a prepared baking sheet and spread into a thin round about 6 inches in diameter. Repeat. (Since the cookies must be shaped while still warm, it is best to bake only 2 at a time.)
4. Bake until the cookies begin to brown around the edges, about 10 minutes.
5. Carefully remove the cookies with a metal spatula, roll into a horn (cone shape), and hold briefly until set. Place on a rack and let cool. (The horns can be stacked inside each other and stored in an airtight container at room temperature for up to 1 week or in the freezer for up to 1 month. Thaw in a covered container or they will become sticky.)
6. Arrange the horns on serving plates and fill with the berries, allowing some to spill out.

VARIATION

Dip the large end of each cookie into melted chocolate.

Hungarian Seven-Layer Cake (Dobostorte)
10 TO 12 SERVINGS

*H*ungary is justly renowned for its baked goods, and *dobostorte*, a seven-layer cake, is one of the best. It was probably inspired during the Ottoman occupation of the country, by Turkish layered pastries such as baklava. You can omit the traditional caramel topping and cover the top with buttercream instead.

CAKE LAYERS
1 cup (2 sticks) unsalted butter or margarine, softened
1 cup sugar
4 large eggs, lightly beaten
1 teaspoon vanilla extract
1½ cups all-purpose flour

CARAMEL GLAZE
1½ cups sugar
¾ cup water
½ teaspoon cream of tartar (optional)

1 recipe chocolate cooked buttercream (page 372)

1. Preheat the oven to 350 degrees. Grease the bottom of several 9-inch round cake pans and dust with flour, tapping out the excess.
2. To make the cake: Beat the butter until smooth, about 1 minute. Add the sugar and beat until light and fluffy, about 5 minutes. Beat in the eggs, one at a time. Add the vanilla. Stir in the flour.
3. Spread about 3 tablespoons of the batter evenly over the bottom of each prepared pan to a ⅛-inch thickness.
4. Bake until the edges of the cake are lightly browned, 7 to 9 minutes. Loosen with a spatula, invert onto a rack, and let cool.
5. Wipe the pans, regrease, flour, and repeat until there are 7 matching layers.
6. To make the caramel: Stir the sugar, water, and if desired, the cream of tartar in a small saucepan over low heat until the sugar dissolves. Stop stirring, increase the heat to medium, and cook, swirling the pan occasionally, until the syrup turns amber in color.

7. Using a lightly greased metal spatula, immediately spread the caramel evenly over one of the cake layers. Let set slightly, then use a greased knife to divide the caramel into 10 or 12 equal wedges indicating where the cake will be sliced. (The caramel will not cut after hardening.)

8. To assemble: Place a cake layer on a serving plate. Spread with a ⅛-inch-thick layer of the buttercream and top with a second cake layer. Repeat with the remaining buttercream and cake layers except the caramel-topped layer. Place the caramel-covered layer on top of the cake and cover the sides with buttercream. Store in the refrigerator for 1 day or in the freezer for several months. Using a very sharp, heavy knife, cut into wedges.

Sachertorte

10 TO 12 SERVINGS

*O*ne of the world's most famous cakes, Sachertorte was created by a Viennese baker named Eduard Sacher in 1832 while he was in the employ of Prince Metternich of Austria. It is traditional to write the word *Sacher* in a slanted script on top of the cake using melted chocolate piped from a parchment paper cone.

CAKE

14 tablespoons (1¾ sticks) unsalted butter or margarine, softened
¾ cup sugar
10 large eggs, separated
7 ounces semisweet chocolate, melted and cooled
1 teaspoon vanilla extract
1¼ cups all-purpose flour or 1½ cups sifted cake flour
½ cup zwieback, rusk, or other plain cookie crumbs
Pinch of salt

TOPPING

½ to 1 cup apricot jam, melted and strained
6 ounces semisweet chocolate, chopped

1. Preheat the oven to 350 degrees. Grease a 9-inch springform pan, line the bottom with wax paper, grease the paper, and dust with flour.
2. Beat the butter until smooth, about 1 minute. Gradually add the sugar and beat until light and fluffy, about 5 minutes. Add the egg yolks, one at a time, and beat until fluffy. Gradually beat in the chocolate and vanilla. Stir in the flour and crumbs.
3. Beat the egg whites on low speed until foamy, about 30 seconds. Add the salt, increase the speed to high, and beat until the whites are stiff but not dry. Fold ¼ of the egg whites into the chocolate mixture to lighten, then fold in the remaining whites.
4. Pour the batter into the prepared pan. Bake until the cake begins to pull away from the sides of the pan, about 1¼ hours. Let cool in the pan for 10 minutes, then remove to a rack and let cool completely.
5. If desired, cut the cake in half horizontally. Spread the center of the cake with ½ cup of the apricot jam and return the top layer.
6. Arrange 4 strips of wax paper on the outer edges of a flat serving plate and place the cake upside down in the center. Spread the top and sides evenly with ½ cup of the apricot jam and let set.
7. In the top of a double boiler over barely simmering water, melt the chocolate. Pour over the middle of the cake and, using a long, narrow metal spatula, spread the chocolate smoothly over the top and sides. Remove the strips of wax paper. If the glaze is dull, place the cake in a 325-degree oven for about 1 minute. Refrigerate until firm. Serve with sweetened whipped cream.

Strawberry-Rhubarb Pie

8 TO 10 SERVINGS

This is my favorite springtime pie. The tartness of the rhubarb perfectly complements the sweetness of the berries.

PÂTE BRISÉE (FLAKY PASTRY)
2 cups all-purpose flour
1 teaspoon salt
¾ cup vegetable shortening (or ½ cup shortening and ¼ cup chilled butter)
About ⅓ cup ice water

FILLING

About 1¼ cups sugar
¼ cup quick-cooking tapioca
¼ teaspoon salt
2 cups (1 pint) halved strawberries
About ½ pound fresh or frozen rhubarb, cut into ½-inch pieces (2 cups)
1 tablespoon unsalted butter or margarine

1. To make the pastry: Combine the flour and salt. Using the tips of your fingers, a pastry blender, or 2 knives in a scissors motion, cut in the shortening until the mixture resembles coarse crumbs. Sprinkle 1 tablespoon of the ice water over a section of the mixture. Gently mix in with a fork to moisten that section. Push the moistened dough aside and continue adding and mixing in the water in this fashion until the dough just holds together. Using your fingertips, lightly press and knead the dough into a ball. Do not overhandle. Cut off ⅓ of the dough and shape both pieces of dough into disks. Cover with plastic wrap and refrigerate for at least 30 minutes or up to 4 days.

2. Preheat the oven to 425 degrees.

3. On a lightly floured surface, roll out the larger piece of dough to a 12-inch round about ⅛ inch thick. Transfer to a 9-inch pie pan and trim the excess dough against the rim of the pan. Cover and refrigerate while preparing the filling.

4. To make the filling: Combine the sugar, tapioca, and salt. Stir in the strawberries and rhubarb and let stand for at least 15 minutes.

5. Spoon the filling into the crust and dot with the butter.

6. On a lightly floured surface, roll out the remaining dough to a 10-inch round. Cut into ½-inch-wide strips and weave into a lattice pattern over the top of the filling.

7. Bake for 20 minutes. Reduce the heat to 350 degrees and bake until the bubbles in the syrup do not burst and the pastry is golden brown, about 40 minutes. Let cool on a wire rack.

Berry Glacé Pie

8 TO 10 SERVINGS

*N*ot baking the filling is the secret of this fresh-tasting pie.

PASTRY

1⅓ cups all-purpose flour
1 tablespoon sugar
½ teaspoon salt
½ cup vegetable shortening (or 4 tablespoons shortening and 4 tablespoons chilled butter)
3 to 5 tablespoons ice water

BERRY LAYER

¾ to 1 cup sugar
3 tablespoons cornstarch or potato starch
2 teaspoons grated lemon zest
Pinch of salt
5 to 6 cups fresh blueberries, raspberries, or sliced strawberries
¾ cup cold water
3 tablespoons fresh lemon juice

OPTIONAL CHEESE LAYER

6 ounces cream cheese, at room temperature
¾ cup confectioners' sugar
1 teaspoon vanilla extract

1. To make the pastry: Combine the flour, sugar, and salt. Using the tips of your fingers, a pastry blender, or 2 knives in a scissors motion, cut in the shortening until the mixture resembles coarse crumbs. Sprinkle 1 tablespoon of the ice water over a section of the mixture. Gently mix in with a fork to moisten that section. Push the moistened dough aside and continue adding and mixing in the water in this fashion until the dough just holds together. Using your fingertips, lightly press and knead the dough into a ball. Do not overhandle. Cover with plastic wrap, flatten into a disk, and refrigerate for at least 30 minutes or up to 4 days.

2. To make the berry layer: Mix the sugar, cornstarch, lemon zest, and salt. In a medium saucepan, bring 2 cups of the berries and the water to a boil over medium heat. Stir in

the sugar mixture and lemon juice. Cook, stirring and mashing the berries with a spoon, until the mixture is thickened and clear, about 3 minutes. Pour into a bowl, press plastic wrap against the surface, and let cool. Stir in the remaining 3 to 4 cups berries.

3. On a lightly floured surface, roll out the dough to a ⅛-inch-thick round. Transfer to a 9-inch pie plate and trim the excess pastry slightly larger than the rim. Fold the edge of the pastry under to double the thickness and crimp or flute the edge. Cover with plastic wrap and refrigerate for at least 45 minutes or up to 4 days.

4. Preheat the oven to 425 degrees.

5. Prick the bottom and sides of the pie shell at ½-inch intervals with the tines of a fork. Line the bottom and sides with aluminum foil, shiny side down, or parchment paper and fill with pie weights or dried beans.

6. Bake until the pastry is set, about 10 minutes. Reduce the heat to 350 degrees and carefully remove the weights and foil. Bake until the pastry is golden brown, about 10 minutes. Let cool on a rack.

7. To make the cheese layer: Beat together the cream cheese, sugar, and vanilla until smooth. Spread evenly in the pie shell.

8. Spoon the berry mixture into the crust, mounding in the center. Refrigerate until set, at least 3 hours. Serve slightly chilled.

Pear Frangipane Tart

8 TO 10 SERVINGS

*F*rangipane is an almond paste named after an Italian who lived in Paris in the early 1600s. Made of equal weights of butter, sugar, and almonds, it is a delicious base for various fresh and cooked fruits.

PÂTE SABLÉE
¾ cup (1½ sticks) unsalted butter or margarine, softened
⅓ cup sugar
1 large egg or 2 large egg yolks
½ teaspoon salt
2 cups all-purpose flour
Ice water as needed

FILLING

½ cup (1 stick) unsalted butter or margarine, softened
½ cup sugar
2 large eggs or 3 large egg whites
4 ounces finely ground blanched almonds (about 1 cup)
3 tablespoons all-purpose flour
2 tablespoons brandy, kirsch, or dark rum
½ teaspoon almond extract
⅛ teaspoon salt
3 to 4 (about 2½ pounds) raw or poached pears, peeled, cored, and sliced
2 tablespoons chilled unsalted butter or margarine, cut into small pieces
⅓ cup apricot jam or currant jelly, melted

1. To make the pastry: Beat the butter and sugar until smooth and creamy. Add the egg and salt. Gradually blend in the flour. (The dough should have the consistency of a sugar cookie dough. If it is too stiff, add a little ice water.) Form the dough into a ball and flatten into a disk. Cover with plastic wrap and refrigerate for at least 1 hour or up to 1 week.

2. On a lightly floured piece of wax paper, roll out the dough to a ⅛-inch-thick round about 2 inches larger than a 10-inch tart pan. (The large amount of sugar makes the dough somewhat difficult to roll and move.)

3. Fit the dough into the tart pan and run a rolling pin over the top to trim the edges. Cover with plastic wrap and refrigerate for at least 1 hour. (The shell can be refrigerated for up to 4 days or frozen for up to 3 months.)

4. Preheat the oven to 375 degrees.

5. Line the bottom and sides of the shell with aluminum foil, shiny side down, and fill with pie weights or dried beans, pressing against the sides. Bake until the pastry is set, about 10 minutes. Remove the weights and foil and bake until the pastry is lightly browned, about 10 minutes. Let cool on a rack. (The tart shell can be prepared a day ahead, covered, and stored at room temperature.)

6. To make the frangipane: Beat the softened butter until smooth. Add the sugar and beat until creamy. Add the eggs, one at a time. Beat in the almonds, flour, brandy, almond extract, and salt (or process in a food processor to form a paste). Refrigerate for at least 15 minutes or up to 3 days.

7. Preheat the oven to 400 degrees.

8. Spread the frangipane over the tart shell. Arrange the pears in overlapping concentric circles on top of the filling, and dot with the butter. Bake until the filling is set and golden brown, about 25 minutes. Set on a rack and let cool. Brush with the melted preserves.

VARIATION

Berry Frangipane Tart: Omit the pears. After baking, arrange 3 to 4 cups (½ to 2 pints) fresh raspberries, blackberries, blueberries, or strawberries over the top.

Italian Rice Tart *(Crostata di Riso)*
8 TO 10 SERVINGS

PÂTE SABLÉE
5 tablespoons unsalted butter, softened
¼ cup sugar
2 large egg yolks or 3 tablespoons lightly beaten whole egg
¼ teaspoon salt
1¼ cups all-purpose flour
Ice water as needed

FILLING
3 cups milk
¼ cup Arborio or short-grain rice
½ cup granulated sugar
2 tablespoons unsalted butter
2 large eggs, lightly beaten
2 tablespoons golden raisins
1 teaspoon grated orange or lemon zest

1. To make the pastry: Beat the butter until smooth. Gradually add the sugar and beat smooth and creamy. Add the egg yolks and salt. Gradually blend in the flour. (The dough should have the consistency of a sugar cookie dough. If it is too stiff, add a little ice water.) Form the dough into a ball and flatten into a disk. Cover with plastic wrap and refrigerate for at least 1 hour or up to 1 week.
2. On a lightly floured surface, roll out the dough into a ⅛-inch-thick round. Line a 9-inch tart or flan pan with the dough and trim the edges. Prick the bottom and sides with the tines of a fork. Cover with plastic wrap and refrigerate for at least 1 hour. (The shell can be refrigerated for up to 4 days or frozen for up to 3 months.)

3. Preheat the oven to 350 degrees.
4. To make the filling: Bring the milk to a simmer. Add the rice, sugar, and butter and simmer, stirring occasionally, until the rice is tender, about 30 minutes. Pour into a bowl and let cool, stirring occasionally.
5. Stir the eggs, raisins, and zest into the rice mixture. Pour into the pastry shell. Bake until the top is golden brown and a knife inserted in the center comes out clean, about 45 minutes. Let cool on a rack.

Figs in Phyllo Purses
IO PURSES

You can also fill the phyllo with poached pears, sautéed apples, or pastry cream.

30 (5-inch-square) phyllo sheets
½ cup (1 stick) unsalted margarine, melted
10 medium fresh figs
About ½ cup Marzipan (page 309) (optional)
Confectioners' sugar

1. Preheat the oven to 375 degrees. Grease a baking sheet with margarine.
2. Place 1 sheet of phyllo on a flat surface and lightly brush with the melted margarine. Top with a second sheet, brush with the margarine, and top with a third sheet. Repeat with the remaining phyllo to make 10 stacks.
3. If desired, cut an X about ¾ of the way through each fig, spread out the sections, and spoon about 1 tablespoon marzipan into each fig.
4. Place a fig in the center of each phyllo stack. Gather the corners of the phyllo to the center and twist to enclose; be careful not to stretch the dough. Brush with the margarine.
5. Place the purses 1 inch apart on the prepared baking sheet. Bake until the purses are crisp and golden, 15 to 20 minutes. Sprinkle with confectioners' sugar and serve warm or at room temperature. (The purses can be stored in the refrigerator for 1 day.)

Russian Cheesecake
10 TO 12 SERVINGS

CRUST
1 cup all-purpose flour
3 tablespoons sugar
1 teaspoon finely grated lemon zest (optional)
¼ teaspoon salt
½ cup (1 stick) chilled unsalted butter or shortening
1 large egg yolk
½ teaspoon vanilla extract

FILLING
1½ pounds cream cheese, at room temperature
1½ cups sugar
2 cups sour cream
1 tablespoon fresh lemon juice
2 teaspoons vanilla extract
¼ teaspoon salt
4 large eggs
⅓ cup chopped dried apricots
⅓ cup chopped pitted dates
⅓ cup chopped pitted prunes or raisins
½ cup (2 ounces) coarsely chopped hazelnuts or walnuts (or ¼ cup each)

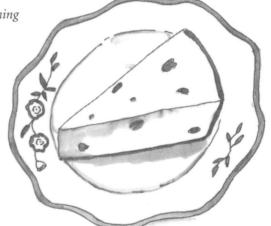

1. To make the crust: Combine the flour, sugar, zest if desired, and salt. Cut in the butter until the mixture resembles coarse crumbs. Stir in the egg yolk and vanilla. Knead the dough until it holds together. Cover with plastic wrap and chill for at least 30 minutes.
2. Preheat the oven to 375 degrees.
3. Press the crust into the bottom and up the sides of a 9-inch springform pan. Bake until it is pale golden, about 10 minutes. Let cool.
4. Preheat the oven to 350 degrees. Place a shallow pan of water on the bottom shelf.
5. To make the filling: Beat the cream cheese until smooth. Gradually beat in the sugar. Blend in the sour cream, lemon juice, vanilla, and salt. On low speed, beat in the eggs, one at a time. Add the dried fruit and nuts.

6. Pour the filling into the crust. Bake until the cheesecake is firm around the edges but still jiggles slightly in the center (it firms during cooling) and the top is lightly browned, about 1¼ hours. Do not test with a knife, which cracks the cake.

7. Turn off the oven, open the door, and let the cake cool in the oven for 30 minutes. Immediately move to the refrigerator and let cool uncovered. Cover with plastic wrap or an inverted bowl and chill overnight. Store in the refrigerator for up to 4 days or in the freezer for up to 2 months. Let stand at room temperature for at least 30 minutes before serving.

Moroccan Almond Coils *(Roses aux Amandes)*
ABOUT 4 DOZEN SMALL ROLLS

*M*oroccans serve these rich pastries, also called *rodanchas* (snails), on special occasions.

12 ounces (about 2¼ cups) blanched almonds
1 cup sugar
2 large eggs, lightly beaten
2 tablespoons rose water, orange blossom water, fresh lemon juice, or water
1 pound (about 24 sheets) phyllo dough
About ¾ pound (3 sticks) unsalted butter or margarine, melted
Confectioners' sugar

1. Preheat the oven to 375 degrees. Grease a large baking sheet.
2. In a food processor, finely grind the almonds with the sugar. Add the eggs and rose water and process until smooth.
3. Lay the stack of phyllo sheets on a flat surface and cut in half lengthwise. As you work, keep the unused phyllo covered with plastic wrap or a damp towel.
4. Place 1 phyllo strip on a flat surface with a narrow end facing you and lightly brush with the melted butter. Spread about 1 tablespoon of the filling across the strip about 1 inch from the end, leaving a 1-inch border on both long sides. Fold the bottom 1 inch of phyllo over the filling, then fold in the uncovered long sides. Roll up jelly-roll

style from the filling end. Holding the roll on both ends, gently push toward the center, creating an accordion effect. (This makes the roll more pliable.) Bend in one end of the roll and continue curling into a coil. (The rolls can be refrigerated at this point for up to 24 hours or frozen for up to 3 months. Do not thaw the frozen pastries; increase the baking time by about 10 minutes.)

5. Pack the coils together on the prepared baking sheet and brush with the butter. Bake until crisp and golden brown, about 30 minutes. Sprinkle with the confectioners' sugar. Serve warm or at room temperature.

Lemon Mousse in a Chocolate Bowl or Cups
ABOUT 6 CUPS

*Y*ou can substitute chocolate mousse (see Chocolate Mousse Cake, page 368) for the lemon mousse. Or put the chocolate mousse in white chocolate bowls.

4 large eggs, separated
½ cup fresh lemon juice (2 to 3 lemons)
1½ tablespoons grated lemon zest
¾ cup sugar
3 tablespoons water
Pinch of salt
1 cup heavy cream
Chocolate Bowls (recipe follows)

1. Lightly beat the egg yolks in a large saucepan. Stir in the lemon juice and zest. Bring to a low boil over medium heat and cook, stirring, for 3 minutes. Let cool.

2. In a small saucepan, stir the sugar and water over low heat until the sugar dissolves. Stop stirring and increase the heat to medium-high. Boil without stirring until the syrup reaches the hard-ball stage or registers 250 degrees on a candy thermometer, about 20 minutes.

3. About 3 minutes before the syrup is ready, beat the egg whites on low speed until foamy, about 30 seconds. Add the salt, increase the speed to high, and beat until soft peaks form.

4. In a slow, steady stream, beat the hot syrup into the egg whites. Continue beating until the whites are cool, stiff, and glossy, about 5 minutes. Fold into the lemon mixture.
5. In a chilled bowl using chilled beaters, beat the cream until soft peaks form. Fold the whipped cream into the lemon mixture. Store in the refrigerator or freezer. To serve, spoon into a chocolate bowl or cups.

CHOCOLATE BOWL

1 MEDIUM BOWL

*A*lmost any scratch-free utensil can be used as a mold for melted chocolate, including bowls, trays, cake pans, muffin tins, and cookie molds. Use chocolate bowls and cups for serving mousse, ice cream, sherbet, pudding, poached pears, chocolate-dipped fruit, cookies, and so on. Untempered chocolate bowls and cups soften as they stand at room temperature and can be eaten with the remains of the filling.

6 ounces semisweet, bittersweet, or white chocolate, chopped
About ¼ teaspoon vegetable oil or shortening

1. Remove the sides of a 9-inch springform pan. Line the sides and bottom of the pan with aluminum foil, then reattach the pieces.
2. In the top of a double boiler over barely simmering water, melt the chocolate and oil, stirring occasionally, until smooth. Or place the chocolate (omit the oil) in a microwave-safe bowl and microwave on medium (50 percent) for dark chocolate or medium-low (30 percent) for white chocolate for 1½ minutes; stir. Continue microwaving until the chocolate is melted and shiny, ½ to 1½ additional minutes. Stir until smooth.
3. Spread the chocolate over the bottom and sides of the prepared pan. Refrigerate until firm, at least 1 hour. Examine the chocolate to see if there are any holes or weak spots; if so, patch with a little melted chocolate and chill again.
4. Release the clasp on the pan and remove the sides and bottom. Carefully peel off the foil. If the bowl starts to break, patch the crack with a little melted chocolate and refrigerate until firm. Store in the freezer.

VARIATION

Chocolate Cups (about 8 cups): Starting from the top and using about 1 teaspoon chocolate at a time, spread the chocolate over the sides, then the bottom of paper cupcake liners (about 1 tablespoon chocolate for each liner). Place the liners in a muffin tin and refrigerate until firm, at least 30 minutes. Carefully peel off the paper and return the cups to the refrigerator.

Chocolate-Dipped Strawberries
ABOUT 24 LARGE STRAWBERRIES

*C*hocolate scorches easily, so it must be melted over low heat. The slightest bit of water will cause the chocolate to seize or clump. Therefore, do not cover when melting, or the condensation may get into the chocolate. A variety of foods, such as banana slices, dried fruits, nuts, cookies, potato chips, or pretzels, can be dipped into melted chocolate. Dry strawberries and other fruits well before dipping. For moist items such as kiwi slices, spoon a little chocolate over them, away from the bowl.

8 ounces semisweet chocolate
Several drops of vegetable oil
2 pints strawberries

1. In the top of a double boiler over barely simmering water, melt the chocolate with the oil, stirring until smooth. Or microwave the chocolate (omitting the oil) on medium (50 percent) until it turns shiny, 2 to 4 minutes, and stir until smooth.
2. Line a large baking sheet with wax paper. Holding the strawberries at the top, dip them into the chocolate and let the excess drip off. Place on the prepared sheet and refrigerate until set. When using fresh fruit, beads of moisture will appear on the chocolate after about 18 hours. Although they affect the appearance, they don't affect the taste.

Cream Dip for Fruit

ABOUT 4 CUPS

1 pound cream cheese, at room temperature
2 cups sour cream
⅔ cup confectioners' sugar
4 teaspoons orange liqueur

> Beat the cream cheese until smooth. Add the remaining ingredients and beat until smooth. Chill for at least 1 hour. Pour the dip into a serving bowl and let your guests dip strawberries and other fresh fruit into it.

An Engagement Cocktail Party

SERVES 50

A Jewish wedding is a two-part process. Before the twelfth century a Jewish couple was betrothed in a ceremony called *erusin* or *kiddushin.* Then, up to a year later, they were wed in a marriage ceremony called *nissuin* or chuppah. However, beginning in the twelfth century, the increasing insecurity of life in Europe all too frequently called for quick relocation, and so the waiting period was abolished and the two ceremonies were joined. This meant there was one banquet instead of two, no small matter in economically pressed times.

In conjunction with the betrothal, the family would agree on the financial conditions of the marriage. After the two parts of the wedding were combined, a separate ceremony called *tenaim shidukin* (conditions of engagement) was established for the families to announce the engagement and agree on their legally binding financial obligations. The terms in the *tenaim,* set in writing and enforced through various edicts and bans, included the date and place of the wedding, the dowry, and inheritance rights.

Today financial stipulations are meaningless to most couples, and so the *tenaim* is generally either ignored or, out of a sense of tradition, signed at the wedding at the *hatan's tish* (groom's table). After the document is signed, the mothers of the bride and groom break a plate (usually safely enclosed in a napkin), reflecting the severity of breaking this legal document as well as the remembrance, even in a moment of joy, of the destruction of the Temple. The pieces, considered lucky, are customarily distributed to unmarried friends.

An increasingly popular custom in certain religious circles of the Ashkenazic community is to officially announce an engagement at a *vort* (verbal agreement). Both families gather to meet each other, listen to friends describe the qualities of the bride and groom, and eat. Sometimes, as for a *tenaim,* the mothers break a plate.

When a Syrian couple decides to wed, the relatives of both families gather for a "coming together party," commonly referred to as a *kinyan* (Hebrew for "acquisition") or *bozra* (Arabic for "negotiating session"). Originally this meeting provided an opportunity for the two families to agree on the financial terms of the union and for the rabbi to legalize it by enacting the *tenaim* between the fathers. Today the couple generally uses the occasion to make the engagement official. Although usually held in a home, sometimes the event is transferred to a hall because the guest list is extensive. The bride's family customarily prepares an elaborate repast for the occasion. Guests send white flowers for decorations, and the crowd is entertained with a *nobeh* (special musical presentation) played on traditional Middle Eastern instruments, including a *qanoon* (zither), *oud* (lute), and *dirbakkeh* (small drum).

Sephardim from the Balkans and Turkey have a similar but less elaborate ceremony, sometimes called *espoziria* (engagement), for the families to meet and agree on financial terms. The hosts customarily offer an extensive assortment of treats, including a *tavla de dulces* (tray of sweets) featuring a large assortment of confections, *dulce de kumquat* (preserved whole kumquats), and various fruit preserves served in glass bowls. Also on the ornate tray are silver teaspoons and glasses of water. A guest samples a spoonful of *dulce,* then deposits the spoon in a glass of water. Turkish coffee accompanies the *dulces.*

The announcement of an engagement is commonly accompanied by a party. I have catered engagement parties for both friends and clients and find that a cocktail party makes an easy way to serve the large number of guests at these affairs.

SPICED ALMONDS
GRAPE NUGGETS
VEGETABLE CHIPS
BLUE CHEESE–WALNUT CRACKERS
BLINIS WITH SMOKED TROUT
CUCUMBER CUPS WITH HORSERADISH CHEESE
CHERRY TOMATOES STUFFED WITH SALMON MOUSSE
MINIATURE BEAN KNISHES
NEW POTATOES WITH CAVIAR
SAVORY CHEESECAKE
PEPPER SLICES WITH TAPENADE
STUFFED MUSHROOMS
BROCCOLI AND CHEESE STRUDEL
CRUDITÉS AND DIPS (PAGE 211)

 Wine and Liquor Suggestions: Chardonnay, Chablis, Soave, or Pinot Noir; vodka and scotch

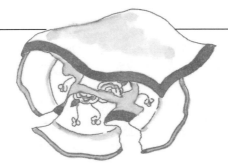

Spiced Almonds

4 CUPS

¼ cup vegetable oil
¼ cup honey
2 teaspoons ground cinnamon
½ teaspoon ground allspice
½ teaspoon ground mace or nutmeg
4 cups (20 ounces) almonds
Salt to taste (optional)

1. Preheat the oven to 300 degrees.
2. Combine the oil, honey, and spices. Add the almonds and toss to coat. Spread in a single layer on a baking sheet.
3. Roast, stirring occasionally, until the almonds are golden and crisp, about 15 minutes. If desired, sprinkle with salt. Serve warm or at room temperature. (The almonds can be stored in an airtight container at room temperature for up to 1 week.)

VARIATION

Omit the spices and add 2 tablespoons chopped fresh rosemary, 2 teaspoons kosher salt, and ½ teaspoon cayenne pepper.

ALMONDS

In Jewish tradition almonds, which come in both bitter and sweet varieties, are a metaphor for marriage, depending on the interdynamics of the couple's relationship. In addition, Ecclesiastes uses the almond, one of only two nuts (the other is pistachios) specifically mentioned in the Bible, as a symbol of human life (12:5). And the numerical value of the Hebrew word for "nut," *egoz*, is seventeen, the same value as *tov* (good). Therefore almonds are ubiquitous in the various Jewish engagement and wedding rites.

Grape Nuggets
ABOUT 50 HORS D'OEUVRES

8 ounces cream cheese, at room temperature
4 ounces blue cheese or about 1 tablespoon curry powder (optional)
About 3 tablespoons sour cream or plain yogurt
Salt to taste
1 pound seedless grapes, removed from the stem
8 ounces almonds, hazelnuts, pecans, pistachios, or walnuts, coarsely chopped

1. Beat the cream cheese and, if desired, the blue cheese or curry powder, or process in a food processor until smooth. Add the sour cream and salt and beat to produce a spreading consistency.
2. Roll individual grapes in the cheese mixture, then in the nuts to coat. Place on a baking sheet lined with wax paper and chill until firm, at least 3 hours. If desired, arrange and stack the nuggets on a serving platter to resemble a bunch of grapes.

Vegetable Chips
ABOUT 6 CUPS

*F*or variety and color, use several types of vegetables.

1 pound (3 medium) baking potatoes or sweet potatoes, thinly sliced
Vegetable oil for deep-frying
Salt to taste

1. Soak the potato slices in cold water for 1 to 2 hours.
2. Heat at least 1 inch of oil to 375 degrees.
3. Drain the potato slices and pat dry. In batches, deep-fry until golden brown on both sides, about 1 minute. Drain on paper towels. Sprinkle with the salt.

VARIATIONS

Beet Chips: Substitute 6 peeled and thinly sliced medium beets for the potatoes, but do not soak. Instead, dust lightly with cornstarch or flour.

Carrot Chips: Substitute 4 thinly sliced (on the diagonal) large carrots for the potatoes, but do not soak.

Celeriac Chips: Substitute 1 peeled and sliced medium celeriac (celery root) for the potatoes and add a little lemon juice to the soaking water.

Parsnip Chips: Substitute 10 medium sliced parsnips for the potatoes, but do not soak.

Rutabaga Chips: Substitute 1 peeled and sliced medium rutabaga for the potatoes.

Sunchoke Chips: Substitute 5 to 6 thinly sliced sunchokes (Jerusalem artichokes) for the potatoes.

Blue Cheese-Walnut Crackers
ABOUT 48 CRACKERS

8 ounces blue cheese, crumbled, at room temperature (about 2 cups)
1¼ cups all-purpose flour
1 cup (4 ounces) chopped walnuts
½ cup (1 stick) unsalted butter, softened
2 large egg yolks
2 to 3 teaspoons ground black pepper

1. In a food processor, process all the ingredients until the dough forms a ball. Divide the mixture in half, wrap each half tightly in wax paper or plastic wrap, and shape into a roll. Refrigerate until firm, at least 3 hours or up to 1 week.
2. Preheat the oven to 400 degrees.
3. Slice the cheese rolls into ¼-inch-thick rounds. Place on an ungreased baking sheet, leaving 1 inch between rounds. Bake until golden, about 10 minutes. Transfer to a rack and let cool. (The crackers can be stored in an airtight container at room temperature for up to 1 week.)

VARIATION

Parmesan-Walnut Crackers: Substitute 4 ounces grated Parmesan cheese for the blue cheese, reduce the walnuts to ½ cup, and add 2 tablespoons milk.

Blinis with Smoked Trout
ABOUT 50 SMALL PANCAKES

½ cup buckwheat flour
½ cup all-purpose flour
1 teaspoon sugar
1 teaspoon baking powder
¼ teaspoon salt
½ teaspoon ground black pepper (optional)
1 large egg, lightly beaten
1 tablespoon unsalted butter or margarine, melted
About ¾ cup milk or water
8 ounces sour cream
About 1 pound smoked trout, cut into small slices

1. Combine the flours, sugar, baking powder, salt, and if desired, the pepper. Stir in the egg. Add the butter and enough milk to make a smooth batter. Place in the refrigerator and let stand for at least 2 hours or overnight.

2. Heat a large griddle or skillet over medium heat until a few drops of water sprinkled on the surface scatter and evaporate. Lightly grease.

3. Drop the batter by teaspoonfuls onto the griddle and fry until bubbles appear on the top, about 2 minutes. Turn and cook until golden brown, about 1 minute. (At this point, the blinis can be cooled, wrapped in foil, and refrigerated. Reheat in a 350-degree oven.)

4. Top each blini with a dollop of sour cream and a slice of trout.

Cucumber Cups with Horseradish Cheese
30 CUCUMBER CUPS

*C*ucumber cups and boats provide an attractive way to present fillings, whether plain or fancy, including cheese spreads, fish salad, or egg salad. A bitter oil frequently accumulates near the ends of a cucumber, and when you peel it, the bitterness can spread. Therefore you should always cut off the ends of a cucumber before peeling.

Cheese spreads are an incredibly versatile item for entertaining. Serve them with vegetables; spread on crackers and bread for canapés; or stuff into hard-boiled eggs, mushroom caps, celery sticks, or hollowed-out cherry tomatoes or radishes. To make a dip, increase the sour cream or yogurt to about 1 cup.

CUCUMBER CUPS
3 medium cucumbers, peeled
Salt for sprinkling
Parsley sprigs, salmon or whitefish caviar, hot pepper jelly,
*   or coarsely chopped smoked salmon*

HORSERADISH CHEESE
8 ounces cream cheese, at room temperature
About 3 tablespoons sour cream or plain yogurt
4 teaspoons horseradish
1 teaspoon minced onion
About ¼ teaspoon salt

1. To make the cucumber cups: Cut the cucumbers crosswise into ½-inch-thick slices. Scoop out the centers with a melon baller, leaving a little of the bottom intact. Sprinkle lightly with salt, invert over paper towels, and let drain for about 1 hour. Rinse and pat dry.
2. To make the horseradish cheese: Beat the cream cheese or process in a food processor until smooth. Add the sour cream and beat to produce a spreading consistency. Stir in the horseradish, onion, and salt. Cover and refrigerate overnight or up to 1 week. Let stand at room temperature at least 30 minutes before serving.
3. Pipe the horseradish cheese from a pastry bag or spoon into the cups, mounding slightly. Chill for up to 4 hours. Top each cup with a sprig of parsley, dab of caviar, dab of jelly, or piece of smoked salmon.

FILLING VARIATIONS

Herb Cheese Filling: Omit the horseradish. Add 3 tablespoons chopped fresh basil, chives, cilantro, dill, oregano, or tarragon and about ¼ teaspoon red pepper sauce or lemon juice.

Blue Cheese Filling: Omit the horseradish. Add 4 to 8 ounces blue cheese.

Curry Cheese Filling: Substitute 1 to 2 tablespoons curry powder for the horseradish.

Smoked Salmon Filling: Omit the horseradish. Add 2 to 3 ounces pureed smoked salmon.

VEGETABLE VARIATIONS

Cucumber Boats: Cut the cucumbers in half lengthwise and scoop out the seeds. Fill with the cheese spread and cut into ¾-inch-thick slices. Makes about 36 hors d'oeuvres.

Endives with Herb Cheese: Separate the leaves of 3 heads of Belgian endive. Spread about 1 teaspoon of the cheese mixture on the wide side of each leaf. Garnish with a watercress leaf or dollop of chopped tomatoes. Arrange on a serving platter. Makes about 40 hors d'oeuvres.

Stuffed Snow Peas: Remove the stems from 12 ounces of snow peas and pull to remove the strings. Blanch the snow peas in a large pot of boiling water for 30 seconds, then drain and plunge into cold water to stop the cooking. Using a small sharp knife, cut along the straight edge of the snow peas to open the pods. Spoon the cream cheese mixture into a pastry bag and pipe into each pod. Makes about 24 hors d'oeuvres.

Cherry Tomatoes Stuffed with Salmon Mousse

24 HORS D'OEUVRES

*A*lthough most cherry tomatoes are red, golden cherry tomatoes are sometimes available and make an interesting contrast to the red ones. Besides salmon mousse, you can fill the cherry tomatoes with tapenade (page 298), avocado mousse (page 211), eggplant puree, or any variation of cream cheese filling (pages 292–293). The salmon mousse is also great by itself.

16 ounces canned salmon, drained, or 8 ounces smoked salmon
½ cup mayonnaise or 12 ounces cream cheese, at room temperature
2 teaspoons fresh lemon juice
2 teaspoons chopped fresh dill or ¾ teaspoon dried (optional)
½ teaspoon paprika
½ teaspoon red pepper sauce
½ teaspoon salt
1 cup heavy cream, whipped, or 1 cup sour cream
24 (about 1 pint) cherry tomatoes

1. In a food processor or blender, puree the salmon, mayonnaise, lemon juice, dill, paprika, red pepper sauce, and salt until smooth. Fold in the whipped cream, cover, and refrigerate for at least 2 hours or up to 1 day.
2. Slice the tops off the tomatoes and remove the seeds. Invert over paper towels to drain.
3. No more than an hour before serving, stuff each tomato with the salmon mixture. (A pastry bag makes this easier.) Serve at room temperature.

Miniature Bean Knishes

ABOUT 36 SMALL PASTRIES

The idea for this recipe originated with a dish prepared by my editor's grandmother—Rebbitzen Miriam Bayla Kaganoff. You can substitute Romanian Garlic Mashed Potatoes (page 337), Mock Chopped Liver (page 52), or 2 cups of your favorite filling for the bean mixture.

PASTRY

2½ cups all-purpose flour
¾ teaspoon sugar
¾ teaspoon salt
¾ cup vegetable shortening
About 7 tablespoons ice water

FILLING

2 tablespoons vegetable oil
1 medium onion, chopped (about ½ cup)
2 cups mashed cooked kidney or other red beans
⅓ cup chopped fresh cilantro or parsley or ⅛ teaspoon red pepper flakes
Salt to taste
Ground black pepper to taste
Egg wash (1 large egg beaten with 1 tablespoon water)

1. To make the pastry: Combine the flour, sugar, and salt. Using the tips of your fingers, a pastry blender, or 2 knives in a scissors motion, cut in the shortening until the mixture resembles coarse crumbs. Sprinkle 1 tablespoon of the water over a section of the mixture. Gently mix in with a fork to moisten that section. Push the moistened dough aside and continue adding and mixing in the water in this fashion until the dough just holds together. Lightly press and knead the dough into a ball. Do not overhandle. Form into a ball, wrap in plastic, and refrigerate for at least 1 hour or up to 2 days.
2. To make the filling: Heat the oil in a large skillet over medium heat. Add the onion and sauté until soft and translucent, 5 to 10 minutes. Add the beans and cook, stirring frequently, until dry, 5 to 10 minutes. Remove from the heat and add the cilantro, salt, and pepper. Let cool.

3. On a lightly floured surface, roll out the dough ⅛ inch thick. Cut into 3-inch rounds. Place a scant tablespoon of the filling in the center of each round and draw the edges together, pinching to close. Refrigerate for at least 40 minutes or overnight.
4. Preheat the oven to 375 degrees. Lightly grease a large baking sheet.
5. Place the knishes, seam side down, on the prepared sheet and brush with the egg wash. Bake until lightly browned, about 20 minutes. Serve warm or at room temperature.

New Potatoes with Caviar
24 APPETIZERS

24 (about 2 pounds total) small new potatoes, unpeeled
Vegetable oil for deep-frying (optional)
½ cup sour cream or crème fraîche
3 ounces whitefish or salmon caviar

1. Cook the potatoes in boiling water or bake in a shallow baking dish at 450 degrees until tender, about 30 minutes.
2. Cut a slice off the top of the potatoes. Using a melon baller or small spoon, scoop out most of the pulp, leaving a shell. For a crisper potato, heat at least 2 inches vegetable oil to 375 degrees and fry the potato shells in batches until golden and crisp. Remove with a slotted spoon and drain on paper towels.
3. Mash the pulp. Fill the shells with the mashed pulp. Top with a dab of sour cream and caviar.

VARIATION
Substitute miniature Potato Latkes (page 94) for the new potatoes.

Savory Cheesecake
24 SERVINGS

This dish could also serve as a flavorful main course for a dairy meal.

CRUST
1¼ cups ground whole-wheat crackers or matza meal
3 tablespoons unsalted butter, melted

FILLING
28 ounces cream cheese, at room temperature
4 large eggs
¼ cup heavy cream or half-and-half
½ cup chopped scallions
¼ cup minced fresh parsley
1 clove garlic, mashed
1 tablespoon fresh lemon or lime juice
1 cup sour cream (optional)
Sliced or chopped vegetables (optional)

1. Preheat the oven to 350 degrees.
2. To make the crust: Mix together the crumbs and butter. Press into the bottom of a 9- or 10-inch springform pan. Bake until lightly browned, 8 to 10 minutes. Let cool.
3. To make the filling: Beat the cream cheese until smooth. Beat in the eggs, one at a time. Blend in the cream, scallions, parsley, garlic, and lemon juice.
4. Pour the filling into the crust. Bake until a knife inserted in the center comes out clean, about 1¼ hours. Turn off the heat and let the cheesecake cool in the oven with the door slightly ajar for 30 minutes. Remove from the oven and let cool completely.
5. Remove the sides from the pan. If desired, spread with the sour cream and garnish with colorful vegetables. Store in the refrigerator and return to room temperature before serving. Cut into 24 small wedges.

VARIATIONS

Mini Cheesecakes (about 36 mini tarts): Press the crust mixture into the bottom of 36 mini (1½-inch) muffin cups, add the filling, and bake until firm, about 10 minutes.

Italian Savory Cheesecake: Add ¼ cup grated Parmesan cheese to the crust and add ¾ cup grated Parmesan cheese, 1 teaspoon dried basil, and ½ teaspoon dried oregano to the filling.

Smoked Salmon Cheesecake: Add ½ pound chopped smoked salmon, ½ cup (about 2 ounces) grated Gruyère or Swiss cheese, and 3 tablespoons grated Parmesan cheese to the filling.

Pepper Slices with Tapenade
24 HORS D'OEUVRES

*T*apenade is a Provençal paste made from olives, anchovies, and capers. Although in this recipe the tapenade is cooked, you could also spread fresh tapenade on *crostini* (small toasts), stuff into hard-boiled eggs or cherry tomatoes, use as a dip for crudités, bread, and crackers, or serve with broiled or grilled fish.

1 large (about 7 ounces) green bell pepper
1 large (about 7 ounces) red bell pepper
1 large (about 7 ounces) yellow bell pepper

TAPENADE
1 pound plum tomatoes, peeled, seeded, and chopped (about 2 cups)
10 to 12 brine-cured black olives, pitted and chopped
¼ cup chopped fresh parsley
3 tablespoons capers, drained and chopped
4 anchovy fillets, chopped
2 to 3 cloves garlic, minced
1½ tablespoons extra-virgin olive oil
½ teaspoon ground black pepper

2 tablespoons extra-virgin olive oil

1. Preheat the oven to 375 degrees. Lightly grease a large baking dish.
2. Cut the peppers in half lengthwise. Remove the seeds and stems. Cut each half into 4 triangles or slices.
3. To make the tapenade: Combine all the tapenade ingredients.
4. Place a heaping teaspoon of the tapenade on each pepper slice. Place in the prepared baking dish and cover with aluminum foil. Bake for 15 minutes. Remove the foil and bake until the peppers are tender but not limp, about 10 minutes. Let cool, then drizzle with the olive oil. (The pepper slices can be stored in the refrigerator for up to 2 days.) Serve at room temperature.

Stuffed Mushrooms

ABOUT 24 HORS D'OEUVRES

*M*ushroom caps are a popular and versatile base for hors d'oeuvres.

1 pound (about 24) large mushrooms
3 tablespoons unsalted butter or margarine
1 medium onion, minced (about ½ cup)
1 clove garlic, crushed
2 tablespoons chopped fresh parsley
1 tablespoon chopped fresh thyme or 1 teaspoon dried
Pinch of grated nutmeg
About ½ teaspoon salt
¼ teaspoon ground black pepper
¼ to ½ cup soft bread crumbs (optional)
¼ cup (½ stick) unsalted butter or margarine, melted

1. Preheat the oven to 350 degrees. Grease a large baking dish.
2. Wipe the mushrooms with a damp cloth or paper towel. Remove the stems from the caps and finely chop the stems.
3. Melt the butter in a large skillet over medium heat. Add the onion and garlic and sauté until soft and translucent, 5 to 10 minutes.

4. Add the chopped mushroom stems and sauté until the liquid evaporates, about 5 minutes. Stir in the parsley, thyme, nutmeg, salt, and pepper. If desired, add the bread crumbs.

5. Stuff the mushroom caps with the mushroom stem mixture. (The stuffed mushrooms can be stored in the refrigerator for 1 day.) Place in the prepared baking dish and drizzle with the melted butter.

6. Bake until browned, about 15 minutes. Serve warm.

Broccoli and Cheese Strudel
ABOUT TWENTY 1-INCH SLICES

2 (10-ounce) boxes frozen chopped broccoli, thawed and drained
8 ounces Cheddar or Swiss cheese, shredded (2 cups)
8 (20- by 12-inch) phyllo sheets
About 6 tablespoons unsalted butter or margarine, melted

1. Preheat the oven to 375 degrees. Grease a large baking sheet.

2. Combine the broccoli and cheese. Place a sheet of phyllo on a flat surface, brush with the melted butter, and top with a second sheet. Repeat layering with 2 more sheets (for a total of 4 sheets).

3. On the 12-inch side of the rectangle, evenly spread half of the broccoli-cheese mixture into a 3- by 10-inch rectangle, leaving a 1-inch border on each side. Fold over the uncovered sides, then roll up jelly-roll style from the broccoli-cheese end. Repeat with the remaining ingredients.

4. Place the strudels on the prepared baking sheet and brush with the butter. Bake until golden brown, about 30 minutes. (The strudel can be cooled, wrapped in foil, and stored in the refrigerator for 1 day or in the freezer for up to 3 months. Reheat in a 350-degree oven for about 10 minutes. Do not thaw frozen strudel; increase the baking time by about 10 minutes.) Let cool for 10 minutes; then, using a serrated knife, cut into 1-inch slices.

SPINNHOLZ

In parts of central Europe, the parents of the bride held a party shortly before the wedding to exchange gifts. The groom sent a girdle, along with other gifts. In turn, the bride sent a *tallit* (prayer shawl), one made with her own hands if possible. During the Middle Ages, Ashkenazim held this reception, called a Spinnholz (from the Latin for "pledges" or a German word for part of a spinning wheel), in the house of the bride's parents, sometimes on the Sabbath corresponding to the groom's *aufruf* (see page 314). The parents entertained family and friends while displaying the bride's trousseau.

A Middle Eastern Wedding Shower

SERVES 12

A bride traditionally immerses herself in a *mikveh* (ritual bath) shortly before her wedding, and to celebrate this occasion, many Sephardic communities hold special parties. (Many Ashkenazim, on the other hand, consider *mikveh* an extremely private matter.) In some areas this event is linked to the henna ceremony (see next page). Although these various prenuptial gatherings for the bride were once generally all-female affairs, today they frequently include both men and women.

In the afternoon anytime up to three days before the wedding, Syrians perform one of their most beloved premarital customs, the *swanne/swehnie* (Arabic for "trays") or *hamman-il-aros* (Arabic for "the bride's bath"). The groom sends his bride-to-be three trays; one is covered with perfumes, soaps, robes, jewelry, candlesticks, and other items for the bride to use at the *mikveh* and to adorn herself. The guests place their presents on another tray. An elaborate luncheon is served that includes pastries, confections, and *sharbat el loz* (almond drink) accompanied by much singing and dancing. Later the mothers and a few close friends accompany the bride to the *mikveh*. After emerging from the *mikveh,* the bride is presented with a silver tray bearing *lebas* (Jordan almonds), *ka'ak ib loz* (a special pistachio confection), marzipan, and coffee surrounded by flowers.

Similarly, in the Balkans and Turkey, the day before the wedding is called El Día de Baño/Banio (Day of the Bath). The mother of the groom throws a party for female relatives and friends called *bogo de baño* (bag for the bath). The celebrants bring gifts of soaps, perfumes, lingerie, and other items appropriate for a new bride. After the bride emerges from the *mikveh*, the mother of the bride holds a smaller party called *café de baño* (coffee of the bath), featuring fancy pastries and coffee. The groom frequently has his own party, called *salidura de boda.*

SEEING RED: HENNA CEREMONIES

My beloved is unto me as a cluster of henna
in the vineyards of Ein-Gedi.—SONG OF SONGS 1:14

Henna (*hinna* in Arabic), a reddish orange dye made from the leaves and roots of a Middle Eastern shrub, is best known in the West as a hair coloring. In parts of the Middle East, however, it has long played a central role in prenuptial ceremonies. Syrians once performed this custom at the *swanne* or added a little henna to the *mikveh* water, but this is rarely done in their community today. Among Moroccans and Yemenites, however, the henna ceremony remains a much-beloved ritual.

It was customarily observed on the night before the wedding, after the bride immersed in the *mikveh,* and was once reserved exclusively for women, although a rabbi frequently stopped by to offer a blessing. Men usually had their own party with the groom. Today the henna ceremony is commonly held about a week before the wedding with both the bride and the groom in attendance.

Moroccans call this occasion Noche de Novia (Night of the New Bride) or Canta de Novia (Chant of the New Bride). Brides from the northern part of the country wear an elaborate dress and head covering called *traje de barbarisco* (robe of the Berbers). This burgundy-colored velvet dress is embroidered with gold and silver threads, symbolizing wealth and happiness. The groom dons a *jalabia* (a white caftan), a black robe with gold embroidery, and a red turban. A five-fingered "hand" is commonly hung around the bride's neck to repulse the evil eye. The bride and groom are led to a place of honor where they exchange jewelry, replacing the custom of the bride's father giving a dowry. Fresh mint, a symbol of luck, is placed on a silver tray; the herb is later used to make tea.

The Yemenite henna ceremony is even more elaborate than those in North Africa. The bride dons a colorful dress and layers of gold and silver jewelry. Of special importance is a jewel-encrusted headdress that can weigh as much as 5 kilograms. The towering headdress is topped with alternating red and white carnations. To one side is hung sweet basil, symbolizing a life of joy, and on the other side is rue, a malodorous plant used to ward off the evil eye. The women carry lit candles, reflecting the light that will soon fill the couple's life together, and baskets containing eggs (wishing for fertility) and flowers (symbolizing a life of beauty).

The henna is spread over the bride's outstretched palms and, in Yemen, the feet as well. It leaves a reddish stain that lasts for about a month and represents the happiness and blessings that will remain with the couple for a lifetime; it also wards off the evil eye. After the ceremony the guests feast on various sweets and other rich foods and partake in dancing, singing, and ululations.

ALMOND SYRUP
PHYLLO CIGARS
OPEN-FACED TEA SANDWICHES WITH EDIBLE FLOWERS
FIVE-FINGERED HAND COOKIES
MARZIPAN
TURKISH DELIGHT
CANDIED ORANGE PEEL
MIDDLE EASTERN APRICOT ROLLS
JORDAN ALMONDS
MINT TEA, SPICED TEA, AND TURKISH COFFEE

Almond Syrup (*Sharbat el Loz*)

ABOUT 1 QUART

*T*his delicate drink is also served at the meal following the fast of Yom Kippur.

4 cups (20 ounces) whole almonds
4½ cups water
8 cups sugar
1 teaspoon almond extract
3 to 6 teaspoons rose water (optional)
Ice water or club soda

1. Bring a large pot of water to a boil, add the almonds, return to a boil, and let boil for several minutes. Remove the almonds and rub off the skins. Spread in a single layer on paper towels and let dry overnight. (You can buy ground blanched almonds for this recipe, but use only freshly ground nuts.)
2. In a food processor or blender, finely grind the almonds. Add the water and blend well. (You might have to do this in several batches.)
3. Pour into a large saucepan and add the sugar. Bring to a boil and cook until the sugar dissolves, about 5 minutes. Remove from the heat and add the almond extract and, if desired, the rose water. Let cool overnight.
4. Strain through cheesecloth and pour into sterilized jars. Store in the refrigerator.
5. To serve, combine about 1 part almond syrup with 2 parts ice water or club soda in a tall glass.

Phyllo Cigars *(Briates/Sigares)*
ABOUT 48 SMALL ROLLS

*A*djust the types and proportions of cheese in the filling according to your taste and what is in your refrigerator. Or substitute 3 cups spinach filling (see Middle Eastern Phyllo Triangles, page 198) or Mock Chopped Liver (page 52) for the cheese filling.

FILLING
2 cups mashed potatoes
8 ounces (1 cup) farmer, pot, or ricotta cheese
8 ounces (about 1½ cups) feta cheese or 8 ounces (2 cups) grated hard cheese,
*   such as kashkavel, Cheddar, Gouda, Monterey Jack, or Muenster*
4 large eggs
About ½ teaspoon salt
¼ cup chopped fresh dill, mint, or parsley, or 1 teaspoon grated nutmeg,
*   or ⅛ teaspoon ground black pepper (optional)*

1 pound (about 24 sheets) phyllo dough
About ¾ pound (3 sticks) unsalted butter or margarine, melted

1. Preheat the oven to 375 degrees. Grease a large baking sheet.
2. To make the filling: Combine all the filling ingredients.
3. Lay the stack of phyllo sheets on a flat surface and cut in half lengthwise. As you work, keep the unused phyllo covered with plastic wrap or a damp towel.
4. To assemble: Place 1 phyllo strip on a flat surface with a narrow end facing you and lightly brush with the melted butter. Spread about 1 tablespoon of the filling across the strip about 1 inch from the end, leaving a 1-inch border on both long sides. Fold the bottom 1 inch of phyllo over the filling, then fold in the uncovered long sides. Roll up jelly-roll style from the filling end. (The rolls can be refrigerated for up to 1 day or frozen for up to 3 months. Do not thaw the frozen pastries; increase the baking time by about 10 minutes.)
5. Place the rolls, seam side down, on the prepared baking sheet and brush with the butter. Bake until crisp and golden brown, about 20 minutes. Serve warm or at room temperature.

Open-Faced Tea Sandwiches with Edible Flowers
3 DOZEN SMALL SANDWICHES

*A*lthough some people hesitate to eat flowers, most readily eat broccoli, which is a cluster of immature flower buds. Not all flowers are edible, so consult an up-to-date guide. Strong-flavored flowers such as nasturtium, mustard green flower, fuchsia, and pink burnet add zest to salads and savory dishes. Mild-flavored blossoms such as violet, pansy, and marigold provide a pretty garnish without adding much flavor. Fragrant flowers such as rose, violet, lavender, lilac, mimosa, jasmine, honeysuckle, and plum blossom add a special touch to desserts. Other edible flowers include bergamot, borage, English daisy, day lily, forget-me-not, geranium, hollyhock, impatiens, and snapdragon. Since flowers may contain pesticides, it is best to get them from your own garden or a re- liable greengrocer—never from a florist.

OLIVE SPREAD
4 ounces (½ cup) cream cheese, at room temperature
2 tablespoons plain yogurt or milk
⅓ cup finely chopped green or black olives
⅓ cup finely chopped almonds, pecans, or walnuts (optional)

FETA SPREAD
3 ounces cream cheese, at room temperature
2 ounces (about ⅓ cup) feta cheese, at room temperature
2 tablespoons mayonnaise or plain yogurt
1 small clove garlic, crushed
⅛ teaspoon dried basil
⅛ teaspoon dried dill
⅛ teaspoon dried marjoram
⅛ teaspoon dried thyme

12 slices sandwich bread, crusts trimmed
Edible flowers, such as violets, pansies, and marigolds

1. To make the olive spread: Combine all the ingredients.
2. To make the feta spread: Combine all the ingredients.
3. Spread 6 of the bread slices with the olive spread and spread the remaining slices with the feta mixture. Cut each slice into thirds. Garnish with the edible flowers.

Five-Fingered Hand Cookies
ABOUT 12 LARGE COOKIES

*I*n North Africa the use of amulets in the shape of a hand dates back to at least the time of the Phoenician colony of Carthage. The custom continues today throughout the Muslim world, while Jews from North Africa commonly make hand-shaped objects to ward the evil eye off newborns and prospective brides and grooms. These hand-shaped cookies are tastier than the traditional metal versions. The cookies can be sprinkled with colored sugar before baking or spread with icing afterward.

2¼ cups all-purpose flour
2 teaspoons baking powder
¾ teaspoon salt
½ cup (1 stick) unsalted butter or margarine, softened
1 cup sugar
1 large egg
3 tablespoons milk or water
1 teaspoon vanilla extract

1. Sift together the flour, baking powder, and salt. Beat the butter until smooth. Gradually add the sugar and beat until light and fluffy, about 5 minutes. Beat in the egg, then the milk and vanilla. Gradually stir in the flour mixture. Form into a ball, wrap in plastic, and chill until firm, at least 1 hour.
2. Preheat the oven to 375 degrees.
3. Sprinkle a flat surface lightly with flour or confectioners' sugar and roll out the dough to a ¼-inch thickness. Place a hand lightly on the dough, fingers slightly spread, and using a pastry wheel or small knife, cut around your hand and fingers. Cut out as many hands as will fit on the dough. Transfer to baking sheets.

4. Bake until the cookies are light golden, 8 to 10 minutes. Let the cookies stand until firm, about 1 minute, then remove to a rack and let cool completely. Store in an air-tight container.

VARIATION

Spice Hand Cookies: Add 1½ teaspoons ground ginger, 1 teaspoon ground allspice, ½ teaspoon grated nutmeg, and ¼ teaspoon ground cloves. Or add ½ teaspoon ground cinnamon, ¼ teaspoon ground allspice, ¼ teaspoon ground cloves, and ¼ teaspoon grated nutmeg.

Marzipan *(Massapan)*
ABOUT THIRTY-TWO ½-INCH CANDIES

*S*ephardim traditionally serve marzipan on Purim, on Passover, and at most family celebrations. It can be formed into simple ½-inch balls or used to create an assortment of treats, including *datils rellenos* (stuffed dates), *nuez con almondratha* (form the marzipan into 1-inch balls and press an almond half or toasted walnut half into the center), *mogados de almendra* (roll into a ¾-inch-thick rope and cut into 1½-inch-long pieces), and *kaak ib loz* (roll into 4-inch-long ropes, form into rings, and press a pistachio into the point of connection).

2 cups sugar
1 cup water
1 to 3 teaspoons fresh lemon juice (optional)
3¼ cups (about 1 pound) blanched almonds, finely ground
⅛ teaspoon almond extract or 4 teaspoons rose water
Several drops food coloring (optional)

1. Boil the sugar, water, and lemon juice until the syrup reaches the soft-ball stage or 236 degrees on a candy thermometer, about 10 minutes. Remove from the heat and stir in the almonds. Stir over low heat until the mixture thickens and pulls away from the sides of the pan, 5 to 10 minutes. Let cool.

2. Moisten your hands with rose water or plain water and knead the marzipan until smooth. Blend in the almond extract and, if desired, the food coloring.

3. Form into ½-inch balls or various shapes, such as fruits, vegetables, flowers, and Stars of David. Let stand at room temperature for at least 24 hours to ripen.

Turkish Delight *(Rahat Lokum)*
ABOUT 64 PIECES

*T*his treat, whose name comes from the Turkish for "giving rest to the throat," is one of the best-known Middle Eastern confections.

3¼ cups sugar
3½ cups water
1 teaspoon fresh lemon juice
Zest of 1 orange, cut into strips
Zest of 1 lemon, cut into strips
½ cup cornstarch
Several drops food coloring (optional)
¾ to 1 cup chopped pistachios or almonds (optional)
Confectioners' sugar

1. In a heavy 4-quart nonreactive saucepan, stir the sugar, 1¾ cups of the water, and the lemon juice over medium-low heat until the sugar dissolves, 5 to 10 minutes. Add the zest, increase the heat to medium-high, and boil until the syrup reaches the thread stage or 225 degrees on a candy thermometer, about 15 minutes.

2. Meanwhile, dissolve the cornstarch in the remaining 1¾ cups water. If desired, stir in the food coloring.

3. Stir the cornstarch mixture into the syrup and cook, stirring constantly, until the mixture reaches the hard-ball stage or 265 degrees on a candy thermometer, about 30 minutes.

4. Strain the mixture into a greased bowl. If desired, stir in the nuts. Pour into a greased baking pan or onto a greased baking sheet and spread to a 1-inch thickness. Let stand overnight. Cut into 1-inch squares. Roll the squares in confectioners' sugar.

Candied Orange Peel *(Dulce de Portokal)*
ABOUT 4 CUPS

*T*his popular confection, also called *ankikos di portokal,* is eaten as candy or added to cakes, cookies, and puddings. You can substitute the peels from etrogs (citrons), grapefruit, lemons, or tangerines.

1 pound thick orange peel, cut into strips (from 4 large oranges)
2 quarts cold water
2¼ cups sugar
1 teaspoon fresh lemon juice

1. Cover the orange peel with 6 cups of the water, bring to a boil, reduce the heat to low, and simmer for 15 minutes. Drain and repeat the process 3 or 4 times or until the peel is only slightly bitter.
2. In a heavy saucepan, cook the sugar, remaining 2 cups water, and lemon juice over medium-low heat until the sugar dissolves. Increase the heat to medium-high, bring to a boil, and cook until syrupy, about 30 minutes.
3. Add the peel and return the syrup to a boil over medium heat. Cover, reduce the heat to low, and simmer until most of the liquid has evaporated and the strips of peel are glazed, about 1 hour. Let cool, pour into a jar, and store in the refrigerator.

VARIATION

Drain the peel. Spread additional sugar over a piece of wax paper, place the peel on the sugar, and toss to coat. Arrange in a single layer and let dry for at least 8 hours. Store in an airtight container at room temperature for up to 2 weeks.

Middle Eastern Apricot Rolls (Mooshmosh)
ABOUT 7 DOZEN ROLLS

1 pound (3¼ cups) dried apricots, washed and drained
½ cup sugar, plus extra for sprinkling
½ cup coarsely chopped blanched almonds or unsalted pistachios

In a food processor or grinder, grind or puree the apricots with the ½ cup sugar. Sprinkle a large piece of wax paper with additional sugar and spread half of the apricot mixture on top in a ¼-inch-thick rectangle. Arrange the nuts along one side of the rectangle, then roll up from the nut side. Repeat with the remaining apricot mixture. Let stand, uncovered, at room temperature for 2 days, then cut into slices. Or mix the nuts into the apricots, roll into ½-inch balls (about 50 balls), and press an additional piece of nut on top of each ball.

Mint Tea (Naa-Naa)
ABOUT 4 CUPS

*M*oroccans learned of tea from the British and loved it to such an extent that mint-flavored tea became the national drink. For iced mint tea, chill and pour over ice cubes.

5 to 6 cups boiling water
2 cups fresh mint leaves
1 tablespoon black tea leaves or 3 tea bags
2 to 4 tablespoons honey or sugar to taste (optional)

Pour some of the boiling water into a teapot, then empty it. Place the mint, tea, and if desired, the honey in the teapot. Add 4 cups boiling water and let steep for 5 to 10 minutes. Strain through a fine sieve.

Spiced Tea

ABOUT 10 CUPS

2 quarts water
2 tablespoons black tea leaves or 6 teabags
2 (3-inch) cinnamon sticks
8 whole cloves
3 whole allspice berries
3 cups pineapple juice or ¼ cup fresh lemon juice
About ¼ cup sugar

Bring the water to a boil. Add the tea and spices, remove from the heat, and let steep for 20 minutes. Strain. Add the pineapple juice and sugar and stir until dissolved. Serve hot or chilled.

AUFRUF/ARUS

Tradition relates that King Solomon built a gate in the Temple where the citizens of Jerusalem would sit on the Sabbath to honor and perform kindnesses for imminent grooms, reciting the blessing "May He whose Presence dwells in this house rejoice you with sons and daughters." Although the gate was destroyed with the First Temple, the custom of honoring the groom on the Sabbath before his wedding remains. Therefore, on the Sabbath before his wedding, the groom is summoned to the *bimah* (platform) to recite the blessing over the Torah reading (in egalitarian congregations, both the bride and groom may be so honored). This is known as an *aufruf* (German for "calling up") by Ashkenazim, Shabbat Haerusin (Sabbath of Betrothal) by Moroccans, and *arus* (betrothal) by Syrians.

On the other hand, many Sephardim call the groom to the Torah reading on the Sabbath following the wedding. The congregation is customarily treated to a *meze allegre* (sweet table) featuring almond foods, such as marzipan, *lebas* (Jordan almonds), and baklava.

Tossing symbolic foods at the bride and groom is an ancient practice to summon fertility and good fortune. Thus, in many congregations, after the prospective groom finishes his *aliyah* (Torah reading), the congregation showers (*bevarfen* in Yiddish) the groom with nuts, dried fruit, and particularly candy, signifying that his married life should be sweet. Afterward, children gather up and enjoy the treats. In order to keep these goodies from sticking to carpets and floors, it is advisable to tie them in small bags. A *kiddush/sabt* customarily follows the services.

An Haute Sheva Brachot

SERVES 10

*A*n ancient Jewish wedding ritual is the *shivat ye'mei hamishteh* (seven days of partying) follow-ing the wedding, first noted in Genesis (29:27), "Wait until the bridal week of this one is over and we will give you that one too," and also seen in Samson's week of feasting (Judges 14:12). Dur-ing this seven-day period, at a meal shared by the newlyweds, a *minyan* (quorum of ten), and someone who did not attend the wedding, the Sheva Brachot (seven blessings) recited under the chuppah (marriage canopy) are repeated.

Once *haute* meant the ostentation of *la grande cuisine,* with an elaborate meal. Perhaps the most notorious one was prepared by Antonin Carême for Czar Alexander; it consisted of sixteen separate courses and ninety dishes. Today sophisticated cuisine is a matter of style and special dishes rather than excess.

ROLLS

WATERCRESS SOUP

CHICKEN LIVERS IN PUFF PASTRY

COMPOSED SALAD WITH POPPY SEED DRESSING

STANDING RIB ROAST

THREE-VEGETABLE PÂTÉ

SEPHARDIC POTATO SLICES

SABRA SORBET IN TULIP CUPS

TEA AND COFFEE

 Wine Suggestions: Merlot or Cabernet Sauvignon

Watercress Soup
10 SERVINGS

3 tablespoons unsalted margarine
1 pound leeks (white and light green parts only), sliced
1 pound boiling potatoes, peeled and chopped
2 quarts chicken broth or water
2 cups (about 2 bunches) firmly packed trimmed watercress

1. Melt the margarine in a large saucepan over medium heat. Add the leeks and sauté until soft, 5 to 10 minutes.
2. Add the potatoes and broth and simmer until tender, 35 to 45 minutes. Add the watercress, reserving a few leaves for garnish, and simmer an additional 2 to 3 minutes.
3. In a blender or food processor, puree the soup without overprocessing; the texture should be a bit rough. Return to the pot and gently reheat. Pour into serving bowls and garnish with watercress leaves.

Chicken Livers in Puff Pastry
10 SERVINGS

2 pounds (4 large sheets) puff pastry
Egg wash (1 large egg beaten with 1 teaspoon water)

FILLING
2 pounds (about 24) chicken livers
Kosher salt
⅓ cup vegetable oil
4 medium onions, sliced
1 pound mushrooms or 3 medium red bell peppers, sliced
1 tablespoon all-purpose flour
Salt to taste

Ground black pepper to taste
1 cup white wine
2 tablespoons chopped fresh parsley

1. Sprinkle a large baking sheet with cold water, letting the excess drip off. Do not dry. Roll the puff pastry to a ¼-inch thickness. Using a sharp fluted or straight-sided 3-inch pastry cutter or biscuit cutter, cut out 20 rounds, leaving a little space between rounds as well as around the outside edges of the pastry. (If the cutter overlaps these areas, it may hinder rising.) Transfer 10 rounds to the prepared baking sheet (these rounds will serve as the bases) and place in the refrigerator while working with the remaining dough.

2. Using a 2-inch cutter, cut out the centers from the remaining 10 rounds to create rings. (Reserve the centers for another use.)

3. Brush the edges of the pastry rounds lightly with cold water and arrange the rings on top. Prick the centers all over with the tines of a fork. Using the back of a paring knife, cut slightly slanted lines around the outside edge of each shell at ⅛-inch intervals. (This seals the rings to the bases. A fluted cutter makes this step unnecessary). Refrigerate for at least 30 minutes. (The shells can be prepared to this point and frozen. Do not thaw; place the frozen shells directly in the oven.)

4. Preheat the oven to 425 degrees.

5. Brush the tops of the pastry shells with the egg wash, being careful not to let any egg touch the sides. (Or the layers will stick, hindering rising.) Place a greased sheet of parchment paper on top. Bake the shells until puffed and lightly browned, about 15 minutes. Remove the parchment paper. Reduce the heat to 375 degrees and bake the shells until crisp and golden brown, about 20 minutes.

6. With a small knife, remove and reserve the top center crust from the shells. While still warm, scoop out and discard any uncooked pastry in the centers. Serve the shells that day or freeze. (To crisp, place thawed shells in a 400-degree oven for about 5 minutes.)

7. To make the filling: Remove any green spots from the livers. Dip into cold water. (This helps to prevent them from hardening.) Pat dry. Sprinkle on both sides with kosher salt. Place on an unheated rack in a broiler pan and broil about 4 inches from the heat on both sides until light brown and blood has dripped off, about 3 minutes per side. Cut in half.

8. Heat the oil in a large skillet over medium heat. Add the onions and mushrooms and sauté until soft, about 15 minutes. Add the flour and stir for 1 minute. Season with salt and pepper.

9. Just before serving, add the wine, then the livers to the onion mixture and sauté un-
    til heated through, about 1 minute. Stir in the parsley.
10. Spoon the liver mixture into the pastry shells and arrange the reserved pastry cen-
    ters on top.

Composed Salad with Poppy Seed Dressing
10 SERVINGS

A composed salad allows you to show off the beauty of the ingredients. The basic idea
is to create a contrast of colors and shapes. Use your imagination in substituting ingredients.

1 pound fresh spinach or other dark greens, torn into bite-size pieces
2 cups alfalfa sprouts
1 medium avocado, peeled and thinly sliced
1 large red onion, halved and thinly sliced
2 medium green bell peppers, halved, seeded, and sliced
2 medium yellow bell peppers, halved, seeded, and sliced
1 medium cantaloupe or large navel orange, halved and thinly sliced
1 small jicama, peeled and julienned
About 4 ounces enoki mushrooms
10 cherry tomatoes
Poppy Seed Dressing (recipe follows)

Mound a handful of spinach in the center of each serving plate and top with a handful
of sprouts. Arrange 2 to 3 slices of the avocado, onion, bell peppers, and cantaloupe
around it. Scatter the jicama and mushrooms all over. Place a cherry tomato over the top.
Drizzle with a little of the poppy seed dressing.

POPPY SEED DRESSING

ABOUT 2 CUPS

1 cup vegetable oil
½ cup sugar
⅓ cup cider vinegar or white vinegar
1 tablespoon minced onion
1 tablespoon poppy seeds
1 teaspoon dry mustard
About ½ teaspoon salt

In a food processor or blender, process all the ingredients until well mixed and thick. Store in the refrigerator. Shake well before using.

Standing Rib Roast

10 SERVINGS

*T*he most tender cuts of meat come from the sections of the animal that are not used for movement and therefore develop little connective tissue. The rib section is the least exercised part of the forequarter and yields the most tender kosher roasts and steaks. A side of beef contains twelve ribs; the seven rib bones extending from six through twelve are cut to make a standing rib roast. The three ribs closest to the loin—called first cut, prime cut, or front cut—are the most tender. The four ribs closest to the chuck—called second cut—contain more muscle and fat but are still tender. Tender cuts are generally cooked by dry heat (broiling and roasting). To ensure tender and juicy prime rib, do not cook at a high temperature or overcook.

1 (7- to 8-pound/4-rib) standing rib roast, preferably first cut
About 1 teaspoon ground black pepper

1. If your butcher does not let the roast hang for a few days, let it stand on a wire rack set in a pan in the refrigerator for at least 1 or up to 4 days. (During this aging period, enzymes in the meat break down the proteins into amino acids, resulting in more flavorful, tender meat.) Remove the roast from the refrigerator about 2 hours before cooking to bring to room temperature.

2. Preheat the oven to 325 degrees. (This produces medium-well-done slices on the exterior and rare slices inside. There will be a weight loss from a 7-pound roast of about 1 pound from melted fat and meat juices, as compared to nearly 2 pounds when the roast is cooked at 425 degrees.)

3. Rub the roast well with pepper. Tie with string running parallel to the bones (to prevent the outer layer of meat from separating from the rib eye and overcooking). Set a wire rack in a shallow baking pan and place the roast, rib side down, on the rack. If desired, insert a meat thermometer into the thickest part without touching the bone or fat. Do not cover.

4. Roast until a meat thermometer registers 130 degrees for rare, about 20 minutes per pound or 2½ to 3 hours total; 150 degrees for medium, 25 to 30 minutes per pound or 2¾ to 3½ hours total. (The meat will continue to cook after it is removed from the oven, so it is actually removed 10 degrees below the desired final temperature of 140 degrees for rare and 160 degrees for medium.)

5. Remove from the oven. Use tongs to move the roast—do not prick with a fork or the juices will escape. Let stand for at least 15 minutes before carving.

6. To carve: Place the roast on its side, steady it with a fork inserted between the ribs, insert the knife between the meat and bones, and cut vertically along the rib. Cut ¼- to ½-inch-thick slices horizontally toward the rib.

Three-Vegetable Pâté

IO SERVINGS

This is an elegant and colorful way to enjoy vegetables.

8 ounces fresh or frozen broccoli, chopped
8 ounces (about 4 medium) carrots, sliced
1 pound rutabaga or celeriac (celery root), peeled and diced,
    or 8 ounces fresh or frozen cauliflower, chopped
3 large eggs
6 tablespoons nondairy creamer
6 tablespoons all-purpose flour
3 tablespoons unsalted margarine, melted
¼ teaspoon salt
Ground black pepper to taste
¼ teaspoon onion powder
Pinch of ground white pepper
Pinch of grated nutmeg

1. Preheat the oven to 350 degrees. Grease a 9- by 5-inch loaf pan, line the bottom with wax paper, and grease the wax paper.
2. Cook each vegetable separately in boiling water until tender. Drain. Puree and place 1 cup of each vegetable in separate bowls.
3. To each vegetable puree, add 1 egg, 2 tablespoons creamer, 2 tablespoons flour, and 1 tablespoon margarine. To the broccoli, add the salt and a pinch of pepper. To the rutabaga, add the onion powder and white pepper. To the carrots, add the nutmeg.
4. To assemble: Evenly spread the carrot mixture in the prepared loaf pan. Carefully spread the rutabaga on top, then the broccoli.
5. Cover with a piece of greased wax paper. Place in a larger pan and add hot water to come halfway up the sides of the loaf pan. Bake until the pâté is set, about 1 hour.
6. Remove the top piece of wax paper. Invert onto a flat surface or serving tray, remove the pan and wax paper, and cut the pâté into slices. Serve warm or at room temperature.

Sephardic Potato Slices (*Kartofis*)
10 SERVINGS

4 pounds (about 8 large) baking potatoes, peeled
8 cloves garlic
About 5 tablespoons olive oil
3 medium onions, chopped
About 1½ teaspoons salt
About ¼ teaspoon ground black pepper

1. Cover the potatoes and 4 cloves of the garlic with water, bring to a boil, reduce the heat to low, and simmer until tender, about 25 minutes. Drain and let cool. Cut the potatoes into ¼-inch-thick slices.
2. Heat the oil in a large skillet over medium-low heat. Add the remaining 4 cloves garlic and sauté until golden. Discard the garlic.
3. Increase the heat to medium-high. In batches, sauté the potato slices until golden on both sides, about 3 minutes per side. Drain on paper towels.
4. Add the onions and sauté until soft and translucent, 5 to 10 minutes. Return the potatoes to the skillet and toss to coat. Sprinkle with the salt and pepper.

Sabra Sorbet

ABOUT 1 QUART

*T*he prickly pear is a 3-inch-long oval-shaped cactus fruit with sweet red flesh mixed with many small black seeds and surrounded by a prickly greenish yellow skin. After the Spanish brought the cactus from the New World, it spread to many parts of the Mediterranean, including the Levant. The fruit eventually became identified with native-born Israelis, as both are tough on the outside but sweet on the inside. Substitute raspberries or plums for part or all of the sabras.

About 12 prickly pears (sabras)
1½ cups water
About 1 cup sugar
3 tablespoons fresh lemon juice
1 to 2 tablespoons vodka (optional)

1. Cut the fruits in half and scoop out the flesh. Mash, then strain out the seeds. (You should have about 3 cups of puree.)
2. In a food processor or blender, puree the sabras, water, sugar, lemon juice, and if desired, the vodka.
3. Pour into ice cube trays and place in the freezer until frozen, at least 2 hours or up to 1 month ahead. Or process in an ice cream machine according to manufacturer's instructions.
4. Place a single layer of cubes in the work bowl of a food processor fitted with the steel blade. Pulse about 10 times, just until smooth. Return to the freezer. (If the sorbet solidifies, process again in the food processor.) Serve scoops of sorbet in Tulips (recipe follows).

Tulips
ABOUT 16 COOKIES

7 tablespoons unsalted margarine, softened
⅔ cup sugar
4 large (⅔ cup) egg whites
1 teaspoon vanilla extract
Pinch of salt
1 cup unbleached all-purpose flour

1. Preheat the oven to 350 degrees. Cut out eighteen 7-inch foil or parchment paper squares and grease or spray with vegetable spray.

2. Beat the margarine until smooth, about 1 minute. Add the sugar and beat until light and fluffy, about 5 minutes. Beat in the egg whites, one at a time. Add the vanilla and salt. Stir in the flour. (The batter can be stored in the refrigerator for up to 3 days.)

3. Spoon 1 heaping tablespoon batter onto the prepared squares and evenly spread into a 5-inch round. (Or omit the foil, bake the cookies on a greased baking sheet, and immediately remove from the sheet with a spatula.)

4. Bake until the cookies begin to brown around the edges, about 8 minutes. Since the cookies must be shaped while still warm, it is best to bake only 2 to 4 at a time.

5. Immediately remove the cookies from the oven and press loosely around inverted custard cups. (If the cookies become too firm to shape, return to the oven for a few seconds to soften.) Let stand until set, about 5 minutes. Carefully peel off the foil. (The cookies can be stored in an airtight container at room temperature for up to 2 days or in the freezer for up to 3 months.) Fill with sorbet, mousse, or fresh berries.

A Special Anniversary Dinner

SERVES 10

*E*very anniversary is important and provides an opportunity to enjoy a romantic dinner for two. Yet momentous occasions such as five, ten, twenty-five, or fifty years call for special recognition with a gathering of family and close friends. Elegance underscores the significance of the occasion, and the menu should include a selection of special dishes. The following offers an elegant repast for an occasion when you want to pull out all the stops.

TWO-COLOR PEPPER SOUP
SALMON TARTARE
ISRAELI ORANGE AND AVOCADO SALAD
INDIVIDUAL BEEF WELLINGTONS
MINT CARROT TZIMMES
GREEN VEGETABLE MEDLEY
MINIATURE WEDDING CAKES
TEA AND COFFEE

 Wine suggestions: Cabernet Sauvignon, Merlot, or Pinot Noir

Two-Color Pepper Soup

10 SERVINGS

A soup with contrasting colors and flavors is a dazzling way to start a special meal. During the spring and summer, serve it chilled; during the fall and winter, serve it hot. Prepare any two of the red, green, and yellow bell pepper soups. Make a memorable presentation with a bright red pepper soup matched with a cumin-accented green bell pepper soup or any thick green soup, such as zucchini, pea, or asparagus. Red pepper soup can also be matched with corn chowder. You can, of course, opt to serve only one color of soup for a tasty start to your meal.

RED BELL PEPPER SOUP

3 tablespoons vegetable or olive oil
1 medium onion, chopped (about ½ cup)
2 pounds (about 4 large) red bell peppers, seeded and chopped
3 cups chicken broth, vegetable broth, or water
1 medium boiling potato, peeled and grated
About ¾ teaspoon salt
Ground black pepper to taste

GREEN BELL PEPPER SOUP

3 tablespoons vegetable or olive oil
1 medium onion, chopped (about ½ cup)
2 pounds (about 4 large) green bell peppers, seeded and chopped
3 cups chicken broth, vegetable broth, or water
1 medium boiling potato, peeled and grated
1 teaspoon ground cumin (optional)
About ¾ teaspoon salt
Ground black pepper to taste
1 tablespoon fresh lemon juice

1. To make the red pepper soup: Heat the oil in a large saucepan over medium heat. Add the onion and sauté until soft and translucent, 5 to 10 minutes. Add the peppers and sauté until softened, about 15 minutes. Add the broth, potato, salt, and pepper. Bring to a boil, reduce the heat to low, and simmer for about 15 minutes. In a blender or food processor, puree the soup until smooth. Strain. Serve hot or chilled.

2. To make the green pepper soup: Heat the oil in a large saucepan over medium heat. Add the onion and sauté until soft and translucent, 5 to 10 minutes. Add the peppers and sauté until softened, about 15 minutes. Add the broth, potato, cumin if desired, salt, and pepper. Bring to a boil, reduce the heat to low, and simmer for about 15 minutes. In a blender or food processor, puree the soup until smooth. Strain. Add the lemon juice. Serve hot or chilled.

3. To assemble: Pour each pepper soup into a separate measuring cup or bottle. From opposite sides of a heated or chilled serving bowl, pour in equal amounts of the soups. If desired, garnish with a sprig of watercress or parsley.

VARIATION

Yellow Bell Pepper Soup: Substitute 2 pounds yellow bell peppers for the green peppers. If desired, add ¼ teaspoon dried thyme or 1 whole clove with the broth.

Salmon Tartare
10 SERVINGS

*B*uy the salmon on the same day you plan to make this raw fish dish, and make sure it's very fresh. Ice-cold vodka or a Chenin Blanc complements the tartare.

3 pounds very fresh salmon fillets, cut into ½-inch cubes
3 tablespoons extra-virgin olive oil
3 tablespoons fresh lemon juice
3 tablespoons chopped capers
3 tablespoons chopped cornichons or sour gherkins
3 tablespoons minced shallots or red onion
3 tablespoons minced fresh chives, ⅓ cup chopped fresh mint,
    or 1½ teaspoons Dijon mustard
Salt to taste
Ground white or black pepper to taste

Process the salmon in a food processor until minced but not pureed, or finely chop by hand. Stir in the remaining ingredients. Cover and refrigerate for at least 1 hour or up to 24 hours. Serve chilled with bread or crackers.

VARIATION

Substitute 3 pounds tuna, red snapper, or bass for the salmon and add 3 tablespoons mayonnaise.

Israeli Orange and Avocado Salad

10 SERVINGS

*F*urther enhance this colorful and refreshing salad by adding any of the following: beets, bell peppers, fresh fennel, jicama, black olives, or strawberries.

1 head romaine or butter lettuce, torn into bite-size pieces
1 bunch watercress or 1 head radicchio, torn into bite-size pieces
6 large navel oranges, peeled and segmented
3 ripe avocados, peeled and sliced
2 medium red onions, thinly sliced

DRESSING

¼ cup extra-virgin olive oil
¼ cup vegetable oil
¼ cup fresh orange juice
2 tablespoons fresh lemon juice or wine vinegar
1 teaspoon grated orange zest
About 1 teaspoon salt
1 tablespoon chopped fresh basil, cilantro, mint, rosemary, or thyme or ½ teaspoon dried

1. Arrange the lettuce and watercress on serving plates and scatter the oranges, avocados, and onions on top.
2. Place all the dressing ingredients in a jar with a tight-fitting lid, shake well, and drizzle over the salad.

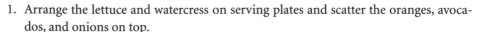

Individual Beef Wellingtons

10 SERVINGS

*F*ollowing the Duke of Wellington's victory over Napoleon at the battle of Waterloo, a British chef created and named a dish of beef and mushrooms wrapped in puffed pastry in his honor. This is a twist on the classic dish. Although it takes a bit of work, the individual Wellingtons can be prepared in stages.

PÂTE BRISÉE

8 cups all-purpose flour
3¾ teaspoons salt
3 cups (1½ pounds) vegetable shortening (or 2 cups shortening
*   and 1 cup chilled unsalted margarine)*
About 1⅓ cups ice water

1 (4-pound) beef rib-eye roast, trimmed of fat
2½ cups Mock Chopped Liver (page 52)
2 large egg whites beaten with 2 teaspoons water
2 large egg yolks beaten with 2 teaspoons water

1. To make the pastry: Combine the flour and salt. Using the tips of your fingers, a pastry blender, or 2 knives in a scissors motion, cut in the shortening until the mixture resembles coarse crumbs. Sprinkle 2 to 3 tablespoons of the ice over a section of the mixture. Gently mix in with a fork to moisten that section. Push the moistened dough aside and continue adding and mixing in the water in this fashion until the dough just holds together. Using your fingertips, lightly press and knead the dough into a ball. Do not overhandle. Divide into 10 equal pieces, flatten into disks, cover with plastic wrap, and refrigerate for at least 30 minutes or up to 4 days.
2. Cut the roast in half lengthwise. Cut the halves crosswise into 5 equal pieces for a total of 10. (For a 3-pound roast, cut into 8 equal pieces.)
3. On a lightly floured surface, roll out each piece of dough into a 10- by 7-inch rectangle, cutting away the excess. (Use the leftover dough to make decorations for the Wellingtons.)
4. Spread ¼ cup of the mock chopped liver in the center of each rectangle and arrange a piece of the meat on top. Brush the edges of the dough with the egg white, fold the dough over the beef, and press the edges to seal.

5. Place the Wellingtons, seam side down, on an ungreased baking sheet. If desired, cut the dough scraps into decorative shapes and secure to the Wellingtons with a little egg white. (The Wellingtons may be covered and stored in the refrigerator for 1 day. Before baking, return to room temperature, at least 2 hours.)
6. Preheat the oven to 400 degrees.
7. Brush the Wellingtons with the egg wash. Bake until the pastry is golden brown and the beef is done, 25 to 26 minutes for rare, 28 to 29 minutes for medium. Serve warm.

Mint Carrot Tzimmes

10 SERVINGS

3 pounds baby carrots or sliced carrots
¼ cup (½ stick) unsalted margarine
About ½ cup sugar or honey
⅓ cup chopped fresh mint or 2 tablespoons dried
⅛ teaspoon ground cinnamon
Pinch of grated nutmeg
Pinch of salt

1. Cook the carrots in boiling salted water or steam until fork-tender, 10 to 15 minutes. Drain.
2. Melt the margarine in a large skillet over medium-high heat. Add the carrots and sauté for 1 minute.
3. Add the sugar, mint, cinnamon, nutmeg, and salt and cook, stirring, until the carrots are glazed, about 5 minutes. Serve warm.

Green Vegetable Medley

10 SERVINGS

1¼ pounds snow peas, trimmed
4 cups shelled fresh green peas or 2 (10-ounce) boxes frozen peas
3 cups ½-inch pieces asparagus or green beans
¼ cup olive oil or unsalted margarine
1 large onion, chopped
½ teaspoon minced fresh tarragon or 2 tablespoons chopped chives
Salt to taste
Ground black pepper to taste

1. Cook the snow peas in lightly salted boiling water until tender-crisp, about 1 minute. Using a slotted spoon, transfer the snow peas to a colander and place under cold running water to stop the cooking and preserve the bright green color. Drain.
2. Add the peas to the same water and cook until tender-crisp, about 3 minutes. (If using frozen peas, thaw but do not cook.) Transfer to a colander and place under cold running water. Drain.
3. Cook the asparagus until tender-crisp, about 3 minutes. Transfer to a colander and place under cold running water. Drain.
4. Heat the oil in a large skillet over medium-high heat. Add the onion and sauté until soft and translucent, 5 to 10 minutes. Add the snow peas, green peas, and asparagus and sauté until heated through. Add the tarragon, and season with the salt and pepper. Spoon into a heated dish and serve warm.

Miniature Wedding Cakes

10 SMALL CAKES

*I*n August of 1997, close family friends Abraham and Juliet Dere of Richmond, Virginia, celebrated their fiftieth wedding anniversary. In honor of the occasion, their family invited more than 150 relatives and friends to a formal dinner party. (Fortunately, I got to enjoy the affair as a guest rather than as caterer.) Although it was a grand evening all around, I was particularly impressed by the charming little wedding cakes served for dessert. Here is my own version of this lovely presentation.

SILVER-WHITE CAKE BATTER

4½ cups all-purpose flour
2⅓ cups sugar
7 teaspoons baking powder
1¾ teaspoons salt
1⅓ cups vegetable shortening
2½ cups nondairy creamer or water
4 teaspoons vanilla extract
10 large egg whites

WHITE BUTTERCREAM

12 cups confectioners' sugar
1½ cups vegetable shortening
2 teaspoons vanilla extract
About 1 cup water

1. Preheat the oven to 350 degrees. Grease two 13- by 9-inch baking pans, line the bottoms with wax paper, grease the wax paper, and dust with flour.

2. To make the batter: Combine the flour, sugar, baking powder, and salt. On low speed, blend in the shortening, creamer, and vanilla. Increase the speed to high and beat for 3 minutes. Add the egg whites, one at a time, and beat until smooth and fluffy, about 2 minutes.

3. Divide the batter between the prepared pans. Bake until a tester inserted in the center comes out clean and the cake springs back when lightly touched, about 40 minutes. Let cool in the pans for 10 minutes, then remove to a rack and let cool completely.

4. To make the buttercream: Beat the sugar, shortening, and vanilla until smooth. Add enough water to make the buttercream of spreading consistency.

5. To assemble: Using a 2½- to 3-inch biscuit cutter or a sharp knife, cut out 10 rounds from the cakes. From the leftover cake, cut out 1-inch rounds.

6. Spread the tops and sides of the cake rounds with the buttercream. Using a metal spatula, carefully arrange the smaller rounds in the center of the larger rounds. If desired, use a pastry bag to add decorations made of buttercream. Top each miniature cake with a 2-inch piece of lace or an edible flower.

A Southern Jewish Family Reunion

SERVES 8 OR 80

*W*hen I first arrived in New York City to attend Yeshiva University, I was astounded at how provincial many northerners could be. Some did not realize that traditional Jews actually lived in the South. Yet I can attest to the existence of Jewish life below the Mason-Dixon Line, including, for more than a century, members of my family.

The Markowitz/Marks family, like most Jewish immigrants in the 1880s, arrived in the United States, seeking the safety and opportunity this country offered in the wake of the pogroms and persecutions that swept eastern Europe following the assassination of Czar Alexander II (events that also spurred the first Aliyah to Israel). Abandoning the small towns of Jassy and Huşi in Romania, the paternal side of my family (two of my great-grandfathers were first cousins) followed the burgeoning stream of eastern European immigrants to New York City, where some of them put down roots. (In a 1900 city directory, my great-great-grandfather, Yacov Yehudah Kupfer, is listed as having a tailor's shop on Forty-second Street.) But prospects were limited in late-nineteenth-century New York, and most of the family soon headed to port cities in the South, settling primarily in two states: Georgia (Brunswick and Savannah) and Florida (Tampa and Miami).

While attending the untimely funeral of my great-grandmother Rose Kupfer Markowitz in 1929, a group of family members decided that they did not want to wait for sad occasions to meet. Each man present put twenty dollars in a hat, and the seed money for the first Marks family reunion was collected. There has been one nearly every year since. The few surviving originators have handed control of the event to younger relatives, leaving it to succeeding generations to maintain the tradition.

The Marks family reunion, which runs from Friday to Sunday, typically consists of the two nonagenarian matriarchs, Toni Markowitz Herscovitz and Cletta Marks, presiding over an assemblage of sixty or more relatives ranging in age from infancy to nearly one hundred years old. Activities include tennis, basketball, and swimming, but center mostly on visiting and eating. The food, except for the Saturday-night banquet, is organized potluck, with everyone contributing favorite dishes.

The menu, reflecting our family history, is a rather unique blend of Romanian and southern American favorites. Surprisingly, there are many similarities between these two forms of cuisine. Cornmeal is a mainstay: cooked as a mush in grits and *mamaliga;* baked in corn bread and *malai;* and used to coat fried vegetable slices (eggplant in the Romanian tradition, green tomatoes in the

southern). Both cultures are partial to highly spiced foods, display a particular fondness for okra, and serve black-eyed peas on New Year's Day. I suppose this correspondence in foods helped to offset somewhat the tension my ancestors must have felt in adapting to what was otherwise an alien environment.

CORNMEAL MUFFINS (PAGE 387)
CRUDITÉS AND DIPS (PAGE 211)
BLACK OLIVES
MOM'S SWEET-AND-SOUR MEATBALLS
LENA'S MATZA-BREADED FRIED CHICKEN WITH HONEY-PECAN SAUCE
ROMANIAN GARLIC MASHED POTATOES
BUBBE'S RICE KUGEL
TONI'S VEGETABLE SLAW
AUNT MARSHA'S OLD-FASHIONED CHOCOLATE CAKE
FLORINE'S SWEET POTATO PIE
BOURBON BALLS
COOKIE ASSORTMENT (PAGES 346–362)
FRESH FRUIT PLATTER (PAGE 217) OR MELON BASKET
ICED COFFEE, ICED TEA, AND SODAS

 Wine and Liquor Suggestions: Chardonnay, Chenin Blanc, and beer

Mom's Sweet-and-Sour Meatballs

*M*y mother serves these at most family functions. There are rarely any leftovers, but when there are, they freeze well.

8 servings	80 servings	
MEATBALLS		
1 pound	5 pounds	ground beef
½ cup	2½ cups	bread crumbs or matza meal
1 medium	5 medium	onions, minced
1 large	5 large	eggs, lightly beaten
3 tablespoons	1 cup	water
1 teaspoon	4 teaspoons	salt
⅛ teaspoon	1 teaspoon	ground black pepper
2 tablespoons	¼ cup	vegetable oil
SWEET-AND-SOUR SAUCE		
2 medium	8 medium	onions, chopped
1 cup	4 cups	chicken broth or water
1 cup	4 cups	tomato sauce or juice
¼ cup	1 cup	granulated or packed brown sugar
2 tablespoons	½ cup	fresh lemon juice or cider vinegar OR
1 teaspoon	4 teaspoons	sour salt
1	4	bay leaves
1 teaspoon	1 tablespoon	salt
⅛ teaspoon	1 teaspoon	ground black pepper
¼ cup	1 cup	raisins (optional)

1. To make the meatballs: Combine the meat, bread crumbs, onion, egg, water, salt, and pepper. Shape into ½-inch balls.
2. Heat the oil in a large saucepan over medium heat. In several batches, brown the meatballs on all sides, about 10 minutes. Remove the meatballs from the pan.
3. To make the sauce: Add the onions to the pan and sauté until soft and translucent, 5 to 10 minutes. Add the broth, tomato sauce, sugar, lemon juice, bay leaf, salt, pepper, and if desired, the raisins. Bring to a boil.

4. Add the meatballs. Cover the pan and simmer over low heat or bake in a 250-degree oven until the flavors in the sauce meld, at least 1 hour. (The meatballs can be cooled, stored in the refrigerator or freezer, and reheated in a 250-degree oven.) Serve warm.

Lena's Matza-Breaded Fried Chicken with Honey-Pecan Sauce

The South boasts numerous versions of deep-fried chicken, but the matza breading gives this one a unique nutty flavor.

8 servings	*80 servings*	
2 (3-pound)	*13 (3-pound)*	*chickens, each cut into 8 pieces*
		salt
		ground black pepper
1 cup	*6 cups*	*all-purpose flour*
2 large	*10 large*	*eggs, lightly beaten*
3 cups	*18 cups*	*matza meal*
		shortening or vegetable oil for deep-frying

HONEY-PECAN SAUCE

1½ cups	*9 cups*	*unsalted margarine*
¾ cup	*4½ cups*	*honey*
¾ cup	*4½ cups*	*chopped pecans*

1. Soak the chicken in water to cover for 1 hour (this helps the flour to stick). Drain. Sprinkle with salt and pepper. Dredge the chicken in the flour, dip in the eggs, then coat with the matza meal. Place on a wire rack and let stand at room temperature for about 30 minutes. (Partially drying the breading prevents the crumbs from falling off and burning, which spoils the fat.)
2. Heat ½ inch shortening or oil to 370 degrees in a 12-inch cast-iron or other heavy skillet over medium heat.

3. In batches, add the chicken and brown on all sides. Cover, reduce the heat to medium-low, and fry, turning the pieces once, until the chicken is fork-tender and the juices run clear when a thigh is pricked with a fork, about 25 minutes.
4. Uncover, turn the chicken pieces skin side up, and cook until the breading is crisp, about 5 minutes. Remove the chicken with tongs and return to the wire rack.
5. To make the sauce: Bring all the ingredients to a boil, stirring to combine. Serve the sauce with the chicken.

VARIATION

Oven-Fried Chicken: Heat a thin layer of oil in a large baking dish in a 350-degree oven. Add the breaded chicken skin side down in a single layer and bake until lightly browned (about 45 minutes). Turn and bake until golden brown (about 10 minutes).

Romanian Garlic Mashed Potatoes

*G*arlic, and plenty of it, is typical of Romanian cooking.

8 servings	80 servings	
3 pounds	18 pounds	baking potatoes, peeled
6 to 7 large	40 to 42 large	cloves garlic, peeled
1 teaspoon	2 tablespoons	salt
¼ cup	1½ cups	olive oil or schmaltz
3 medium	18 medium	onions, chopped
		salt to taste
		ground white pepper to taste

1. Rinse the potatoes in cold water. Place the potatoes and garlic in a large pot (or pots), add cold water to cover by 1 inch, then add the salt. Bring to a low boil, reduce the heat to medium-low, and simmer until the potatoes are fork-tender, about 25 minutes. (Overcooking breaks down the starch cells, resulting in a gummy texture.)
2. Meanwhile, heat the oil or schmaltz in a large skillet (or skillets) over medium heat. Add the onions and sauté until lightly colored, about 20 minutes.

3. Drain the potatoes, reserving the cooking liquid. Return the potatoes and garlic to the warm cooking pot and mash with a potato masher over low heat. Add the onions, salt, and pepper. Using a whisk or wooden spoon, stir in enough of the reserved cooking liquid to make the potatoes fluffy. (The potatoes can be kept warm in a bowl set in a pan of simmering water for 1 hour.)

Bubbe's Rice Kugel

*M*y maternal grandmother, from the Lithuanian side of the family, prepared this moist, slightly creamy pudding during her visits to our house. Although she sometimes added canned fruit cocktail or maraschino cherries, I prefer this raisin-and-apple version.

8 servings	80 servings	
4 cups	6 quarts	water
2 cups	12 cups	long-grain white rice
1 teaspoon	2 tablespoons	salt
6 large	36 large	eggs
¾ cup	4 cups	granulated or packed brown sugar
⅓ cup	2 cups	melted unsalted margarine or vegetable oil
1 teaspoon	2 tablespoons	vanilla extract
⅔ cup	4 cups	raisins
3 medium	18 medium	apples, peeled, cored, and chopped (optional)
1 teaspoon	1 tablespoon	ground cinnamon

1. Preheat the oven to 350 degrees. Grease a 13- by 9-inch baking pan (or 6 pans).
2. Bring the water to a boil. Add the rice, cover, reduce the heat to low, and simmer until tender, about 15 minutes. Fluff with a fork.
3. Add the eggs, sugar, margarine, vanilla, raisins, and if desired, the apples to the rice. Pour into the prepared baking pan and sprinkle lightly with the cinnamon.
4. Bake until golden, about 1 hour. Serve warm or at room temperature.

Toni's Vegetable Slaw

*H*orseradish adds an eastern European touch and zip to this salad.

8 servings	80 servings	
1 medium	*6 medium*	heads green cabbage, shredded (2 or 12 pounds)
1 tablespoon	*⅓ cup*	kosher salt OR
1½ teaspoons	*2 tablespoons*	table salt
2 medium	*12 medium*	carrots, shredded
1 medium	*6 medium*	green bell peppers, seeded and shredded
1 medium	*6 medium*	red bell peppers, seeded and shredded
1 medium	*6 medium*	onions, minced
1 cup	*6 cups*	mayonnaise
3 tablespoons	*1 cup*	cider vinegar or white vinegar
1 tablespoon	*½ cup*	sugar
2 teaspoons	*¼ cup*	prepared white horseradish
		salt to taste
		ground black pepper to taste

1. Place the cabbage in a colander and toss with the salt. Let stand until the cabbage begins to wilt, about 1 hour. Rinse and pat dry. (Salting extracts the excess water from the cabbage, thereby preventing a watering down of the dressing as the coleslaw sits.) The cabbage can be stored in a plastic bag in the refrigerator for up to 1 day.
2. Combine the cabbage with the remaining ingredients. Cover and refrigerate for at least 6 hours. (Coleslaw keeps about 4 days in the refrigerator unless onions are added, and then it lasts only up to 2 days.)

Aunt Marsha's Old-Fashioned Chocolate Cake

14 TO 16 SERVINGS

*T*his is a moist, dense, intensely flavored cake. Cocoa gives cakes a fuller chocolate flavor than chocolate does. For a large crowd, triple the recipe and make a tiered cake.

1¼ cups boiling water
⅔ cup nonalkalized (not Dutch-process) unsweetened cocoa powder
1 teaspoon vanilla extract
2¼ cups all-purpose flour
1¼ teaspoons baking soda
1 teaspoon salt
¼ teaspoon baking powder
¾ cup vegetable shortening
1⅔ cups sugar
2 large eggs

CHOCOLATE FROSTING

½ cup (1 stick) unsalted margarine, softened (or ¼ cup margarine and ¼ cup shortening)
4 cups (1 pound) confectioners' sugar, sifted
½ cup unsweetened cocoa powder or 2 ounces unsweetened chocolate, melted and slightly cooled
2 teaspoons vanilla extract
⅛ teaspoon salt
About ¼ cup water

1. Preheat the oven to 350 degrees. Grease and flour two 9-inch round cake pans or one 13- by 9-inch baking pan.
2. Pour the water over the cocoa powder and stir until smooth. Let cool, then stir in the vanilla.
3. Sift together the flour, baking soda, salt, and baking powder. Beat the shortening and sugar until light and fluffy, about 5 minutes. Beat in the eggs, one at a time. Stir in the flour mixture and cocoa mixture.
4. Divide the batter between the prepared pans. Bake until a wooden tester inserted in the center comes out clean, about 35 minutes. Let the cake cool in the pans for 10 minutes, then remove to racks and let cool completely. (The cake can be wrapped in plastic wrap and stored at room temperature for 1 day or frozen for several months.)

5. To make the frosting: Beat the margarine until smooth. Add the confectioners' sugar and beat until light and fluffy. Add the cocoa powder, vanilla, and salt and beat until smooth. Add enough water to produce a spreading consistency.

6. To assemble: If desired, split the cakes horizontally to make 4 layers. Spread the frosting between the layers, then frost the top and sides. (Dipping the knife into cold water makes spreading frosting easier.)

Florine's Sweet Potato Pie

ONE 9-INCH PIE

In the South, where this is also called sweet potato pudding, it is considered tastier than the better-known pumpkin pie.

PÂTE BRISÉE

1⅓ cups all-purpose flour
½ teaspoon salt
½ cup shortening (or 5 tablespoons shortening
    and 3 tablespoons chilled unsalted margarine)
3 to 5 tablespoons ice water

FILLING

2 cups (about 1¼ pounds) mashed cooked sweet potatoes
¾ cup granulated or packed brown sugar
3 large eggs, lightly beaten
1¼ cups nondairy creamer
1 to 2 tablespoons bourbon or orange juice
1½ teaspoons vanilla extract
½ teaspoon ground cinnamon
½ teaspoon salt
⅛ teaspoon ground allspice
⅛ teaspoon grated nutmeg

1. To make the pastry: Combine the flour and salt. Using the tips of your fingers, a pastry blender, or 2 knives in a scissors motion, cut in the shortening until the mixture resembles coarse crumbs. Sprinkle 1 tablespoon of the ice water over a section of the mixture. Gently mix in with a fork to moisten that section. Push the moistened dough aside and continue adding and mixing in the water in this fashion until the dough just holds together. Using your fingertips, lightly press and knead the dough into a ball. Cover with plastic wrap, flatten into a disk, and refrigerate for at least 30 minutes or up to 4 days.
2. On a lightly floured surface, roll out the dough to a 12-inch round about ⅛ inch thick. Fold in half or into quarters and fit into a 9-inch pie pan. Gently press into the pan. Trim the excess dough against the rim of the pan. Flute or crimp the edges. Refrigerate for at least 30 minutes.
3. Place a baking sheet in the oven to preheat. Preheat the oven to 425 degrees.
4. To make the filling: Blend together all the ingredients in order given. Pour into the prepared crust.
5. Place the pie on the preheated baking sheet and bake for 20 minutes. Reduce the heat to 350 degrees and bake until a knife inserted halfway between the center and edge comes out clean, about 45 minutes. If the edge of the pastry browns before the filling is set, cover with a 9- by 1½-inch foil circle. Let the pie cool on a wire rack.

VARIATION

Streusel Sweet Potato Pie: Combine ½ cup all-purpose flour, ½ cup packed light brown sugar, ½ cup finely chopped pecans or almonds, and ½ teaspoon ground cinnamon. Cut in 2 tablespoons unsalted margarine to produce coarse crumbs. Sprinkle over the filling before baking.

Bourbon Balls

ABOUT 60 SMALL CONFECTIONS

2½ cups (about 8 ounces) graham cracker crumbs or vanilla wafer crumbs
½ to 1 cup ground almonds, pecans, or walnuts
1 cup confectioners' sugar
2 tablespoons unsweetened cocoa powder or 2 ounces bittersweet or semisweet chocolate, melted
¼ to ⅓ cup bourbon
2 tablespoons light corn syrup or honey
About 1 cup confectioners' sugar, chopped nuts, or grated chocolate (optional)

1. Combine the crumbs, nuts, sugar, and cocoa powder. Mix in the bourbon and corn syrup.
2. Shape the mixture into 1-inch balls. If desired, roll the balls in the confectioners' sugar, chopped nuts, or grated chocolate. Place in an airtight container and let stand at room temperature for at least 1 day before serving.

VARIATION

Rum Balls: Substitute ¼ to ⅓ cup rum for the bourbon.

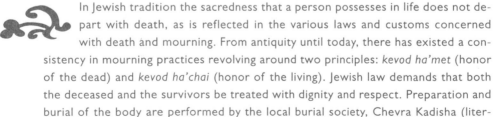

YAHRZEIT/MELDADO

In Jewish tradition the sacredness that a person possesses in life does not depart with death, as is reflected in the various laws and customs concerned with death and mourning. From antiquity until today, there has existed a consistency in mourning practices revolving around two principles: *kevod ha'met* (honor of the dead) and *kevod ha'chai* (honor of the living). Jewish law demands that both the deceased and the survivors be treated with dignity and respect. Preparation and burial of the body are performed by the local burial society, Chevra Kadisha (literally, Holy Brotherhood). It is the duty of the entire community to see to the needs of the relatives.

According to talmudic dictum, "A mourner is forbidden to eat of his own bread on the first day of mourning" (Moed Katan 27:B). Therefore friends prepare a *seudat havraah* (meal of condolence) for the mourners returning from the cemetery, the meal serving as another step in helping the mourners recover from their loss. Round foods, connoting no beginning and no end, are the most common Jewish mourning fare. Three ancient symbols of mourning—bread (II Samuel 3:35 and Jeremiah 16:7), eggs (Talmud Baba Bathra 16:B), and lentils (Genesis 25:34)—play the predominant roles at this meal. Ashkenazim usually serve bagels, rolls, and hard-boiled eggs. Among Jews from Salonika the meal consists of bread, eggs, and olives. Like their Muslim neighbors, Iranian Jews serve *halva* (grain confections) and *kuku* (omelets) at a house of mourning. Other foods served to mourners in the Middle East include round cakes, fish, chickpeas, and coffee.

Various Jewish communities hold special ceremonies to recognize the anniversary of a relative's death. Ashkenazim commemorate this occasion with a Yahrzeit, marked by lighting a twenty-four-hour candle and reciting the Kaddish prayer. Although some relatives commemorate this date by fasting, among Hasidim it has become common to sponsor a Kiddush in the synagogue. Sephardim hold a Meldado at which various sections of the Mishnah are read, including those beginning with letters spelling out the deceased's and his or her mother's name. Afterward, various foods, including *biscochos de levadura* (bread rings) or *biscochos de huevo* (unsweetened egg cookies), raisins, hard-boiled eggs, and chickpeas, are served, along with sweetened drinks, allowing the participants to recite various blessings. Extra food is prepared for distribution to the poor. Syrians hold Ariyat (readings) at various stages of the mourning process, reciting passages of the Zohar and eulogies. After the ceremony those present join the mourners in a dinner; after the Ariyat of *sheloshim* (thirty days), a sweet buffet follows. Moroccans conduct a Mishmara to study the Zohar and Pirkei Avot (Ethics of the Fathers) and to read Hosea 14:2–10 in memory of a man and Samuel 2:1 in memory of a woman. Afterward, a dinner is served featuring traditional foods of mourning, and blessings are recited in memory of the deceased.

The Baker's Bible

Cookie Assortment

*A*mong the vast assortment of baked goods, none projects a more comforting feeling than cookies—spontaneously conjuring up memories of childhood and a sense of abundance. They can be pleasingly plain or tarted up in the most decorative manner. They can be thin and delicate or thick and hearty. They can be teeth-shatteringly crisp or soft and chewy. I like to offer an assortment of at least five different types and shapes of cookies attractively arranged on a platter or tray.

TIPS FOR COOKIE-MAKING SUCCESS

- Use clean, heavy, unwarped baking sheets with low or preferably no sides. Do not use pans with sides higher than ½ inch, which restrict the airflow. Shiny baking sheets are preferable, as dark sheets tend to brown cookie bottoms. If you have only dark sheets, place another sheet underneath the one you are using.

- In order to allow proper air circulation, the cookie sheet should be at least 2 inches shorter in width and length than your oven.

- To ensure uniform, evenly browned cookies, spoon or pipe out equal amounts of dough and space evenly on the baking sheets. A small ice cream scoop is one of the best utensils for measuring equal amounts. Leave 1 to 2 inches between high-fat cookies (they spread more than less fat ones) and place at least 1 inch from the edges of the baking sheet.

- Heat is attracted to the part of the baking sheet containing the cookies, so that partially filled sheets can result in burned cookies. To compensate, place an inverted baking pan on the unoccupied part of the baking sheet.

- Due to the short baking time and high baking temperature for cookies, be on the alert for signs of browning. Golden brown edges indicate doneness. If the cookies are browning unevenly, reverse the baking sheet in the oven. If the bottoms show signs of burning, quickly slip another sheet underneath. If using more than one sheet in the oven at a time, shift the sheets halfway through baking to ensure even browning.

- Brown sugar and molasses cookies brown more quickly and burn more readily than those made with granulated sugar.

- Dough placed on warm baking sheets will spread more, producing a crisper cookie; therefore, cooling the baking sheets between batches will produce softer cookies.

STORING COOKIES

When I began baking professionally, several caterers sought my services, including one in Queens. Two subways and a bus ride later, I found myself at his spacious synagogue kitchen and proceeded to whip up a host of baked goods, including hundreds of cookies. By the time I finished, it was after three in the morning and nearly everyone else had left. I did not plan on waiting around until everything cooled, so I left instructions for the cookies to be stored in the freezer. Unfortunately, they were placed in the refrigerator and, as a result, became soggy. Needless to say, neither the caterer nor I was happy. So take a lesson in storing food: freeze—never refrigerate—baked cookies. Freeze delicate or frosted cookies on a baking tray before wrapping. Cookies last in the freezer for at least 6 months and thaw in about 30 minutes at room temperature.

For short-term storage, place soft cookies in an airtight container and crisp cookies in a loosely covered container at room temperature for up to 3 days. Sugar is hygroscopic, meaning it attracts moisture from the air. Thus, due to their high proportion of sugar and low proportion of moisture (about 10 to 12 percent), cookies tend to absorb whatever moisture is in the environment. Therefore, do not store soft and crisp cookies in the same container, or the crisp cookies will soften. To keep cookies crisp, place a sugar cube in the container to absorb any moisture. To recrisp cookies, place in a 300-degree oven for several minutes.

To keep cookies soft, place a slice of apple or bread in the container, discarding it after a day or two before it becomes moldy. The moisture in these items—bread contains a high proportion of moisture (up to 38 percent)—and low proportion of sugar raise the humidity in the container. As a result, the sugar in the cookies absorbs the excess humidity, keeping them soft.

DUTCH BUTTER COOKIES
CRANBERRY AND PISTACHIO MANDELBROT
POPPY SEED COOKIES
HUNGARIAN SOUR CREAM COOKIES
NUT CRESCENTS
HERMITS
CHOCOLATE-COCONUT PETITS FOURS
MONSTER MINT-FILLED CHOCOLATE COOKIES
COOKIE BONBONS
TURTLE COOKIES
CHOCOLATE PRETZELS
RAINBOW SLICES/NEAPOLITAN COOKIES
FRUIT SLICES

Dutch Butter Cookies (Joodse Boterkocke)

ABOUT FIFTY 2-INCH-LONG COOKIES

*F*ollowing the Dutch declaration of independence from Spain in 1581, the Netherlands became a haven for Sephardim and Conversos (Jews forcibly converted). These exiles merged their Iberian fare with the local cuisine, creating dishes such as these rich cookies, which the Dutch call Jewish butter cookies. Since the dough of this tender cookie contains no leavening, it holds its basic shape during baking.

1 cup (2 sticks) butter or margarine, softened
⅔ cup sugar or ¾ cup confectioners' sugar
2 large egg yolks
1 teaspoon vanilla extract
¼ teaspoon salt
2 cups all-purpose flour

1. Beat the butter until smooth, about 1 minute. Gradually add the sugar and beat until light and fluffy, about 5 minutes. Beat in the egg yolks, vanilla, and salt. Blend in the flour. Wrap the dough in plastic and refrigerate for at least 2 hours or up to 3 days.
2. Preheat the oven to 375 degrees.
3. Pipe the dough through a pastry bag fitted with a star tip onto ungreased baking sheets, placing the cookies 1 inch apart, or shape into 1-inch balls and flatten.
4. Bake until set but not browned, 8 to 10 minutes. Let the cookies stand until firm, about 1 minute, then transfer to a rack and let cool completely.

VARIATIONS

Almond Butter Cookies: Add 1 cup finely ground blanched almonds and substitute 1 teaspoon almond extract for the vanilla. If desired, press a whole almond in the center of each cookie.

Anise Butter Cookies: Substitute 1½ teaspoons anise flavoring for the vanilla.

Butterscotch Butter Cookies: Substitute ¾ cup packed brown sugar for the granulated sugar.

Cherry Butter Cookies: Shape the dough into 1-inch balls, press your thumb into the center of each ball, and press a halved candied cherry into each thumbprint.

Chocolate-Dipped Butter Cookies: Melt 8 ounces semisweet or bittersweet chocolate in the top of a double boiler. Dip the tips of the cooled cookies into the chocolate, place on baking sheets lined with wax paper, and chill until set, about 30 minutes. Store in the freezer.

Cranberry and Pistachio Mandelbrot

ABOUT 3 DOZEN ½-INCH-THICK COOKIES

This cookie is harder and keeps longer than versions made with oil or butter. Since it contains whole eggs, it is crunchier than versions containing only egg yolks. A recipe that calls for only egg whites (from 6 large eggs), no yolks, results in an extremely hard cookie. You can substitute raisins or other dried fruit for the cranberries and almonds or hazelnuts for the pistachios.

2 cups all-purpose flour
1 teaspoon baking powder
¼ teaspoon salt
2 large eggs, lightly beaten
1 cup sugar
½ teaspoon vanilla extract
½ cup dried cranberries
½ cup pistachios

1. Preheat the oven to 350 degrees. Line a large baking sheet with parchment paper or wax paper or grease and flour the sheets.
2. Sift together the flour, baking powder, and salt. Beat the eggs and sugar until light and creamy. Add the vanilla. Stir in the flour mixture. Add the cranberries and pistachios.
3. Divide the dough in half (it will be a little sticky). Place the dough in an oblong on the prepared sheet. Using floured hands, shape each oblong into a log about 10 inches long and 2 inches wide, leaving 3 inches between the logs. Pat to smooth the surface.
4. Bake until the logs are firm and lightly browned, 30 to 40 minutes. Let cool slightly on the baking sheets, about 10 minutes.

5. Reduce the heat to 325 degrees.
6. Using a serrated knife, cut the logs diagonally into ½-inch-thick slices. Arrange the slices, cut side down, on the baking sheet. Bake, turning once, until golden brown and dry, about 7 minutes per side. Transfer to racks and let cool completely. (Mandelbrot harden as they cool. Store in an airtight container for up to 1 month.)

Poppy Seed Cookies *(Mohn Kichlach)*
ABOUT 3 DOZEN COOKIES

*A*lthough Americans tend to relegate poppy seeds to the role of garnish for bread, central Europeans use them as a flavoring in a host of dishes, such as this beloved cookie.

1½ cups all-purpose flour
½ teaspoon baking powder
3 large eggs
3 tablespoons sugar
½ cup vegetable oil
¼ teaspoon salt
3 to 4 tablespoons poppy seeds
Additional oil for brushing
Additional ¼ cup sugar for sprinkling

1. Preheat the oven to 375 degrees. Grease several baking sheets.
2. Sift together the flour and baking powder. Beat the eggs lightly. Gradually add the sugar and beat until light and creamy, 5 to 10 minutes. Add the oil and salt and beat about 10 minutes. Blend in the flour mixture. Add the poppy seeds.
3. On a lightly floured surface, roll out the dough to a ⅛-inch thickness. Brush with additional oil and sprinkle with the additional sugar. Cut into 2½- by 1½-inch diamonds.
4. Bake until lightly browned, about 25 minutes. Let the cookies stand until firm, about 1 minute, then remove to a rack and let cool completely. Store in an airtight container.

Hungarian Sour Cream Cookies (*Pogacha/Pogachel*)

ABOUT THIRTY 4-INCH OR SEVENTY 2½-INCH COOKIES

Sour cream results in a tender cookie with a slight tang.

2¼ cups all-purpose flour
½ teaspoon baking powder
½ teaspoon salt
½ cup (1 stick) unsalted butter or shortening, softened
  (or ¼ cup butter and ¼ cup shortening)
⅔ cup sugar
2 large egg yolks or 1 large egg
¼ cup sour cream
1½ teaspoons vanilla extract

1. Sift together the flour, baking powder, and salt. Beat the butter until smooth. Gradually add the sugar and beat until light and fluffy, about 5 minutes. Beat in the egg yolks, one at a time. Add the sour cream and vanilla. Gradually stir in the flour mixture. Form the dough into a ball, wrap in plastic, and refrigerate until firm, at least 1 hour.
2. Preheat the oven to 375 degrees.
3. Divide the dough in half. Sprinkle a flat surface lightly with flour or confectioners' sugar and roll out the dough halves to a ⅛- to ¼-inch thickness (the thinner the cookie, the crisper it will be). Cut out the desired shapes and place the cookies on ungreased baking sheets.
4. Bake until light golden, 8 to 11 minutes. Let the cookies stand until firm, about 1 minute, then remove to a rack and let cool completely. Store in an airtight container.

Nut Crescents

ABOUT SIXTY-FIVE 1½-INCH COOKIES

These delicate cookies are also called *kupferlin* in Austria and Hungary, *nusskipferlin* in Germany, *kourambiedes* in Greece, and *polvorones* in Mexico. Although the omission of eggs and leavening results in an incredibly tender cookie, it also makes them very fragile. Confectioners' sugar, which contains cornstarch, makes for a crisper, even more tender cookie than one made with granulated sugar.

1 cup (2 sticks) unsalted butter or margarine, softened
⅔ cup confectioners' sugar or ⅓ cup granulated sugar
1 tablespoon water, rum, or lemon juice
1 teaspoon vanilla extract
¼ teaspoon salt
2 cups all-purpose flour
1 to 1½ cups (4 to 6 ounces) finely chopped pecans, walnuts, almonds,
    husked hazelnuts, macadamia nuts, or pistachios
Additional ¾ cup confectioners' sugar for dusting

1. Beat the butter until smooth, about 1 minute. Gradually add the sugar and beat until light and fluffy, about 5 minutes. Add the water, vanilla, and salt. Stir in the flour and nuts. Cover and refrigerate the dough for at least 1 hour or up to 3 days.
2. Preheat the oven to 350 degrees.
3. Shape 1-inch pieces of the dough into crescents and place 1 inch apart on ungreased baking sheets.
4. Bake until lightly browned, 15 to 20 minutes. Let the cookies stand until firm, about 1 minute, then transfer to a rack and let cool completely. When cool, roll the cookies in the additional confectioners' sugar.

Hermits

ABOUT 3 DOZEN 2-INCH COOKIES

1¾ cups all-purpose flour
½ teaspoon baking soda or 1 teaspoon baking powder
½ teaspoon ground cinnamon
½ teaspoon grated nutmeg
½ teaspoon salt
½ cup (1 stick) unsalted butter or margarine, softened
1 cup packed brown sugar
1 large egg
1 teaspoon vanilla extract
¼ cup brewed coffee, cooled
¾ cup (3½ ounces) raisins
¾ cup (3 ounces) chopped dried apricots or dates
¾ cup chopped nuts

1. Sift together the flour, baking soda, cinnamon, nutmeg, and salt. Beat the butter until smooth, about 1 minute. Add the sugar and beat until light and fluffy, about 5 minutes. Beat in the egg, then the vanilla. Stir in the coffee and the flour mixture. Add the dried fruit and nuts. Wrap the dough in plastic and refrigerate for at least 4 hours or up to 3 days.
2. Preheat the oven to 375 degrees.
3. Drop the dough by level tablespoonfuls onto ungreased baking sheets, 2 inches apart. Flatten slightly.
4. Bake until golden brown, 8 to 12 minutes. Let the cookies stand until firm, about 1 minute, then remove to a rack and let cool completely.

Chocolate-Coconut Petits Fours

32 SMALL CAKES

*M*y mother once mentioned that these were among her favorite bakery treats while growing up in Cleveland. Later, while visiting my sister's family in Melbourne, Australia, I discovered that they are called Lamingtons down under, where they are a national dessert. In any case, this genoise provides the basis for dainty and elegant cakes. Or you can substitute a 13- by 9-inch yellow or white butter cake.

GENOISE
¾ cup all-purpose flour
¼ cup cornstarch
1 teaspoon baking powder
¼ teaspoon salt
¼ cup hot water
1 tablespoon unsalted butter or margarine
3 large eggs
1 teaspoon vanilla extract
½ cup sugar

COATING
4 cups (1 pound) confectioners' sugar
½ cup unsweetened cocoa powder, preferably nonalkalized
½ cup milk or nondairy creamer
1 tablespoon unsalted butter or margarine
12 ounces (about 4 cups) shredded coconut

1. Preheat the oven to 350 degrees. Grease an 11- by 7-inch baking pan, line with wax paper, grease the wax paper, and dust with flour.
2. To make the genoise: Sift together the flour, cornstarch, baking powder, and salt. Pour the hot water over the butter and stir until melted. Beat the eggs until slightly thickened. Add the vanilla. Gradually add the sugar and beat until very thick, about 5 minutes. Gently fold in the flour mixture, then the butter mixture.
3. Pour the batter into the prepared pan. Bake until the cake springs back when lightly touched, 25 to 30 minutes. Let cool in the pan for 5 minutes, then invert onto a rack, remove the wax paper, and let cool completely.

4. Trim off the hard sides or uneven edges of the cake. Cut into 2½- by 1½-inch pieces. Cover with plastic wrap and freeze. (Freezing allows for easier handling.)
5. To make the coating: Sift together the confectioners' sugar and cocoa powder. In the top of a double boiler, stir the milk and butter until it is melted. Stir in the cocoa mixture.
6. To assemble: Dip the cake pieces into the chocolate glaze to coat all the sides, letting the excess drip off. Carefully roll in the coconut to cover on all sides. Place on a rack and let stand until firm, about 1 hour.

Monster Mint-Filled Chocolate Cookies
2 VERY LARGE COOKIES

COOKIE DOUGH
1½ cups all-purpose flour
2 teaspoons baking soda
1 teaspoon ground cinnamon
¼ teaspoon salt
⅔ cup vegetable shortening
½ cup sugar
1 large egg
¼ cup light corn syrup
6 ounces semisweet or bittersweet chocolate, melted

FILLING
¼ cup (½ stick) unsalted butter or margarine, softened
¼ teaspoon peppermint extract
2 cups (8 ounces) confectioners' sugar
2 to 3 tablespoons milk or water
Additional sugar for rolling

1. Preheat the oven to 350 degrees.
2. To make the dough: Sift together the flour, baking soda, cinnamon, and salt. In a large bowl, beat the shortening, sugar, and egg until creamy, about 5 minutes. Add the corn syrup and chocolate. Gradually blend in the flour mixture.

3. Divide the dough into 4 equal pieces and form into balls. Roll each ball in the additional sugar. Place on a large baking sheet and flatten slightly, leaving 3 inches between balls.

4. Bake until set, about 25 minutes. Let the cookies stand until firm, about 1 minute, then transfer to a rack and let cool completely. (Store in an airtight container at room temperature for up to 3 days or in the freezer for several months.)

5. To make the filling: Beat the butter and peppermint extract until smooth, about 1 minute. Gradually add the confectioners' sugar and beat until light and fluffy. Stir in enough milk or water to produce a spreading consistency.

6. Spread the filling on the top (rounded) side of 2 cookies and press together with the top side of a second cookie.

Cookie Bonbons
ABOUT 2 DOZEN COOKIES

*M*olding sugar cookie dough around a filling results in a fancy treat.

COOKIE DOUGH
½ cup (1 stick) unsalted butter or margarine, softened
(or ¼ cup butter or margarine and ¼ cup shortening)
¾ cup confectioners' sugar or ½ cup granulated sugar
1½ teaspoons vanilla extract
⅛ teaspoon salt
1½ cups all-purpose flour

FILLINGS
Well-drained maraschino cherries
Whole nuts
Chocolate chunks
Candied fruit chunks, such as cherries, mango, or pineapple chunks
Pitted date halves

TOPPINGS
Confectioners' sugar, confectioners' sugar glaze,
*   or melted semisweet or bittersweet chocolate*
Chopped nuts or flaked coconut (optional)

1. To make the dough: Beat the butter until smooth, about 1 minute. Add the sugar and beat until light and fluffy, about 5 minutes. Stir in the vanilla and salt. Add the flour to make a smooth dough. Cover and refrigerate for at least 1 hour or up to 3 days.
2. Shape the dough into 1-inch balls and flatten each ball into a round. Place the desired filling in the center and press the dough around it to enclose completely. Chill for at least 15 minutes.
3. Preheat the oven to 350 degrees.
4. Place the cookies 1 inch apart on ungreased baking sheets. Bake until firm but not browned, about 15 minutes. Transfer to a rack and let cool completely. Sprinkle with confectioners' sugar or dip the tops into confectioners' sugar glaze or melted chocolate and, if desired, sprinkle with nuts or coconut.

Turtle Cookies
ABOUT 4 DOZEN COOKIES

1 cup (2 sticks) unsalted butter or margarine, softened
⅔ cup packed brown sugar
2 large egg yolks or 1 large egg
1 teaspoon vanilla extract
¼ teaspoon salt
1½ cups all-purpose flour
About 192 pecan halves (about 14 ounces)

GLAZE
2 ounces unsweetened chocolate
2 tablespoons unsalted butter or margarine
2 cups confectioners' sugar
1 teaspoon vanilla extract
About 3 tablespoons hot water

1. Beat the butter until smooth, about 1 minute. Add the brown sugar and beat until light and fluffy, about 5 minutes. Beat in the egg yolks, vanilla, and salt. Blend in the flour. Wrap the dough in plastic and refrigerate for at least 1 hour or up to 3 days.
2. Preheat the oven to 350 degrees.
3. Shape the dough into 1-inch balls. Arrange 4 pecan halves in an X shape on an ungreased baking sheet, leaving about 1 inch in the center. Place 1 dough ball in the center of the X. Repeat with the remaining pecans and dough.
4. Bake until lightly browned, about 10 minutes. Let the cookies stand until firm, about 1 minute, then transfer to a rack and let cool completely.
5. To make the glaze: Melt the chocolate and butter, stirring until smooth. Stir in the confectioners' sugar and vanilla. Add enough hot water to make a pouring consistency. Drizzle the cooled cookies with the chocolate glaze and let stand on the rack until the glaze is set.

Chocolate Pretzels
4 DOZEN COOKIES

2 cups all-purpose flour
½ cup unsweetened cocoa powder
¼ teaspoon salt
1 cup (2 sticks) unsalted butter or margarine, softened
1 cup confectioners' sugar
1 large egg
1 teaspoon vanilla extract

1. Sift together the flour, cocoa powder, and salt. Beat the butter until smooth, about 1 minute. Add the sugar and beat until light and fluffy, about 5 minutes. Beat in the egg and vanilla. Blend in the flour mixture. Wrap the dough in plastic and refrigerate for at least 1 hour or up to 3 days.
2. Preheat the oven to 375 degrees.
3. Shape the dough into 1-inch balls and roll each ball into a 9-inch-long rope. Form the ropes into rings and place on ungreased baking sheets with the ends at the top. Pull one end down over the bottom of the ring, with the end overlapping the bottom by

about ¼ inch from the end of the rope. Repeat with the second end to form a pretzel shape.

4. Bake until set but not browned, about 8 minutes. Let the cookies stand until firm, about 1 minute, then transfer to a rack and let cool completely.

Rainbow Slices/Neapolitan Cookies
ABOUT 8 DOZEN COOKIES

1 cup (2 sticks) unsalted butter or margarine, softened
1 cup sugar
8 ounces (about ¾ cup) almond paste (page 361), crumbled
4 large eggs, separated
1 teaspoon almond extract
⅛ teaspoon salt
2 cups all-purpose flour
Several drops red, green, and yellow food coloring
½ cup apricot preserves, melted and strained
3 ounces semisweet or bittersweet chocolate

1. Preheat the oven to 350 degrees. Grease three 13- by 9-inch baking pans, line with wax paper or parchment paper, and grease the paper.
2. Beat the butter until smooth, about 1 minute. Add the sugar and beat until light and fluffy, about 5 minutes. Beat in the almond paste. Beat in the egg yolks, almond extract, and salt. Blend in the flour.
3. Beat the egg whites on low speed until foamy, about 30 seconds. Increase the speed to high and beat until stiff but not dry. Fold ¼ of the egg whites into the almond mixture, then fold in the remaining whites.
4. Divide the batter into thirds (about 1½ cups each). Fold a few drops of red coloring into one third and spread evenly over 1 pan. Repeat with the green and yellow coloring.
5. Bake until the edges of the cake begin to color, about 15 minutes. Invert onto wire racks and let cool completely.
6. Place a cake layer on a flat surface and spread with half of the preserves. Top with a second layer, spread with the remaining preserves, then top with the third layer.

Cover with plastic wrap, place a board or other large flat surface on top, and weight down. Refrigerate overnight.

7. In the top of a double boiler over barely simmering water, melt the chocolate, stirring until smooth. Or microwave on medium (50 percent power) until the chocolate turns shiny, 2 to 4 minutes. Spread the melted chocolate over the top of the cake and let stand for 30 minutes. Cut into 1- by ½-inch bars.

Almond Paste (*Alemendrada*)
ABOUT 1 POUND OR 1¾ CUPS

1¾ cups (8 ounces) blanched almonds
2 cups (8 ounces) confectioners' sugar
*   or 1 cup plus 2 tablespoons granulated sugar*
Pinch of salt
½ teaspoon almond extract
*   or 1 to 3 teaspoons orange blossom or rose water*
About 1 large egg white

In a food processor, finely grind the almonds with the sugar and salt. Add the almond extract or flavored water. Add enough egg white to make a cohesive paste and knead until smooth, about 3 minutes. Wrap and refrigerate overnight, but preferably for 24 hours. (Almond paste can be stored in the refrigerator for at least 6 weeks and in a freezer for up to a year. If almond paste hardens, microwave on HIGH for several seconds until pliable.)

Fruit Slices
ABOUT 60 COOKIES

1 cup (2 sticks) unsalted butter or margarine, softened
1 cup sugar
2 large eggs
2 teaspoons vanilla extract
½ teaspoon salt
3 cups all-purpose flour
1½ teaspoons grated lemon zest
Several drops yellow food coloring
1½ teaspoons grated lime zest
Several drops green food coloring
1½ teaspoons grated orange zest
Several drops orange food coloring
Additional sugar for rolling

1. Beat the butter until smooth, about 1 minute. Add the sugar and beat until light and fluffy, about 5 minutes. Beat in the eggs, one at a time. Add the vanilla and salt. Stir in the flour.
2. Divide the dough into 4 equal pieces. For the lemon slices, combine 1 piece of dough with the lemon zest and yellow food coloring. For the lime slices, combine 1 piece of dough with the lime zest and green food coloring. For the orange slices, combine 1 piece of dough with the orange zest and the orange food coloring. (The fourth piece of dough remains plain.) Wrap the pieces of dough in plastic and refrigerate for at least 1 hour or up to 3 days.
3. Place the colored dough pieces on sheets of wax paper or aluminum foil and shape into logs 2 inches in diameter and 6 inches long.
4. Divide the plain dough into thirds. Roll each piece into a 6- by 4-inch rectangle. Wrap the rectangles around the logs, pressing the edges to seal. Roll in the additional sugar. Chill until firm, at least 4 hours.
5. Preheat the oven to 400 degrees.
6. Using a sharp knife, cut the logs into ⅛-inch-thick slices. Cut each slice in half. Place 1 inch apart on ungreased baking sheets.
7. Bake until firm but not browned, about 8 minutes. Let the cookies firm up on the baking sheet for about 1 minute, then transfer to a wire rack and let cool completely.

Cakes

Growing up in a kosher household in the South without the benefit of a kosher bakery or even packaged mixes (if they can actually be considered a benefit) meant that baked goods were always made from scratch. Cakes were used to mark special occasions, such as birthdays, weddings, anniversaries, and holidays. There were honey cakes for Rosh Hashanah, sponge cakes and nut tortes for Passover, cheesecakes for Shavuot, and butter cakes for birthdays.

My mother, not one to follow directions, never quite mastered this area of cuisine, which requires strict attention. (It is for good reason that professional bakers refer to recipes as formulas; they are chemical equations. And anyone who has ever taken high school chemistry knows what happens when an equation is not properly followed.) Sometimes my mother's cakes turned out a bit lopsided, deflated, or occasionally a little overdone, but they were always appreciated. On the other hand, many southern women (my mother was born in Ohio), both Jewish and gentile, possess a passion for baking and create cakes worthy of blue ribbons. I can still practically taste the coconut cakes layered with tangy lemon curd, lane cakes packed with a filling of chopped fruit, coconut, and a hint of Kentucky bourbon, jam cakes slathered with caramel icing, and intense chocolate cakes that eschewed any dairy products that would have inhibited the flavor of the cocoa. In the synagogue the women whipped up such delicacies as *marmorgugelhupf* (marble cake) and assorted *kuchen*—apple, pear, hazelnut, and cinnamon-raisin. Alas, today *kiddush* generally consists of store-bought products laden with chemicals and lacking in personality and flavor. Progress does not always equate with taste.

TIPS FOR CAKE-MAKING SUCCESS

- There are two basic types of cakes, categorized by the method used to prepare the batter: butter and egg-foam. In the former, butter or shortening is beaten with sugar to incorporate air, which raises the batter. Chemical leavenings such as baking powder and baking soda are frequently added. Egg-foam cakes, such as sponge and chiffon, depend solely on beating air into eggs for leavening. Tortes are egg-foam cakes that contain little or no flour.

- Use the right size pan. If the pan is too large for the amount of batter, the sides of the cake will be done before the center. The preferable pans for baking cakes are aluminum (not disposable) with straight sides. Grease the pans with shortening and

dust with flour or, for chocolate cakes, cocoa powder—the fat keeps the batter from touching the pan and sticking; the flour keeps the fat in place.

- To measure flour for cakes, unless otherwise indicated, lightly stir the flour to settle it and spoon it into a "dry" measure (they come in sets ranging from ¼ to 1 cup), filling it above the rim. Then level the top with a flat instrument such as the back of a knife. Do not tamp.

- Cake pans should be placed at least 3 inches away from the sides of the oven and from each other. The part of the cake too close to the oven sides or other pans is exposed to more heat, which sets it before the cooler parts, and the result is a lopsided cake.

- Slice cakes just prior to the party or serving, keeping the cut surfaces together to preserve freshness as well as create a more attractive presentation. If the guests are to help themselves, be sure to provide sufficient cake servers.

DECORATING CAKES

The addition of sweet fillings and toppings—such as buttercream, ganache, and whipped cream—transforms a simple baked good into a layer cake and a special treat. Frostings not only decorate a cake and add flavor but also act as a protective coating to extend its freshness. Use a stiff consistency to make flowers, a medium consistency for borders, and a thin consistency for writing and leaves.

Pastry bags are conical bags that narrow near one end. Plastic or polyester-coated canvas bags are best because fat can seep through plain canvas bags. If you do not have a pastry bag, use a sturdy plastic bag and cut off a corner. To pipe frostings, you will need an 8- to 10-inch bag. Squeezing the frosting through a hollow metal tip fitted to the pastry bag produces various designs depending on the tip. Each tip is numbered to reveal which design it makes. Couplers are two-part plastic caps designed to hold the decorating tip in place.

To fill a pastry bag, unscrew the sections of the coupler, insert the larger part of the coupler, narrow end first, through the end of the pastry bag, attach the desired tip onto the coupler, and screw on the coupler ring. Fold the top half of the bag inside out and down to create a collar. Holding the bag under the collar in one hand, fill the bag no more than halfway, pushing the frosting down toward the tip. Unfold the collar, twist the top of the bag to close, and press the frosting downward. Hold the twisted end between your thumb and index finger and use other hand to squeeze and guide the pastry bag.

TIPS FOR DECORATING CAKES

- To soften butter or margarine quickly, beat it in a bowl set over hot water or work it with your hands until pliable.

- Cakes should be completely cooled before frosting.

- To ensure evenly aligned cake layers, make a narrow vertical cut down the side of the cake before cutting it into horizontal layers. Then, after filling, simply align the cut marks.

- To handle and transport a frosted cake easily, frost it on a piece of thick cardboard.

- Cover the edges of the cake plate with strips of wax paper to keep the plate clean. After the cake is frosted, pull away the paper.

- If the frosting on a cake thickens too much to spread, dip the spatula in hot water.

- Brush any crumbs from the surface of the cake before frosting. To prevent getting crumbs in the frosting, place a larger amount of frosting than needed (a 9-inch round requires about 1 cup of buttercream) in the center of the cake layer. Using a back-and-forth motion while keeping the spatula flat against the surface, spread the frosting to the edges, then remove the excess frosting. An offset spatula has a slender, flexible blade that is lower than the handle, making for easier spreading of frosting.

- Dipping a knife in cold water makes spreading icing easier.

- If the frosting is very soft, place the covered cake layer in the freezer for several minutes before adding the upper layers.

- To give frosting a silky look, blow a hair dryer over the frosted surface of the cake until it is smooth and shiny.

- Candy thermometers are helpful in determining the temperature of sugar syrups used for some buttercreams. There are two types of candy thermometers: a glass tube containing mercury (the more accurate one) and a metal stem fitted with a 1-inch dial.

CARROT CAKE
APPLESAUCE SPICE CAKE
CHOCOLATE MOUSSE CAKE
BASIC BUTTERCREAM
BASIC COOKED BUTTERCREAM

Carrot Cake
10 SERVINGS

In this cake, the oil and the moisture in the carrots serve as the liquid. Using oil results in very moist and tender cake that can be stored in the refrigerator without any deleterious effects.

1 pound carrots, shredded (3¼ cups)
1 cup granulated sugar
1 cup packed brown sugar (light or dark)
2 cups unbleached all-purpose flour
2 teaspoons ground cinnamon
½ teaspoon ground ginger
1 teaspoon baking powder
1 teaspoon baking soda
1 teaspoon salt
1 cup vegetable oil
4 large eggs, lightly beaten
1 teaspoon vanilla extract
1 cup raisins or chopped pitted dates (optional)
1 cup shredded coconut (optional)
1 cup coarsely chopped walnuts or pecans (optional)

FROSTING
2 pounds cream cheese, at room temperature
8 ounces unsalted butter, softened
2 teaspoons vanilla extract
1 pound (4 cups) confectioners' sugar

1. Preheat the oven to 350 degrees. Grease and lightly flour two 9-inch round pans or one 13- by 9-inch baking pan.
2. Combine the carrots and sugar and let stand for 30 minutes. (This extracts moisture from the carrots, resulting in a more intense flavor and darker color.)
3. Sift together the flour, cinnamon, ginger, baking powder, baking soda, and salt. Stir in the oil. Beat in the eggs, one at a time. Add the vanilla. Stir in the carrot mixture and, if desired, the raisins, coconut, and/or walnuts.

4. Pour the batter into the prepared pans. Bake until a tester inserted in the center comes out clean and the cake begins to shrink slightly, 35 to 40 minutes for 9-inch pans, 40 to 50 minutes for a 13- by 9-inch pan.

5. Let cool in the pans for 15 minutes, then remove to a rack and let cool completely. (The cake can be stored in the refrigerator for up to 1 week or in the freezer for up to 3 months.)

6. To make the frosting: Beat the cream cheese, butter, and vanilla until light and fluffy. Gradually beat in the confectioners' sugar until smooth. Spread over the cake. If desired, garnish with marzipan carrots or toasted coconut.

Applesauce Spice Cake
10 TO 12 SERVINGS

2½ cups all-purpose flour
1½ teaspoons baking soda
¼ teaspoon baking powder
1½ teaspoons salt
1 teaspoon ground cinnamon
½ teaspoon ground allspice or cloves
½ teaspoon grated nutmeg
2 cups granulated or packed brown sugar (or 1 cup each)
½ cup vegetable shortening
2 large eggs
1½ teaspoons vanilla extract
1½ cups (12 ounces) applesauce
½ cup water
1 cup raisins or chopped pitted dates (or ½ cup each)

FROSTING
4 cups (1 pound) confectioners' sugar
6 tablespoons unsalted margarine, softened
About ¼ cup maple syrup or orange juice

1. Preheat the oven to 350 degrees. Grease two 9-inch round cake pans or one 10-inch tube or Bundt pan. If using cake pans, line the bottoms with parchment paper or wax paper, grease the paper, and dust with flour.
2. Sift together the flour, baking soda, baking powder, salt, and spices. Beat the sugar and shortening until light and fluffy, about 5 minutes. Beat in the eggs, one at a time. Add the vanilla. Stir in the flour mixture, then the applesauce and water. Stir in the raisins.
3. Divide the batter between the prepared pans. Bake until a tester inserted in the center of the cake comes out clean and the cake springs back when lightly touched, 25 to 35 minutes for the 9-inch rounds, about 55 minutes for the tube or Bundt pan. Let cool in the pans for 10 minutes, then remove to a rack and let cool completely.
4. To make the frosting: Beat together the sugar, margarine, and enough maple syrup or orange juice to make a spreading consistency. Frost the top and sides of the cake.

Chocolate Mousse Cake
10 TO 12 SERVINGS PER CAKE

*T*he chocolate cakes are cut horizontally into thirds, with each layer providing the base for one finished mousse cake. Each chocolate cake, therefore, yields enough layers for three mousse cakes. The chocolate mousse in this recipe can also be served as a dessert in a large bowl or in individual serving bowls.

CHOCOLATE CAKE LAYER

1 mousse cake	*6 mousse cakes*	
½ cup	*1 cup*	*all-purpose flour*
2 tablespoons	*¼ cup*	*unsweetened cocoa powder*
½ teaspoon	*1 teaspoon*	*baking powder*
Pinch	*⅛ teaspoon*	*salt*
4 large	*8 large*	*eggs*
½ cup	*1 cup*	*sugar*

CHOCOLATE MOUSSE

1 mousse cake	6 mousse cakes	
12 ounces	4½ pounds	semisweet or bittersweet chocolate, chopped
3 tablespoons	1 cup	sugar
¼ cup	1½ cups	water
6 large	36 large	eggs, separated
1 teaspoon	2 tablespoons	vanilla extract
2 tablespoons	¾ cup	rum, brandy, kirsch, or brewed coffee
Pinch	¼ teaspoon	salt

1. To make the cake: Preheat the oven to 375 degrees. Grease an 8-inch springform pan (2 pans for 60 servings), line with wax paper, grease the wax paper, and dust with flour.

2. Sift together the flour, cocoa powder, baking powder, and salt. Beat the eggs and sugar until thick and creamy, 5 to 10 minutes. Sift the flour mixture over the egg mixture and gently fold in.

3. Pour the batter into the prepared pan (or pans), tilting the pan to level the surface. Bake until the cake springs back when lightly touched and the edges begin to pull away from the sides of the pan, 35 to 45 minutes.

4. Let cool in the pan for 10 minutes, then loosen the edges with a sharp knife and invert onto a wire rack. Remove the wax paper and let the cake cool completely. (The cake can be covered in plastic wrap and stored at room temperature for up to 2 days or in the freezer for up to 4 months.)

5. To make the mousse: In the top of a double boiler set over barely simmering water, heat the chocolate, sugar, and water, stirring occasionally, until the chocolate is melted and the mixture is smooth. Remove from the heat and beat in the egg yolks, one at a time. Add the vanilla and rum.

6. Beat the egg whites on low speed until foamy, about 30 seconds. Add the salt, increase the speed to high, and beat until the whites are stiff but not dry. Fold ¼ of the egg whites into the chocolate mixture, then gently fold in the remaining whites.

7. To assemble: Using a serrated knife, cut the cake horizontally into thirds. (When making 1 cake, save the other 2 layers for another use.) For each mousse cake, snugly fit a cake layer into an 8-inch springform pan. Pour the mousse on top and place in the freezer for at least 2 hours or up to 1 month. Allow the cake to soften at room temperature about 30 minutes before serving. If desired, garnish with dollops of whipped cream or nondairy topping and Chocolate-Dipped Strawberries (page 284).

VARIATION

Black Forest Cake: For each cake, spread 3 of the cake layers with canned cherry pie filling. Frost the top and sides of the cake with sweetened whipped cream. Sprinkle the top of the cake with chocolate shavings.

Basic Buttercream
ABOUT 2 CUPS

*T*his version of buttercream is firm enough to hold its shape, yet does not set hard, which complements sturdy butter cakes. For a creamier buttercream, increase the butter to 1 cup (2 sticks) and reduce the milk or water to about 1 tablespoon. For a stiffer consistency, add a little more confectioners' sugar. This makes enough to frost a 2-layer 8-inch cake, a 13- by 9-inch cake, or 2 dozen cupcakes.

½ cup (1 stick) unsalted butter or margarine, softened (or ¼ cup butter and
*   ¼ cup vegetable shortening)*
1 pound (about 4 cups) confectioners' sugar, sifted
2 teaspoons vanilla extract
About ¼ cup water, cream, milk, juice, or liqueur

Beat the butter until smooth, about 1 minute. Add the sugar and beat until light and fluffy, about 5 minutes. Do not overbeat, or the frosting will be too soft to pipe. Beat in the vanilla and enough of the water to make a smooth buttercream of spreading consistency.

VARIATIONS

Almond Buttercream: Substitute 2 teaspoons almond extract for the vanilla.

Apricot Buttercream: Substitute ¼ cup apricot liqueur or strained apricot preserves for the liquid.

Banana-Rum Buttercream: Increase the butter to 1½ cups (3 sticks). Add ¾ cup mashed ripe bananas mixed with 1 teaspoon lemon juice and use ¼ cup rum for the liquid.

Chocolate Buttercream: Add 3 ounces melted and slightly cooled unsweetened or bittersweet chocolate or ⅔ to ¾ cup unsweetened cocoa powder.

Lemon Buttercream: Substitute 1 teaspoon finely grated lemon zest for the vanilla and use ¼ cup lemon juice for the liquid.

Mocha Buttercream: Add ⅓ cup unsweetened cocoa powder and use 3 to 4 tablespoons strong coffee for the liquid.

Orange Buttercream: Substitute 1 tablespoon finely grated orange zest for the vanilla and use ¼ cup orange juice for the liquid.

Peanut Butter Buttercream: Omit the liquid. Reduce the confectioners' sugar to 2 cups. Add ½ cup creamy peanut butter.

Peppermint Buttercream: Substitute ¼ teaspoon peppermint extract for the vanilla.

Basic Cooked Buttercream
ABOUT 4 CUPS

*T*he sugar syrup and egg yolks result in a creamy texture and less sweet flavor that complements egg-foam cakes. As a rule of thumb, spread lighter cakes such as genoise with a thinner layer of buttercream than sturdier butter cakes. This recipe makes enough to frost a 3-layer 8-inch cake or 2-layer 9-inch cake. You can divide the plain buttercream into half or thirds and flavor each part differently.

1⅓ cups sugar
⅔ cup water
8 large egg yolks
2 cups (4 sticks) unsalted butter or margarine, softened
2 teaspoons vanilla extract or 3 to 4 tablespoons liqueur

1. Over low heat, stir the sugar and water until the sugar dissolves. Increase the heat to medium-high and boil, without stirring, until the syrup reaches the soft-ball stage or 238 degrees on a candy thermometer, about 10 minutes.

2. Meanwhile, beat the egg yolks until pale and thick, about 4 minutes. In a slow, steady stream, pour the hot syrup into the eggs, beating continuously as you pour. (Do not let the syrup touch the beaters, or it will spin into threads.) Continue beating until the mixture thickens and cools to room temperature, 10 to 15 minutes.

3. Beat in the butter or margarine, 2 tablespoons at a time, until absorbed. Gradually beat in the vanilla. (Do not add the flavoring too quickly, or the buttercream will curdle.) Chill until of spreading consistency, at least 2 hours or up to 1 week. Return to room temperature before using, about 1 hour.

HINT: If the buttercream curdles, beat in a little more softened butter or margarine.

VARIATIONS

Ivory Cooked Buttercream: Reduce the egg yolks to 2 and add 4 beaten egg whites.

Almond Cooked Buttercream: Add 1 cup toasted and finely ground blanched almonds.

Banana Cooked Buttercream: Stir in ⅔ cup mashed banana mixed with ½ teaspoon lemon juice.

Berry Cooked Buttercream: Add ⅔ cup blackberry, raspberry, or strawberry puree.

Chocolate Cooked Buttercream: Add ½ cup unsweetened cocoa powder or 8 ounces melted and cooled semisweet or bittersweet chocolate. For Mocha Buttercream: Add 2 tablespoons instant coffee or espresso powder dissolved in 2 teaspoons hot water.

Hazelnut Cooked Buttercream: Add 1 cup toasted, skinned, and finely ground hazelnuts.

Lemon Cooked Buttercream: Add 1 tablespoon finely grated lemon zest and 1 tablespoon fresh lemon juice.

Orange Cooked Buttercream: Add 4 teaspoons finely grated orange zest and 1 tablespoon fresh orange juice or 1 teaspoon orange oil.

Quick Breads

Quick breads are batters and doughs that rise without yeast. They are similar to cakes, except they contain a smaller proportion of sugar and generally rely solely on chemical leavenings for rising. If you are a novice baker, quick breads are a good place to start because they are relatively easy. A quick bread is also the perfect treat for a baker on the go, as there is no kneading, beating, or rising time and almost all the ingredients can be found in the average cupboard.

Unbleached all-purpose flour provides the best texture and flavor; cake flour results in flat, oily breads. The amount of sugar in the batter may be adjusted according to personal preference as well as the tartness of the flavorings. Preparation should take no longer than 10 minutes, and baking time is generally an hour for loaves and a half hour for muffins. The most demanding part may be waiting for the bread to cool before eating—it will slice more easily and taste better when cooled.

TIPS FOR MAKING QUICK BREADS

- Use dull metal or glass loaf pans. Since heat passes through glass pans, reduce the baking temperature by 25 degrees.

- The preferable utensil for mixing quick bread batters is a whisk, which helps to aerate the batter, but a fork can also be used. For best results, all ingredients should be at room temperature. Overbeating the flour creates long threads of gluten, which cannot properly absorb the liquid, and the result is a tough, flat cake instead of light, moist bread.

- Grease only the bottom of the pan to prevent the raised rim that forms around the edges of the bread. Do not fill the pan more than two-thirds full, or the batter may overflow during baking.

- In order not to lose any of the leavening power, bake quick breads soon after mixing. Do not overbake. Remove from the oven when the tops are golden brown and a toothpick inserted in the center comes out clean. Do not worry if the bread cracks down the middle. This is normal for most quick breads.

- Do not cool a quick bread in the pan for too long or you will end up with a soggy loaf. Let the bread rest in the pan for only 5 to 10 minutes, then remove to a wire rack. When cooled, wrap the quick bread in plastic or foil and store at room temperature or in the freezer. Quick breads freeze well.

APPLE QUICK BREAD
BANANA QUICK BREAD
HONEY–SUNFLOWER SEED QUICK BREAD
OATMEAL QUICK BREAD
PUMPKIN QUICK BREAD
STRAWBERRY QUICK BREAD
ZUCCHINI QUICK BREAD
SCONES

Apple Quick Bread
2 LARGE LOAVES

3 cups all-purpose flour, preferably unbleached
1 teaspoon baking soda
¾ teaspoon salt
1½ teaspoons ground cinnamon
½ teaspoon grated nutmeg
¼ teaspoon ground allspice or cloves
1 cup vegetable oil
1 cup granulated sugar
1 cup packed brown sugar
3 large eggs, lightly beaten
4 cups peeled, cored, and grated apples (3 large apples)
1 cup raisins or chopped pitted dates
1 cup chopped almonds, pecans, or walnuts (optional)

1. Preheat the oven to 350 degrees. Grease and flour the bottom of two 9- by 5-inch loaf pans.
2. Sift together the flour, baking soda, salt, and spices. Combine the oil, sugars, and eggs. Add the flour mixture all at once and stir just to mix. Stir in the apples, raisins, and if desired, the nuts.
3. Pour into the prepared pans. Bake until the bread is lightly browned and a wooden tester inserted in the center comes out clean, about 1 hour 10 minutes. Let cool in the pans for 10 minutes, then turn out onto a rack and let cool completely.

Banana Quick Bread
1 LARGE LOAF

1½ cups mashed ripe bananas (about 3 medium)
1 tablespoon fresh lemon juice or rum
2 cups all-purpose flour, preferably unbleached
1 teaspoon baking soda
1 teaspoon salt
2 teaspoons ground cinnamon
½ teaspoon grated nutmeg
¼ teaspoon ground allspice or cloves
¼ cup wheat germ (optional)
¾ cup vegetable oil
1 cup granulated or packed brown sugar or ½ cup each
2 large eggs, lightly beaten
1 teaspoon vanilla extract
1 cup chopped walnuts, chopped pecans, blueberries,
    chopped pitted dates, or chocolate chips (optional)

1. Preheat the oven to 350 degrees. Grease and flour the bottom of one 9- by 5-inch loaf pan.
2. Mash the bananas with the lemon juice. Sift together the flour, baking soda, salt, and spices. If desired, add the wheat germ. Combine the bananas, oil, sugar, eggs, and vanilla. Add the flour mixture all at once and stir just to mix. If desired, add the nuts.
3. Pour into the prepared pan. Bake until the bread is lightly browned and a wooden tester inserted in the center comes out clean, about 1 hour 10 minutes. Let cool in the pan for 10 minutes, then turn out onto a rack and let cool completely.

Honey-Sunflower Seed Quick Bread
2 MEDIUM LOAVES

3 cups all-purpose flour
1 tablespoon baking powder
1½ teaspoons ground ginger

¾ teaspoon ground cinnamon
1 teaspoon salt
1¼ cups milk, nondairy creamer, or water
1 cup honey
2 large eggs, lightly beaten
6 tablespoons unsalted butter or margarine, melted
½ cup sunflower seeds
1 cup raisins, chopped pitted dates, chopped dried figs, or chopped dried apricots (optional)

1. Preheat the oven to 350 degrees. Grease the bottom and halfway up the sides of two 8½- by 4½-inch loaf pans.
2. Sift together the flour, baking powder, ginger, cinnamon, and salt. Beat together the milk, honey, eggs, and butter. Add to the flour mixture all at once and stir just to mix. Stir in the sunflower seeds and, if desired, the raisins.
3. Pour into the prepared pans, tapping to remove any air bubbles. Bake until the bread is lightly browned and a wooden tester inserted in the center comes out clean, about 50 minutes. Let cool in the pans for 10 minutes, then turn out onto a rack and let cool completely.

Oatmeal Quick Bread
I LARGE LOAF

2 cups all-purpose flour, preferably unbleached
1 cup rolled oats
¾ cup packed brown sugar
4 teaspoons baking powder
1 teaspoon ground cinnamon
1 teaspoon salt
1¼ cups milk or water
2 large eggs, lightly beaten
½ cup vegetable oil or melted shortening
½ teaspoon vanilla extract
1 cup raisins, coarsely chopped cranberries, or chopped pitted dates

1. Preheat the oven to 350 degrees. Grease and flour the bottom of one 9- by 5-inch loaf pan.
2. Combine the flour, oats, sugar, baking powder, cinnamon, and salt. Combine the milk, eggs, oil, and vanilla. Add the flour mixture all at once and stir just to mix. Stir in the raisins.
3. Pour into the prepared pan, tapping to remove any air bubbles. Bake until the bread is lightly browned and a wooden tester inserted in the center comes out clean, about 1 hour. Let cool in the pan for 10 minutes, then turn out onto a rack and let cool completely.

Pumpkin Quick Bread
I LARGE LOAF

*Y*ou can double the recipe and bake in a 10-inch tube pan.

1½ cups all-purpose flour, preferably unbleached
1 teaspoon baking soda
½ teaspoon baking powder
½ teaspoon salt
¾ teaspoon ground cinnamon
½ teaspoon ground mace or nutmeg
¼ teaspoon ground cloves
⅛ teaspoon ground allspice or ginger
1 cup (8 ounces) pure-pack canned pumpkin
1 cup granulated or packed brown sugar
½ cup vegetable oil
2 large eggs, lightly beaten
¼ cup water
½ teaspoon vanilla extract
½ cup chopped pecans or walnuts
½ cup raisins or chopped pitted dates

OPTIONAL TOPPING

2½ tablespoons sugar
1½ teaspoons all-purpose flour
½ teaspoon ground cinnamon
1½ teaspoons butter or margarine

1. Preheat the oven to 350 degrees. Grease and flour the bottom of one 9- by 5-inch loaf pan or two 1-pound coffee cans.
2. Sift together the flour, baking soda, baking powder, salt, and spices. Combine the pumpkin, sugar, oil, eggs, water, and vanilla. Add the flour mixture all at once and stir just to mix. Stir in the nuts and raisins. Pour into the prepared pans.
3. To make the optional topping: Combine the sugar, flour, and cinnamon. Cut in the butter to produce coarse crumbs. Sprinkle over the top of the loaf.
4. Bake until the bread is lightly browned and a wooden tester inserted in the center comes out clean, about 1 hour. Let cool in the pan for 10 minutes, then turn out onto a rack and let cool completely.

VARIATION

Apple-Pumpkin Bread: Add 1 cup peeled and grated apples.

Strawberry Quick Bread
I LARGE LOAF

1½ cups (8 ounces frozen) hulled and sliced strawberries
1 cup sugar
1½ cups all-purpose flour, preferably unbleached
1 teaspoon ground cinnamon
½ teaspoon baking soda
½ teaspoon salt
½ cup plus 2 tablespoons vegetable oil
2 large eggs, lightly beaten
1 teaspoon orange or vanilla extract
½ cup chopped pecans or walnuts (optional)

1. Mix the strawberries with ¼ cup of the sugar, mash slightly, and let stand at room temperature for 1 hour.
2. Preheat the oven to 350 degrees. Grease and flour the bottom of one 9- by 5-inch loaf pan.
3. Sift together the flour, cinnamon, baking soda, and salt. Blend together the strawberries, remaining ¾ cup sugar, oil, eggs, and orange extract. Add the flour mixture all at once and stir just to mix. If desired, add the nuts.
4. Pour into the prepared pan. Bake until the bread is lightly browned and a wooden tester inserted in the center comes out clean, about 1 hour. Let cool in the pan for 10 minutes, then turn out onto a rack and let cool completely.

VARIATION

Strawberry-Applesauce Bread: Reduce the strawberry puree to ½ cup and the oil to ½ cup and add 1 cup applesauce.

Zucchini Quick Bread
I LARGE LOAF

1½ cups all-purpose flour, preferably unbleached
¾ cup granulated or packed brown sugar
2 teaspoons baking powder
½ teaspoon salt
½ teaspoon ground cinnamon
¼ teaspoon ground allspice or ginger
¼ teaspoon grated nutmeg
1 large egg, lightly beaten
½ cup vegetable oil
1 teaspoon vanilla extract
1 cup (about 4 ounces) shredded zucchini
½ cup raisins
½ cup coarsely chopped pecans or walnuts (optional)

1. Preheat the oven to 350 degrees. Grease and flour the bottom of one 9- by 5-inch loaf pan.
2. Sift together the flour, sugar, baking powder, salt, and spices. Beat together the egg, oil, and vanilla. Add the flour mixture all at once and stir just to mix. Stir in the zucchini, raisins, and if desired, the nuts.
3. Pour into the prepared pan. Bake until the bread is lightly browned and a wooden tester inserted in the center comes out clean, about 1 hour. Let cool in the pan for 10 minutes, then turn out onto a rack and let cool completely.

VARIATION

Zucchini-Carrot Bread: Reduce the zucchini to ½ cup and add ½ cup grated carrots.

Scones

Scones are among the most popular quick breads in Great Britain. Delicate and cake-like due to the addition of eggs, they are richer than American-style biscuits. Scones are easy to make, even under less than professional conditions. Indeed, during a week-long camping and canoeing trip with a group of friends in upper Quebec, I made batches of them several times for breakfast. If they turned out delicious over an open fire, think how good they can be baked in an oven.

Scones are usually split open horizontally and spread with butter, jam, lemon curd, or whipped cream. Or reduce the amount of sugar in the dough (to 1 teaspoon for 2 cups flour), omit the raisins, and top with lox and scrambled eggs.

Eight 3-inch or twelve 2-inch	*Forty-eight 3-inch or seventy-five 2-inch*	
2 cups	12 cups	all-purpose flour
1 tablespoon	6 tablespoons	baking powder
3 tablespoons	1 cup	sugar
½ teaspoon	2 teaspoons	salt
¼ cup	1½ cups	unsalted butter or margarine, chilled
2 large	12 large	eggs, lightly beaten
⅓ cup	2 cups	heavy cream or milk
¾ cup	3¼ cups	dried currants or raisins
		egg wash (1 or 2 large eggs beaten with 1 or 2 tablespoons water)
		additional sugar for sprinkling

1. Preheat the oven to 400 degrees. Grease a large baking sheet.
2. Combine the flour, baking powder, sugar, and salt. Cut in the butter until the mixture resembles coarse crumbs.
3. Combine the eggs and cream. Stir into the flour mixture just to combine, adding more cream if necessary to make a dough that just holds together. Add the currants.
4. Place the dough on a lightly floured surface and pat into a ½-inch thickness. Cut the dough into wedges or, using a 2- or 3-inch cutter, cut out rounds (dip the cutter in flour to prevent sticking). Reroll and cut the remnants (these scones will be a little tougher).
5. Place the scones on the prepared baking sheet close together. (Some cooks like to bake their scones immediately, while others let them stand for 1 hour.) Brush the tops with the egg wash and sprinkle lightly with the additional sugar. Bake until the scones are golden brown, 15 to 20 minutes. Serve warm. To keep warm, cover the baked scones with a tea towel.

Muffin Assortment

*T*hese small quick breads make an excellent breakfast food, afternoon snack, or dessert. The ideal muffin is well-rounded, light, and evenly textured. For special events I like to serve at least three types of muffins piled into baskets.

The following recipes are for standard muffins. For mini muffins (about 30 muffins per recipe), spoon the batter into 1¾-inch-wide (1-ounce) muffin cups and bake for 8 to 12 minutes. For jumbo muffins (about 6 muffins per recipe), spoon the batter into 4-inch-wide (6-ounce) muffin cups or custard cups and bake for 25 to 30 minutes. Muffins can be sealed in plastic bags and stored in the freezer for up to 3 months.

TIPS FOR MUFFIN-MAKING SUCCESS

- An ice cream scoop, ladle, or measuring scoop makes filling muffin cups easy.

- If not all the cups in a muffin tin are filled with batter, fill the empty ones with water to ensure an even conduction of heat.

- To prevent the bottoms of fruit muffins from becoming soggy, spoon about 1 tablespoon plain batter into the bottom of each muffin cup, then add the fruit to the batter and fill the muffin cups.

APPLE MUFFINS
BRAN MUFFINS
CHOCOLATE MUFFINS
CORNMEAL MUFFINS
GINGERBREAD MUFFINS
KITCHEN SINK MUFFINS
LEMON—POPPY SEED MUFFINS
OATMEAL MUFFINS
PAPAYA MUFFINS
PUMPKIN MUFFINS
SUN-DRIED TOMATO MUFFINS

Apple Muffins
12 MEDIUM MUFFINS

1¼ cups all-purpose flour, preferably unbleached
1 teaspoon baking soda
½ teaspoon ground cinnamon
¼ teaspoon salt
1 cup granulated or packed brown sugar (or ½ cup each)
½ cup vegetable oil
1 large egg, lightly beaten
2 tablespoons fresh lemon juice
1½ teaspoons vanilla extract
1 teaspoon grated lemon zest
1½ cups (about 2 medium) peeled and grated apples
½ cup raisins or chopped pitted dates (optional)
Additional sugar for sprinkling

1. Preheat the oven to 375 degrees. Grease and flour the bottoms only of 12 standard-size muffin-tin cups.
2. Sift together the flour, baking soda, cinnamon, and salt. Combine the sugar, oil, egg, lemon juice, vanilla, and zest. Add to the flour mixture all at once and stir only to blend. Do not overmix. Stir in the apples and, if desired, the raisins.
3. Spoon the batter into the muffin cups and sprinkle the tops with the additional sugar. Bake until the muffins are golden brown and a wooden tester comes out clean, 20 to 25 minutes. Let the muffins cool in the pan for several minutes, then remove to a wire rack.

VARIATION

Apple–Sour Cream Muffins: Substitute 1 cup sour cream for the oil and lemon juice.

Bran Muffins
12 MEDIUM MUFFINS

1 cup milk
1 cup unprocessed bran or 3 cups bran flakes cereal
1¼ cups all-purpose flour, preferably unbleached
½ cup granulated or packed brown sugar (or ¼ cup each)
1 tablespoon baking powder
½ teaspoon salt
¼ cup vegetable oil or melted vegetable shortening
1 large egg, lightly beaten
1 teaspoon vanilla extract
1 cup raisins or chopped pitted dates

1. Preheat the oven to 375 degrees. Grease and flour the bottoms only of 12 standard-sized muffin-tin cups.
2. Pour the milk over the bran and let stand for at least 5 minutes.
3. Sift together the flour, sugar, baking powder, and salt. Combine the bran mixture, oil, egg, and vanilla. Add to the dry ingredients all at once and stir only to blend. Do not overmix. Stir in the raisins.
4. Spoon the batter into the muffin cups. Bake until the muffins are golden brown and a wooden tester comes out clean, about 25 minutes. Let the muffins cool in the pan for several minutes, then remove to a wire rack.

Chocolate Muffins
12 MEDIUM MUFFINS

1 cup boiling water
½ cup unsweetened nonalkalized (not Dutch-process) cocoa powder
1¾ cups all-purpose flour, preferably unbleached
¾ cup sugar
2 teaspoons baking powder
½ teaspoon salt
¼ teaspoon baking soda
¼ cup vegetable oil or melted vegetable shortening
1 large egg, lightly beaten
1 teaspoon vanilla extract
1 cup coarsely chopped walnuts, chocolate chips, or chopped pitted dates (optional)
Additional sugar for sprinkling

1. Pour the water over the cocoa powder and stir until smooth. Let cool.
2. Preheat the oven to 400 degrees. Grease and flour the bottoms only of 12 standard-size muffin-tin cups.
3. Sift together the flour, sugar, baking powder, salt, and baking soda. Combine the cocoa mixture, oil, egg, and vanilla. Add to the dry ingredients all at once and stir only to blend. Do not overmix. If desired, stir in the nuts.
4. Spoon the batter into the muffin cups and sprinkle the tops with the additional sugar. Bake until the muffins are golden brown and a wooden tester comes out clean, 20 to 25 minutes. Let the muffins cool in the pan for several minutes, then remove to a wire rack.

VARIATION

Chocolate-Banana Muffins: Reduce the water to ½ cup and the cocoa to ⅓ cup. Increase the oil or shortening to ⅓ cup and add ⅔ cup mashed ripe bananas.

Cornmeal Muffins

12 MEDIUM MUFFINS

1¼ cups cornmeal, preferably stone-ground
1 cup all-purpose flour, preferably unbleached
¼ to ⅓ cup granulated or packed brown sugar
1 tablespoon baking powder
½ teaspoon salt
1 large egg, lightly beaten
1 cup milk or water
⅓ cup unsalted butter, margarine, or shortening, melted and cooled
1 to 1½ cups blueberries, fresh corn kernels, or chopped pecans (optional)

1. Preheat the oven to 400 degrees. Grease and flour the bottoms only of 12 standard-size muffin-tin cups.
2. Combine the cornmeal, flour, sugar, baking powder, and salt. Combine the egg, milk, and melted butter. Add to the dry ingredients all at once and stir only to blend. Do not overmix. If desired, stir in the blueberries.
3. Spoon the batter into the muffin cups. Bake until the muffins are golden brown and a wooden tester comes out clean, about 20 minutes. Let the muffins cool in the pan for several minutes, then remove to a wire rack.

VARIATION

Buttermilk Corn Muffins: Substitute 1 cup buttermilk or plain yogurt for the milk. Reduce the butter to ¼ cup and the baking powder to 2 teaspoons. Add ½ teaspoon baking soda (or reduce the baking powder to ½ teaspoon and add 1½ teaspoons baking soda).

Gingerbread Muffins
12 MEDIUM MUFFINS

2 cups all-purpose flour, preferably unbleached
1 tablespoon ground ginger
1 teaspoon ground cinnamon
½ teaspoon grated nutmeg
1 teaspoon baking powder
1 teaspoon baking soda
½ teaspoon salt
1 cup milk
½ cup packed brown sugar
¼ cup vegetable oil or melted vegetable shortening
¼ cup unsulfured (light) molasses
1 large egg, lightly beaten
1 teaspoon vanilla extract
1 cup raisins or chopped pitted dates
Additional sugar for sprinkling

1. Preheat the oven to 400 degrees. Grease and flour the bottoms only of 12 standard-size muffin-tin cups.
2. Sift together the flour, spices, baking powder, baking soda, and salt. Combine the milk, sugar, oil, molasses, egg, and vanilla. Add to the dry ingredients all at once and stir only to blend. Do not overmix. Stir in the raisins.
3. Spoon the batter into the muffin cups and lightly sprinkle the tops with the additional sugar. Bake until the muffins are golden brown and a wooden tester comes out clean, 20 to 25 minutes. Let the muffins cool in the pan for several minutes, then remove to a wire rack.

Kitchen Sink Muffins

12 MEDIUM MUFFINS

2 cups all-purpose flour, preferably unbleached
1 tablespoon baking powder
2 teaspoons ground cinnamon
¾ teaspoon salt
1 cup vegetable oil
1 cup sugar (or ½ cup granulated sugar and ½ cup packed brown sugar)
3 large eggs, lightly beaten
1 teaspoon vanilla extract
1 cup shredded apple
1 cup shredded carrots
1 cup shredded zucchini
¾ cup raisins or chopped pitted dates
½ cup chopped almonds, pecans, or walnuts
½ cup shredded coconut
Additional sugar for sprinkling

1. Preheat the oven to 400 degrees. Grease and flour the bottoms only of 12 standard-size muffin-tin cups.
2. Sift together the flour, baking powder, cinnamon, and salt. Combine the oil, sugar, eggs, and vanilla. Add to dry ingredients all at once and stir only to blend. Do not overmix. Stir in the remaining ingredients except the additional sugar.
3. Spoon the batter into the muffin cups and lightly sprinkle the tops with the additional sugar. Bake until the muffins are golden brown and a wooden tester comes out clean, 20 to 25 minutes. Let the muffins cool in pan for several minutes, then remove to a wire rack.

Lemon-Poppy Seed Muffins
12 MEDIUM MUFFINS

2 cups all-purpose flour, preferably unbleached
1 tablespoon baking powder
¾ teaspoon salt
1 cup sugar
1 cup water
¼ cup vegetable oil or melted vegetable shortening
1 large egg, lightly beaten
1 tablespoon lemon extract
1 teaspoon grated lemon zest (optional)
¼ cup poppy seeds
Additional sugar for sprinkling

1. Preheat the oven to 400 degrees. Grease and flour the bottoms only of 12 standard-size muffin-tin cups.
2. Sift together the flour, baking powder, and salt. Combine the sugar, water, oil, egg, lemon extract, and if desired, the zest. Add to the dry ingredients all at once and stir only to blend. Do not overmix. Stir in the poppy seeds.
3. Spoon the batter into the muffin cups and lightly sprinkle the tops with the additional sugar. Bake until the muffins are golden brown and a wooden tester comes out clean, 20 to 25 minutes. Let the muffins cool in the pan for several minutes, then remove to a wire rack.

Oatmeal Muffins
12 MEDIUM MUFFINS

1⅓ cups all-purpose flour, preferably unbleached
1 tablespoon baking powder
½ teaspoon salt
1 cup rolled oats
1 cup milk

⅔ cup granulated or packed brown sugar
3 tablespoons vegetable oil or melted shortening
1 large egg, lightly beaten
1 teaspoon vanilla extract
1 to 1½ cups coarsely chopped cranberries, chopped pitted dates, or raisins
Additional sugar for sprinkling

1. Preheat the oven to 400 degrees. Grease and flour the bottoms only of 12 standard-size muffin-tin cups.
2. Sift together the flour, baking powder, and salt. Add the oats. Combine the milk, sugar, oil, egg, and vanilla. Add to the dry ingredients all at once and stir only to blend. Do not overmix. Stir in the cranberries.
3. Spoon the batter into the muffin cups and lightly sprinkle the tops with the additional sugar. Bake until the muffins are golden brown and a wooden tester comes out clean, about 20 minutes. Let the muffins cool in the pan for several minutes, then remove to a wire rack.

Papaya Muffins
12 MEDIUM MUFFINS

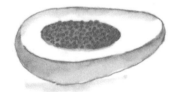

2 cups all-purpose flour
1 cup sugar
1 tablespoon baking powder
¾ teaspoon salt
½ teaspoon ground allspice
½ teaspoon ground cinnamon
½ teaspoon ground ginger
1 cup (about 1 medium) mashed ripe papaya
¼ cup (1 stick) unsalted butter or margarine, melted
2 large eggs, lightly beaten
1 teaspoon vanilla extract
½ cup raisins or chopped pitted dates
¼ cup chopped pecans or walnuts

1. Preheat the oven to 400 degrees. Grease and flour the bottoms only of 12 standard-size muffin-tin cups.
2. Combine the flour, sugar, baking powder, salt, and spices. Stir together the papaya, melted butter, eggs, and vanilla. Add to the dry ingredients all at once and stir only to blend. Do not overmix. Stir in the raisins and nuts.
3. Spoon the batter into the muffin cups. Bake until the muffins are golden brown and a wooden tester comes out clean, 20 to 25 minutes. Let the muffins cool in the pan for several minutes, then remove to a wire rack. Serve warm or at room temperature.

Pumpkin Muffins
12 MEDIUM MUFFINS

2 cups all-purpose flour, preferably unbleached
1 teaspoon baking soda
1 teaspoon ground cinnamon
½ teaspoon ground cloves
¼ teaspoon grated nutmeg
½ teaspoon salt
1 cup pure-pack canned pumpkin
¾ cup sugar
¼ cup unsulfured (light) molasses
¼ cup milk or water
½ cup vegetable oil or melted vegetable shortening
1 large egg, lightly beaten
½ teaspoon vanilla extract
1 cup coarsely chopped cranberries, chopped pitted dates, or raisins
Additional sugar for sprinkling

1. Preheat the oven to 400 degrees. Grease and flour the bottoms only of 12 standard-size muffin-tin cups.
2. Sift together the flour, baking soda, spices, and salt. Combine the pumpkin, sugar, molasses, milk, oil, egg, and vanilla. Add to the dry ingredients all at once and stir only to blend. Do not overmix. Stir in the cranberries.

3. Spoon the batter into the muffin cups and lightly sprinkle the tops with the additional sugar. Bake until the muffins are golden brown and a wooden tester comes out clean, 20 to 25 minutes. Let the muffins cool in the pan for several minutes, then remove to a wire rack.

Sun-Dried Tomato Muffins
ABOUT 12 MEDIUM MUFFINS

2 cups all-purpose flour
⅔ cup grated Parmesan cheese
1 tablespoon sugar
1 tablespoon baking powder
¾ teaspoon salt
½ teaspoon ground black pepper
½ teaspoon ground dried rosemary
1 cup milk
¼ cup vegetable oil or melted shortening
1 large egg, lightly beaten
⅓ cup drained and chopped sun-dried tomatoes
¼ cup chopped fresh parsley
1 clove garlic, minced

1. Preheat the oven to 400 degrees. Grease and flour the bottoms only of 12 standard-size muffin-tin cups.
2. Combine the flour, Parmesan, sugar, baking powder, salt, pepper, and rosemary. Stir together the milk, oil, and egg. Add to dry ingredients all at once and stir only to blend. Do not overmix. Stir in the tomatoes, parsley, and garlic.
3. Spoon the batter into the muffin cups. Bake until the muffins are golden brown and a wooden tester comes out clean, 20 to 25 minutes. Let the muffins cool in the pan for several minutes, then remove to a wire rack.

Index